Understanding

MEDIA
CULTURES

Nick Stevenson

Understanding

MEDIA
CULTURES

Social Theory and Mass Communication

Second Edition

SAGE Publications
London • Thousand Oaks • New Delhi

SAGE Publications Ltd
6 Bonhill Street
London EC2A 4PU

SAGE Publications Inc
2455 Teller Road
Thousand Oaks, California 91320

SAGE Publications India Pvt Ltd
32, M-Block Market
Greater Kailash I
New Delhi 110 048

British Library Cataloguing in Publication Data

A catalogue record for this book is available
from the British Library

ISBN 0 7619 73621
ISBN 0 7619 7363X (pbk)

Library of Congress catalog card number available

Typeset by Keystroke, Jacaranda Lodge, Wolverhampton.
Printed in Great Britain by The Cromwell Press Ltd,
Trowbridge, Wiltshire

Contents

Contents

Contents

Preface for the second edition

The main aim of this new edition has been to revise and expand the text to take account of recent media theory and research, and the development of new media. Since the first publication of this book in 1995, there has been a great deal of fresh thinking in this respect. This has given rise to a considerable amount of debate as to whether society has now entered into an information age unlike any other. However we theorise this transition it has posed new and of course old questions within the sociology of the media. Not surprisingly those who are trying to think about the impact of new media have increasingly looked to developments in sociology and social theory to help them in this task. Hence the central aim of my book remains the same as it was in 1995. That is I attempt to demonstrate why a grounding in social theory remains key for the study of the media. This claim remains consistent whether we are talking of new or old media. Whether I successfully make this case remains for the reader to judge.

There are a number of people I should like to thank for help in the preparation of the manuscript. Firstly, and above everyone else, I would like to praise my publisher Julia Hall. Without her vision and commitment this book would not have happened. Secondly, I would like to acknowledge my debt to a number of colleagues and friends whose conversations and insights have helped along the way. They are: Micheal Kenny, Anthony Elliott, Alex MacDonald, David Moore, Paul Ransome, Joke Hermes, Ann Gray, John Downey, Maurice Roche, John B. Thompson, Sharon MacDonald, Peter Jackson, Jagdish Patel, Gaye Flounders, Chris Docx, Chris Baber, Anthony Giddens, Andrew Gamble, Dave Hesmondhaugh, David Rose, Matthew Dickson, Robert Unwin, Jim McGuigan, Claire Annesley, and Kate Brooks. Finally, I would like to thank my partner Lucy James for putting up with my tastes in television, magazines, radio, newspapers, Internet, and cinema. While we remain divided on Radio One and Wim Wenders we have found solace in Ally McBeal. In addition, Lucy has devoted a considerable amount of time to reading through the chapters that are enclosed within. This book owes a great deal to her continual support. However, this new edition is dedicated with love to our daughter Eve Anna James.

Nick Stevenson, Nottingham

people within the narrowest horizons grow stupid at the point where their interest begins, and then vent their rancour on what they do not want to understand because they could understand it only too well, so the planetary stupidity which prevents the present world from perceiving the absurdity of its own order is a further product of the unsublimated, unsuperseded interest of the rulers.

(Adorno, 1974:198)

You either shut up or get cut up. It's only inches on the reel to reel. And the radio is in the hands of such a lot of fools trying to anaesthetise the way you feel. Radio is the sound salvation. Radio is cleaning up the nation. They say you better listen to the voice of reason. But they don't give you any choice 'cause they think that it's treason. So you had better do as you are told. You better listen to the radio.

('Radio, Radio', Elvis Costello)

Introduction

One

What is the significance of media cultures today? The emergence of global forms of mass communication, as most would recognise, has reworked the experiential content of everyday life. But how important is the field of communications when compared with other fields of research? What is the relationship between the study of mass media and other aspects of social practice? How have different media of communication reshaped relations of time and space? Do media cultures reaffirm today's dominant social relations? What kinds of identities are currently being fostered by electronic communication? Who are the key thinkers of whom we should be aware in thinking about these issues? Here I hope to contribute towards our shared understanding of such questions, while broadly indicating the shape some answers might take.

This book began as an attempt to think about the relationship between mass communication and social theory. This soon brought to mind a paradox. Much of the social theory I read dealt with issues of work, sexuality, structure and **agency, ideology, commodification**, the unconscious, time and space, citizenship, **globalisation** and other aspects. But within many of these texts the media of mass communication seemed to have marginal status. Most current writing seemingly acknowledges its increasing significance within modernity before passing over into a discussion of the reshaping of the economic base or the institutional transformations in the political sphere. This seemed wrong. My own life made me aware of the importance that certain elements of media had within my leisure time, in talk amongst friends, as gifts to be exchanged, in maintaining connection with absent others, and in opening out a sense of the public. Yet I was also aware of a number of perspectives that treated the media as all-important. Here the influence of the media of mass communication seemed pervasive and could be blamed for the major ills of society. While at least these perspectives recognised the significance of the media, they were treated as unproblematically as they were by those who ignored their influence. Rightist and leftist thinkers alike have similarly conceptualised the media as being the cause of social breakdown and the ideological cement that glues an unjust society together. Such views might seem to have some plausibility, but are generally overly reductive and essentialist.

In this book I will develop an informed debate with those aspects of social theory that have taken the media seriously. Admittedly this largely ignores the reasons why social theory has been so slow to investigate its importance. In this my argumentative strategy has been to drive a wedge between the two positions outlined above. First, I am concerned to link the media of mass communication to other social practices contained within the public and the private. As such, the book will engage with those positions that view media practice as connected to a field of historical and spatial practice. Secondly, the media of mass communication constitute social practices in themselves that are not reducible to other formations. The act of broadcasting a radio programme, reading a magazine or watching television is a significant social practice in itself. This book, then, is also concerned with the specificity of media practices. These need to be maintained against the temptation to crush them into a generalised **discourse** on economics, politics or culture. But here I am aware of a further paradox. When social theory finally got round to noticing the importance of mass media the television age was the emergent cultural process. For this reason, apart from Marshall McLuhan (1994) and Jürgen Habermas (1989), most of the theoretical considerations under review neglect other media of communication. This is not a tendency I shall be able to reverse here. Arguably social theory became interested in the impact of the mass media once it became impossible to ignore. This meant that until the television age it had had only a negligible impact upon sources of social criticism. Classical nineteenth-century social theory tended to treat it as a marginal phenomenon that lacked importance beside issues of capitalism, bureaucracy and authority, and anomie. Current postmodern perspectives have sought most dramatically to reverse this emphasis. In postmodernity, the mass media are conceptualised both as technologically interrelated and as promoting a historically unstable domain of popular **intertextuality**. Television's dominance has arguably been replaced by a complex technological field of compact disc players, personal computers, magazine culture and video cassette recorders. Now, amongst the rapid technological development of media forms, it is easy to forget the permanence and continued structural priority that television and the press retain. However, these domains are currently being transformed by the impact of new technologies of communication that are ushering in a new society that is challenging older more established research paradigms.

2

Two

Why media cultures? Originally I thought of calling the book 'Social Theory and Mass Communication'. Luckily I was quickly advised by a friend of mine that this sounded desperately dull, and certainly not the kind of book she would read! This again seemed wrong given the importance of the themes covered by the text. Further, such a title, I thought, did not even serve my own purposes very well. What I intend to communicate by media cultures can be summarised in three senses. The first is the obvious point that much of modern culture is transmitted by the media of mass communication. The various media disseminate classical opera and music, tabloid stories about the private lives of politicians, the latest Hollywood gossip and news from the four corners of the globe. This has profoundly altered the phenomenological experience of living in modernity, as well as **networks** of social power. The other two points are more academically inclined. Secondly, most of the theorists I have discussed within this text build up a picture of the media out of a wider analysis of modern cultural processes. If say, we want to understand Habermas's (1989) writing on the public sphere, we might also look at his analysis of money and power. Similarly, Baudrillard's (1993a) concern with **simulation** and **implosion** is not detachable from his other-cultural concerns, and his own intellectual biography. Hence, while I concentrate upon particular theorists' interpretations of mass communication, their views are always integrated into wider cultural concerns. In doing this I have become aware of the durability of certain intellectual traditions. Academic culture is probably one of the most international of those currently in operation. The exchange of travelling theory has certainly made geographical impacts, and yet national trends remain evident. In the main this book concentrates upon contributors from Australia, Britain, Canada, France, Germany, Spain and the USA. I am aware this gives the text a Eurocentric bias. Yet the traditions of hermeneutics, post-structuralism, **critical theory** and **Marxism** evident here are not *owned* by specific nationalities. But the way in which these ideas have circulated is not as free-floating as talk of a pervasive global **culture** might suggest. For instance, despite the impact of French intellectual culture, and to a lesser extent German traditions of critical theory, British cultural studies has mostly ignored contributions that emerged originally within Canada. Baudrillard's overtly French social theory, which has made a huge impact, is perhaps responsible for reminding us of the importance of certain branches of Canadian thought in respect of Innis and McLuhan. Had I more rigorously traced through these crosscurrents, I would have produced a different book. This adds a third dimension to media cultures – there are histories of intellectual exchange of those who have theorised about the media to be written. Again this is not our concern. However, attentive readers might want to bear this in mind while reading the text. It is less with the intellectual contexts of the main contributors that I am concerned than with the production of ideas and discourses. But still further qualification is required. My main aim is not to present an overview of all the perspectives in social theory that currently mention mass communications. This has been done excellently elsewhere.[1] I also wanted to avoid presenting the material in an overly unified way that did not open out areas of critical dispute and engagement. What has emerged is a *selected* engagement with specific intellectual fields of criticism and theoretical practice. In this I have prioritised traditions of theorising and thinking that have sought to offer a critique of mass communications. But even here some currents are hardly dealt with, and others are quickly passed over. For instance, I could have offered a chapter on the Chicago school or the contributions of American Marxism. That I have not speaks of my own location in current debates on mass communication and my anchoring in a specific context. Of course such a recognition does not mean that this book has not been written with a diverse spectrum of readers in mind, and to recognise my cultural specificity need not relativise the theoretical labour that is in evidence here. Every effort has been taken to present the arguments in a way that might be able to persuade others of their rightness. I want to offer an engagement with the strands of intellectual debate that both excited and stimulated me. I also chose to concentrate upon intellectual traditions about which I thought I had something to say. For omissions I offer no apologies. This is after all not an attempt to have the final word. What I hope I have achieved is a critical space that allows different traditions to be compared, and a clear account of their interconnections and omissions. Whether I have chosen wisely and achieved this aim is for the reader to decide.

Three

One of my most powerful childhood memories was watching the flickering black and white images of the first people on the moon. I can vaguely remember watching the television images of those vulnerable astronauts with intense excitement. The explorations into space seemed to capture the imaginations of my family and schoolfriends alike. This, along with the fall of the Berlin Wall, the Gulf War, the events of September 11th and Live Aid, was probably one of the most memorable events transmitted by the mass media during my lifetime. I feel sure other readers will have their own. Yet how could social theory help me to understand the social significance of this event? Most mainstream theoretical analysis would quickly dismiss my interest in the moon landing as either unimportant, or as somehow not as *real* as my position within a family or social class. This is unacceptable. Such arguments are at best avoidance and, at worst, unimaginative and sterile. If we take some of the theoretical perspectives offered within this book we will soon realise that my schoolboy projections can be variously interpreted.

In this text I draw a broad distinction between three paradigms of mass communication research. The first two chapters offer an investigation of both British and German research that has taken mass communications to be an important source of social power. These viewpoints are mainly concentrated with a **political economy** of mass communication, and related concerns with ideology and the **public sphere**. The debates have generally been preoccupied with the links between mass media, democracy and capitalism. The set of debates represented here by British and American Marxism and the Frankfurt school can be referred to as a *critical* approach to mass communication. The third chapter presents a discussion of more interpretative approaches in respect of the **audience**'s relationship with media cultures. The aim is to open out concerns with the everyday practices in which most of us participate. The research presented here is concerned with processes of unconscious identification, power relations within the home and the semiotic production of meaning. The second paradigm can usefully be called *audience* research. These themes set the scene for the discussion of technological means of communication in Chapter 4. McLuhan's distinctive analysis has been neglected by social theorists seeking to comment on the media of mass communication. In this respect media implosion, **hybridity** and the restructuring of time and space have much to contribute. This is evident in the important discussions of Jack Goody (1977) and Anthony Giddens (1991) of oral, print and electric cultures. Chapter 5, through a discussion of Baudrillard (1993a) and Jameson (1991), takes McLuhan's concern with technological media a stage further. They map out a distinctive intellectual terrain around **postmodernism** in the effort to explain emerging cultural practices. As in the previous two sections, there is much disagreement and intellectual tension between the perspectives that are presented. Yet they are united in their representation of a fragmented, discontinuous and simulated popular culture. Chapters 4 and 5 represent research into mass communications that concentrates upon the *media* of transmission. Finally, the second edition of this book has lead to the preparation of a completely new chapter which aims to debate the significance of an **information society** and the development of new **mediums of communication**. As should become evident, this chapter represents the increasing convergence of the three paradigms of research.

The emphasis throughout is on the fact that media cultures are irredeemably plural. This necessitates the maintenance of the three research paradigms in that they all highlight different aspects of media culture. There is little point in attempting to produce a grand theory, as it would most likely be unable to account for every aspect of media practice. But, on the other hand, the fragmented particularism of certain aspects of poststructuralism often fail to see the connections between different levels of theoretical and media practice. This is to be avoided. I want to present a complex view of the field that is constantly evolving without ever being completed. If these reflections are followed, the various theoretical discourses represented in this book might all be able to tell me a great deal about my early concern with fuzzy spacemen.

Feminist and critical theorists, like Jessica Benjamin (1988) and Jürgen Habermas (1989), would probably draw attention to the way in which instrumental and masculine forms of reason were increasingly dominating the life-world through popular representations of the Apollo flights. The captivation of my family would be explained in terms of the dominance of certain ideological frames of reference. The space age was allowed to emerge in a world that had inadequate forms of birth control and where extreme poverty still existed. The race for the moon also legitimised the cold war and the production of weapons for mass destruction. Further, the often sexual imagery that was used to discuss the ventures into space spoke of a masculine obsession with the domination and differentiation from a feminine other. It enunciated a masculine escape from the responsibilities we collectively hold towards this planet and other human beings. On the moon there were no others, allowing for the projection of fantasies of absolute control. Finally, the popular science programmes which emerged along with the Apollo rocket launches managed to bracket off certain critical concerns with the relationship between the life-world and technical reason. Instead of technical concerns being subordinate to a communicative or feminist ethics, they came to dominate such reflections.

Such concerns take us only so far. The second paradigm, that of audience research, would have wanted to record who became interested in these space flights, and how. For instance, did I primarily watch the moon walks with my father, and did my sister and mother feel excluded from a masculine scientific culture? Or perhaps these concerns are wide of the mark? I'm sure I can remember these programmes being treated with a certain scepticism by all family members. Surely, they reasoned, the money could be put to better use, and why did we have to listen to all those boring scientists before we got to hear about the daily lives of the astronauts? What did they eat? How did they pass the time? When could we be sure they were safe? These questions might have pointed to popular concerns being different from the official representations fostered by the media.

Finally, the perspectives of the third paradigm bring different questions to bear. McLuhan (1994) would undoubtedly have pointed to the way in which technical media could stretch space and time to bring media representations into my living room, and to the way in which scientific culture and everyday impressions had imploded. Science was no longer the specialised concern of an elite culture but was popularly shared by everyone. Baudrillard (1983) would have pointed to the extent to which space was a simulated event. For instance, he might argue that notions of space travel are socially constructed through regimes of interpretation formed in different historical periods. He could also argue that popular representations of rocket launches were the modern-day equivalent of the pioneer spirit which ideologically helped the Europeans colonise native Americans. The popular idea of space also drew upon American comic books, science fiction films and 1950s radio serials. Space is intertextual and does not exist separately from popular forms. Further, Baudrillard could argue that the institution of one-way forms of communication helped impose this culture on the people. The majority of the population would, on this reading, have paid only the most distracted forms of attention to the out-of-focus pictures coming in from the moon. Jameson (1991), on the other hand, would probably agree with Baudrillard that notions of space were represented through popular codes, but without denying that they were also real events. Unlike other Marxist thinkers, he might be less concerned with the colonisation of a critical public sphere, and more with the search for a popular utopian moment. This was certainly evident in my own experience. Despite being eight years old, I can still remember the intense feelings I had of watching this historic event, and the overwhelming sense of hope and optimism that was caught up with the landing on the moon. These projections connected, at the end of the 1960s, with a general sense that science and technology could be harnessed to improve the quality of life of most of those who lived on the planet. That this has since failed to emerge leads me back to more critical currents of theorising.

This somewhat impressionistic analysis does not do justice to the complexity of the concerns evident within this text. Any serious detailed study cannot be summarised in a few nostalgic sentences about the events of 1969. However, the following discussion attempts to lay the perspectives open so that they can be applied by students, academics and lay readers alike. In doing so, it might be possible to demonstrate that social theory and mass communications has much to contribute to our understanding of the modern world. By exploring a specific set of theoretical issues I aim to show how this is so. In this sense the book is meant to have a critical as well as a democratic function. This is important given the growing importance of media cultures within most people's everyday lives. It is undoubtedly the case that the practice of media cultures in the modern world is being rapidly transformed. These changes are being driven along by a multitude of social forces which include new ownership patterns, new technology, global- isation, state policy and audience practices to name but a few. These dramatic shifts require wide ranging forms of debate both inside and outside of academic circles. Arguably the very nature of our culture is changing and this will present both current and future generations with new possibilities and dangers. In the following chapters I aim to outline the beginnings of a new project for cultural studies in this respect. This involves the need to reconnect cultural to economic and political practices in such a way that their specificity is respected. This has many precedents in the history of cultural and media studies, although it has been lost in the recent developments within postmodernism, **discourse** theory and semiotics. Here I will try to provide some of the theoretical tools that are required if we are to analyse adequately the changes taking place in media practice and cautiously point to ways in which this venture could be reconnected with more democratic currents and concerns. This should give the reader some of the tools necessary to do media analysis of their own, outline wider structural changes that impact on media cultures and provide a broad critical knowledge of the subject area. However the major aims of this book are to present a clearly written account of a complex field of theoretical practice and to defend the normative relevance of democratic media cultures in increasingly troubled times. If I can do this then my venture will have been worthwhile.

Chapter
1

Marxism and Mass Communication Research

Debates within Political Economy and Ideology:

Raymond Williams, Glasgow University Media Group
and Stuart Hall

Marxism, Political Economy and Ideology

Historically Marxism has offered an analysis of the media of mass communication that has sought to emphasise their role in the social reproduction of the status quo. Whereas liberalism has argued that the mass media have an essential role to play in the maintenance of free speech, Marxism has charged that unequal social relations have helped form ideological images and representations of society. In this sense, Marxism's strength has been to suggest that there is indeed a link between questions of ownership and the cultural content of media production. Marxists have rightly criticised liberal accounts for assuming that the free exchange of ideas could take place in conditions of class domination. However, Marxism's limitations are also considerable. It has neglected other modes of domination not reducible to class, such as race and gender, and has under-theorised the role of the state. It was noticeable that in European state-administered, socialist societies the flow of information and civil society generally was centrally controlled. This along with Marxism's current **identity** crisis poses difficult questions concerning its continued role as a critical theory. While these issues form the backcloth of our discussion, they cannot be fully debated here. Despite these limitations, British Marxist perspectives still have much to contribute to our understanding of media cultures. Raymond Williams made considerable attempts to learn from democratic **liberalism** by asking what a system of free communication might look like. Further, through a debate with post-structuralism, Stuart Hall sought to explain symbolic modes of domination that are not rooted in social class. Finally, the Glasgow University Media Group (GUMG) offers empirical examples of **bias** towards class perspectives in news production.

This chapter traces two central themes through contemporary debates within British Marxism on the theme of mass communication: the patterns of ownership and control evident within the cultural industries, and their role in the formation of cultural content and subjectivity. The question of political economy remains crucial to critical attempts to develop a theory of mass communication. The study of modern cultural forms, I will argue, presupposes an analysis of the institutional structures that produce and distribute them. Such theoretical manoeuvres have sought to investigate structured relations of power embedded within relations of ownership and control, place these material relations within a historical context, and unravel the impact of commercial and public institutions upon discursive practices (Golding and Murdock, 1991). Of those under review only Raymond Williams has substantively contributed to our understanding in this context. While issues of political economy engage members of the GUMG and Stuart Hall, such concerns never occupy centre stage.

If the contributions of the GUMG and Stuart Hall have little of note to offer in terms of locating the media within institutional frameworks, the same could not be said of issues related to ideology and the formation of subjectivity. The question of ideology within British Marxist mass communication research is intimately bound up with the history of Western Marxism (Anderson, 1979). Here ideological forms of analysis are employed to explain the continuation of structures of domination within late capitalism. In this respect, while it is recognised, to borrow Enzensberger's famous phrase, that the so-called *consciousness industry* exhibits a certain 'leakiness' (Enzensberger, 1976b: 23), the emphasis is squarely placed upon forms of manipulation. In an earlier essay on this theme, Enzensberger (1976a) had claimed that the 'mind industry' could not be conceptualised in terms of the circulation of commodities, as its main concern was to ideologically sell the existing order. In a sharp reply to the perceived ideologism of the media analysis of much of the New Left, Dallas Smythe (1977) sought to correct the drift into Left idealism. For Smythe, the first question Marxists should ask themselves is, what economic function does the communications industry fulfil? The answer to this question can only be supplied once we grasp the economic rather than ideological dimension of capitalist cultural forms. According to Smythe, time under monopoly capitalism is separated between work (time spent in the production of commodities) and leisure (time which is sold to advertisers). Audiences are bought by advertisers on the basis of income, age, sex, ethnic and class specifications. Hence the work performed by the audience is to learn how to buy the goods on offer, thereby decisively shaping 'free time' in the interests of consumer capitalism. The economic foundation of contemporary culture, he concludes, remains a considerable 'blind spot' for Western Marxism.

While I want to return to these issues later, Dallas Smythe surely bends the stick too far. As Graham Murdock (1978) points out, Dallas Smythe considerably overstates the importance of the selling of audiences to advertisers. There remain a number of cultural industries such as cinema, popular music, comic books and popular fiction, not to mention public service broadcasting, with only a minimal dependence on advertising revenue. In addition, mass communication theory not only needs to provide a critical analysis of how the dual media of money and power help shape the institutions of communication, but how these structures systematically distort society's understanding of itself. To theoretically grasp the execution of mass forms of culture one needs to integrate an analysis of institutional power with issues related to media content and bias (GUMG) and the discursive and psychic formation of human identity (Hall). Williams, the GUMG and Hall provide essential contributions to ongoing debates between social theory and mass communications, without ever producing such a synthesis.

Raymond Williams:
Communications and the Long Revolution

The work of Raymond Williams remains one of the richest sources of cultural criticism available within British Marxism. The corpus of his writing contains substantial contributions to literary and cultural criticism and political theory, as well as mass communications. In this Williams is part of a wider change evident within Left thinking in postwar society. Along with other writers on the New Left, Williams is aware that the economism evident within Marxist thought inadequately accounts for the growth in the importance of democratic and commercial cultures. In addition, artistic practice severed from the social conditions of its production and reception by traditional criticism, was thought to contain a certain critical immanence. These concerns prompted a lifelong project that would seek to form an understanding of ordinary and aesthetic cultures, and in turn their relationship with social institutions.

His first major work, *Culture and Society* (1961), probably remains his best known. The term 'culture', within Williams's presentation, is discussed by a historically sequenced collection of writers ranging from Burke to Orwell. Williams aims to argue, by critically tracing through a predominantly Romantic tradition around 'culture', that the term potentially retains both immanent and critical uses. Williams in effect merges what might be called an anthropological and an artistic definition of culture. For Williams, 'culture' signified the dual meaning of a 'way of life' (Williams, 1961: 137) and notions of human perfection that provide a critical court of appeal (Williams, 1961: 65–84). Williams writes:

> A culture has two aspects; the known meanings and directions, which its members are trained to; the new observations and meanings, which are offered and tested. We use the culture in these two senses; to mean a whole way of life – the common meanings; to mean the arts and learning – the special process of discovery and creative effort. (Williams, 1988: 4)

Williams's book, *The Long Revolution* (1965), develops a more institutionally grounded approach to cultural transformations, while retaining some of his earlier leanings. The long revolution refers to the slow historical unfolding of three interrelated changes taking place in the economic, political and cultural spheres since the industrial revolution. The gradual broadening of access to the education system, along with the growth of the reading public, the popular press, and the use of standard English, provides the backcloth for a culture in common. The dialectic of the long revolution is constituted through the contradiction between the forces of production that had been liberated by capitalism and the communicative nature of human beings. The social reproduction of dominating social relations between capital and labour prevents cultural forms from being utilised in an emancipatory fashion. The realisation of the essentially learning and creative nature of the people could only be captured through a socialist transformation of society (Williams, 1965: 118). The problem Williams faced was that the labour movement, whom he had identified as the central agency for change, had become incorporated into the capitalist system.

The aims of the long revolution can best be highlighted by referring back to Williams's dual definition of culture. First Williams wished to create the material conditions for an enlightened, educated, participatory democracy. This could only be carried through once the social relationships within economic, political and cultural institutions had been radically democratised. In addition, Williams argued that 'our' literary cultural heritage and new forms of cultural production should be opened up to the critical practice of everyone, rather than restricted to a privileged few. The dominant values of capitalism sought to promote a shallow, synthetic popular culture that either relegated 'serious' art to the margins, or reinforced the elitist notion that high culture ideologically belonged to the upper classes (Williams, 1962: 115). This particular perspective represents a reworking of F.R. Leavis's notion that in all historical periods it was left to a minority to maintain, criticise and contribute to 'culture'.[1] This is an important change of emphasis for Williams, as he had previously accepted the necessary role that certain cultural elites would play in preserving a literary culture from 'mechanical ways of thought, feeling and conjecture' (Williams, 1952). But Williams's literary origins do play an important role in shaping his disposition towards the media of mass communication.

In his little classic, *Communications* (1962), he continues with many of the themes of the long revolution. This text was originally written by Williams to initiate discussion on future policy directions within the Labour party. Although critical debate on the future of the mass media failed to materialise, the book remains an outstanding example of what I shall call *democratic realism*. In proposing to reform society's communicative structure, Williams desired to create the conditions for free, open and authentic expression. To do this one has to provide artists, commentators, performers and reviewers with a social setting that ensures their autonomous control over the means of expression. Williams offers an 'ideal type' of free communication when he writes:

> A good society depends upon the free availability of facts and opinions, and on the growth of vision and consciousness – the articulation of what men have actually seen and known and felt. Any restriction of the freedom of individual contribution is actually a restriction of the resources of society. (Williams, 1962: 1245)

Williams outlines four brief models against which this ideal type is to be tested: (1) authoritarian, (2) paternal, (3) commercial and (4) democratic.

An *authoritarian* communicative institution simply transmits the instructions of ruling groups. Inherent within this approach is the undertaking as a matter of policy to exclude other or conflicting perspectives. Here Williams has in mind the mass communication systems of 'actually existed socialism'. The transmission of electronically coded messages and the print media were largely centrally controlled by the state, which tightly restricted the expression of dissent within civil society. As Williams clearly perceived, Marxism's emphasis upon property relations within the economic sphere led to a theoretical neglect of the relations between state and civil society. This strain within Marxism can be connected to the tendency in practice to replace civil society with the state (Keane, 1988). Any radical democratic politics worth the name, Williams insisted, would have to protect the free circulation of information from state **surveillance**.

Paternal social structures, on the other hand, are oriented around the desire to protect and guide, rather than the assertion of the right to rule. For example, the BBC was built upon the ideal of the maintenance of high standards, which largely reflected the ethos and taste of England's dominant social groups. Lord Reith, the first Director-General of the BBC (British Broadcasting Corporation), defended this approach by arguing that a more democratic media would inevitably lead to lower standards. According to Williams, the Reithian public service model had an inbuilt tendency to view the people as masses (Williams, 1962: 108). The expression 'the masses' is used to signify a way of thinking about the people that denies their cultural plurality. Reith's view of public service sought to educate the people into a rich, high culture away from homogeneous Americanised popular culture. For Williams, Reithian paternalism had much in common with the commercial culture it was meant to oppose. Whereas the market sought to target consumer types, the reproduction of high and low categories within paternal approaches divides 'our culture into separate areas with no bridges between them' (Williams, 1962: 108). Williams's revised version of the public service model would attempt to embrace a more pluralistic model of the people, while institutionally underpinning democratic communicative relations.

Commercial cultural industries offer a certain amount of freedom in that a plurality of cultural forms can be bought and sold in the marketplace. But, as Williams (1980) makes clear in an essay on capitalism and advertising, commercial systems often obscure the distinction between human wants for goods and services and the need for democratic selfgovernment. Advertising is able to play this particular ideological trick by offering 'magical' solutions to the more authentic problems of 'death, loneliness, frustration, the need for identity and respect' (Williams, 1980: 190). In addition, commercial structures promote a further illusion in that certain exclusions are built into capitalistic methods of cultural distribution. That is, commercial forms of cultural dissemination inevitably exclude works unlikely to sell quickly and reap a profitable return.

The *democratic* model of cultural production has much in common with the commercial system outlined above, given its emphasis upon free communication. However, according to Williams, certain rights of free communication should be insulated and protected from the dominance of capital in the marketplace. Williams proposes that the media of mass communications be taken out of the control of commercial and paternal institutions, such as those underwritten by capital and the state, and both democratised and decentralised. Once institutionally separate from the government and the market this would provide cultural contributors with the social context for free expression. Open democratic forms of 'talk' would have no necessary end point, given that all of those who contribute must remain open to 'challenge and review' (Williams, 1962: 134). This utopia of free communication, Williams believed, would undoubtedly promote stronger community relations and bonds. The reform of the national system of communication would also allow a democratic public forum for the presentation of previously excluded experiences and perspectives. Here in particular, Williams had in mind an emergent generation of artists, such as Tony Garnett, Ken Loach and John McGrath, all of whom were developing a new realist structure of feeling within cinema and television. Through the progression of the long revolution such contributors would eventually displace the superficiality of much popular culture. In short, Williams felt strongly that the new forms of communication (press, television, radio, cinema) could produce a democratic climate for serious engagement and the genuine attention to human needs.

Williams's writing can be described as *democratic realism* not only because of his commitment to the institutional changes outlined in the long revolution, but also because of his defence of a realist aesthetic. However, unlike Lukacs's famous remarks on realism and art, Williams does not argue that the social should be represented as though it were a reflection in a mirror (Jameson, 1977). For Williams, as we shall see in his later writing on cultural materialism, artistic practices do not reflect reality, but actively produce it through material and symbolic forms. Cultural production can be described as realist through what Williams describes as an 'attitude to reality' (Williams, 1989a: 228). The cultural contributor should make an attempt to capture 'what is really going on', while seeking to connect with the structure of feeling of the audience. For the democratic realist, communication can be conceived as successful only if social processes have been presented truthfully, and in a way in which the audience can understand. For example, Spike Lee's recent film *Malcolm X* could be described as a form of democratic realism. The film portrays the radical black civil rights leader Malcolm X within a historical framework centred around black people's struggle against racism. The narrative is evidently an attempt to symbolically reinterpret 'real' social processes, and to connect with the sensibilities of modern audiences. Such an approach should strive towards what Williams and Orrom (1954) call 'total expression'. Total expression is achieved when the audience leaves a performance, or puts down a novel, with an idea of what the author intended. This is not achieved either by the denial of the importance of specific cultural forms and styles, or by retreat into a purely aesthetic disposition on the part of the artist. Instead the cultural producer is compelled to work within certain conventions and structures of feeling that best enable them to communicate with others.

Cultural Materialism and Hegemony

Raymond Williams's later writing struck up a closer engagement with Western Marxism and post-structuralism. In response to these two theoretical trends he cultivated a more material account of cultural processes. The theory of cultural materialism was intended to critique Marxist notions of base and superstructure along with the reifying forms of abstraction he found evident in certain strands of post-structuralism (Williams, 1979b: 27).

Theoretical arguments around base and superstructure have emerged as one of the central problems in Marxist theory. This notion is usually taken to mean that the base (economy) has an explanatory priority over, or sets external limits upon, the superstructure (cultural and political institutions). Most recent Marxist analysis on this subject, usually inspired by Gramsci (1971), Althusser (1977, 1984) and Poulantzas (1978), seeks to argue that the superstructure has at least a *relative* autonomy from the economic base. Norman Geras (1987) best describes this phenomenon in his polemic against Post-Marxism. Geras usefully asks us to figuratively reimagine the base and superstructure model by picturing the author chained to a post. The chain does not prevent Geras from playing the violin or watching television, but it does restrain him from going shopping or attending a jazz concert. In this respect, Geras chained to a post, could be said to have a relative autonomy similar to that of the superstructure in relation to the base. Williams, on the other hand, and despite his closer association with Marxism, remains sceptical of the base and superstructure metaphor. Such an argument (1) reduces the superstructure to a reflection of the base; (2) abstracts from historical process; (3) characterises human needs as economic rather than social; and (4) isolates cultural questions from issues related to economic organisation. As I have outlined these arguments elsewhere (Stevenson, 1995), I shall concentrate upon Williams's first and primary objection.

Williams claims that to label a phenomenon superstructural is to assign it to a lesser degree of reality. The superstructure, in this reading, becomes a dependent realm of ideas that reflects the material economic base. The diminishing of the superstructure to an idealist realm runs counter to Williams's desire to make cultural practices material. Williams's theory of cultural materialism holds that all social practices are made up of significatory and material elements. He writes that culture is made up of two main features:

> (a) an emphasis on the 'informing spirit' of a whole way of life, which is manifest over the whole range of social activities but is most evident in 'specifically cultural' activities – a language, styles of art, kinds of intellectual work; and (b) an emphasis on a 'whole social order' within which a specifiable culture, in styles of art and kinds of intellectual work, is seen as the direct or indirect/product of an order primarily constituted by other social activities. (Williams, 1982: 11–12)

Williams demonstrates his argument with a discussion of Marx's writing in the *Grundrisse* (Williams, 1982). Marx, according to Williams, argues that a worker who constructs a piano out of raw materials is involved in a productive activity, whereas a pianist playing the piano is not. This is because the worker, in a way that could not be said of the pianist, is directly involved in the social reproduction of capital. Williams, contrary to Marx, insists that the practice of playing the piano is simultaneously material and symbolic. The idea here is to make listening to music as much of a productive practice as working for McDonald's.

Like many on the British Left, the search for a non-reductive Marxism led Williams to Gramsci. Williams first became acquainted with Gramsci's work on hegemony during the 1960s and 1970s (Forgacs, 1989; Ransome, 1992). In brief, a ruling group can be said to be hegemonic if it transcends more limited economic concerns and provides the people with moral and intellectual leadership. Hegemony is best thought of as a continuous battleground, where the bourgeoisie and the working class construct economic, political and cultural alliances with other social groups. The aim here is to progressively isolate the opposing camp while tilting the balance of public interests and perceptions towards your own side. Gramsci's view of ideology is interesting in this sense. Ideology is represented as the social *cement* that binds together different class alliances. According to Gramsci, we can judge ideology to be effective if it is able to connect with the 'common sense' of the people and mobilise them for change.

The clearest outline of what Williams means by hegemony is provided in *Marxism and Literature* (1979b).[2] In keeping with Gramsci, Williams defines hegemony as a continuous historical process that is always shifting and never static or systematic in its formation. In Williams's terms, hegemonic practices can be either dominant, residual or emergent, although, as Williams makes plain, no social order could ever incorporate the whole range of human experience. Consequently certain social practices, like teaching Marxism within a university or working for an AIDS organisation, are inherently contradictory and occasionally oppositional in that such practices simultaneously challenge and reaffirm the dominant hegemony. While this is undoubtedly a comforting theory for Leftists working in education and health, its historical bent fits well with Williams's work on culture generally.[3]

The hegemonic, in Williams's analysis, is a combination of three cultural processes: traditions, institutions and formations. Traditions are constantly invented and reinvented by nation states, while being presented as fixed, final and neutral. The material production and reproduction of invented traditions are largely dependent upon institutions like the mass media. The growth in popularity of the British royal family – the most ideologically timeless of Britain's institutions – was facilitated by largely uncritical media coverage. When the BBC first instituted the monarchy's Christmas broadcast in 1932, they helped create a symbolically 'stable' national community through the fatherly figure of George V (Cannadine, 1983: 142). The cultural transmission of traditions through institutions, like mass communications and the education system, helps to form a dominant consensus in contemporary society. Other than dominant institutions and traditions, hegemonic modes of domination are also dependent upon formations within civil society. Formations are certain conscious movements and tendencies (like literary movements) that largely work within dominant meanings and values. Formations like the early modernist movement misrecognise themselves as oppositional while reaffirming certain dominant perceptions. Williams's posthumously published *The Politics of Modernism* (1989c), further emphasises this point. He characterises early twentieth-century modernism as politically ambiguous. The avant-garde aimed to shock and deride the bourgeoisie by trading on a robust individualism that denied all connection with others. For Williams the denial of the human need for community is typical of Rightist modes of thinking, and can be linked to certain neo-liberal strains of thought. As this example illustrates, so-called 'oppositional' tendencies are often far more complex ideological constructs than they first appear.

Raymond Williams and Material Culture:
Television and the Press

Williams's writing can be understood as a growing attempt to represent cultural practices as material. In this he displaces his earlier emphasis on the long revolution's need to maintain a transcendental literary culture oriented around 'certain absolutes or universal values' (Williams, 1962: 57). His second work on the media, which is primarily concerned with television, is perhaps the primary example of the application of cultural materialism to historical analysis. Williams's analysis works on three levels: (1) the material social relations that determine the development of television; (2) an analysis of the flow or rhythms of television content; (3) a critique of the assumptions that lie behind some of the research on television 'effects'. Of these three tiers of analysis, Williams seemingly privileges the first.

1. For Williams, the primary question is how did television come to inhabit a central part of our cultural lives? This cannot be adequately answered through a technological paradigm. For instance, one unsatisfactory response to Williams's question would be to concentrate on the scientific research that invented television. This way of viewing technology abstracts the spread of television from social needs, purposes and practices. In Williams's account the growth of mass television can be said to be *overdetermined* by the economy, the state and what he calls mobile privatism (Williams, 1974). Of the multiplicity of causes analysed by Williams the most crucial remains private capital, whose interests dominate the development of communication technology. The cultural form of television, like that of radio, had to be adapted for a market that was shaped by a home-based consumerism. In other words, television technology had to fit the needs of the 'private' conditions of reception, while being small enough to be easily transportable. The first television sets were often enclosed within pieces of furniture designed to fit comfortably into people's front rooms. This condition, which Williams often referred to as mobile privatism, was to some extent counterbalanced by the state's policy of public broadcasting. The *steering mechanisms* shaping the development of television in Britain (although the same could not be said of the USA) were both public and private. While the commercialisation of television meant that it would be consumed

in private, its public regulation provided the state with a means to promote its own legitimacy. The idea of public service broadcasting, which can be either paternal or democratic, grew out of a state-defined national culture. However, since the 1950s the most important development within broadcasting systems has been the expansion of American communications. There has been a transformation from national and state-controlled broadcasting to global and commercial forms of television. This situation has created a world market in film, television and video. Williams argues that the development of culturally emergent satellite and cable systems should be viewed dialectically. The capitalist world market in cultural production, which has eroded the dominance of the British state, will, through the dumping of cheap television, prohibit the making of local products. Alternatively, a more 'socialised' approach to new communicative systems could seek to undermine the dominance of large-scale capital and nation states, through more local forms of control. Public service broadcasting, while maintaining links to the national and the international, would thereby become progressively localised and democratised.

2. Williams addresses the 'experience' of watching television by looking at the distribution of television programmes across networks and what he calls television flow. A content analysis of commercial and public television reveals that the latter provides programmes of a more social and educative nature. But, what both types of television have in common is that programming is organised into a sequential flow in an attempt to capture an audience for an evening's entertainment. Ien Ang describes flow as 'a coming and going of programmes without their individuality leaving any specifically deep impression' (Ang, 1985: 22). This phenomenon is best captured through the experience of passively watching television rather than critically engaging with a specific programme. That television has become a medium of privatised relaxation is a missed opportunity. Instead, Williams proposes that the opening up of the channels of communication could provide a critical forum for a more robust form of public discourse.

3. Much of the audience research reviewed by Williams was based on similarly reified assumptions to that of technological determinism. This research paradigm, at the time of writing, had become dominated by the search for scientifically isolated 'effects'. Such an enterprise was bound to fail. This was due, for the most part, to the problem of separating the impact of television from the viewer's contextual location within social relations. Also, the oversimplified models of cause and effect, evident within this analysis, often assumes that the institutional organisation of television is not worth studying. While Williams thought that audience research could be further developed, these issues did not have the political importance retained by the social organisation of mass communication (Williams, 1974:123).

Williams's writing has been crucial in providing a history of the British press (Williams, 1965, 1978, 1989c). His contribution, similar to that on television, combines a historical approach with a desire to bridge both radical and liberal perspectives on the press. While Williams considers the independence of the national press from the state to be important in maintaining its critical freedom, liberal perspectives have too often ignored the controlling power of large conglomerates. The twentieth century has witnessed two major developments in the national press: the disappearance of the popular radical press and the cultural polarisation of the press. While the fate of the radical press has been discussed elsewhere (Curran and Seaton, 1985), the idea of the erosion of a mid-range press is particularly important for Williams (1987). Colin Sparks (1992b) has argued that the growing separation between the popular and quality press provides tabloid readers with an overly personalised account of institutional processes. The further cultural fragmentation of high and low-quality forms of information are connected to a growing atomism and political passivity amongst the working class (Williams, 1985). Such developments, for Williams, obviously have negative consequences for any future shared participatory democracy.

Raymond Williams and Communication Theory

In this section I want to examine Williams's arguments in more detail. I shall consider four main points: (1) the notion of base and superstructure; (2) Williams's conception of ideology and hegemony; (3) the contemporary relevance of democratic realism; and (4) the importance of Williams's literary background.

1. Marxists seeking to uphold a notion of base and superstructure are usually articulating a theoretical position closer to that of Dallas Smythe (1977) than to Enzensberger (1976b), and in this Nicholas Garnham (1986a) is no exception. The economic, in thinking about cultural production, Garnham argues, remains firmly determinant. Our first question – he agrees with Dallas Smythe – when coming to analyse the cultural industries remains the economic function they perform for capital. The media of mass communication have historically been closely bound up with the economic base's ability to create a surplus through more direct forms of production. The shape of the superstructure has been formed historically through the economic because 'it is these social relations that determine the distribution of the surplus' (Garnham, 1986a: 29). Current investment in the cultural industries can be conceptualised as the product of a rising surplus, and a search for new areas of investment. On this reading, the superstructure does not inhabit an autonomous level of development, but is concretely tied to the economic. Williams's analysis, therefore, is correct to stress the materiality of social practices, but fails to recognise the determinacy of the economic.

Terry Eagleton (1989) has objected, in opposition to Williams, that 'base and superstructure' is not an ontological thesis. To refer back to Williams's example concerning the piano player and the worker; one could readily admit that playing the piano is as real as making a piano. But 'base and superstructure' rests upon questions of determination rather than ontology. As Geras (1987) and Garnham (1986a) put it, 'base and superstructure' seeks to unravel the levels of relative autonomy enjoyed by political and cultural practices. While Eagleton is undoubtedly correct on this point, Williams's argument was also intended to illustrate that discussion centred around base and superstructure was inherently reductive. Garnham's point that Williams avoids issues of economic determinism is similarly misleading. Williams's second book on mass communication illustrates that the determinacy of the base has to be traced through historically, and that it cannot be presumed (Williams, 1974). The problem is less that Williams wished to avoid issues centred around determinacy, and more that he found some of Marxism's analytical framework wanting. On determinacy, Williams writes:

> We have to think of determination not as a single force, or a single abstraction of forces, but as a process in which real determining factors – the distribution of power or of capital, social and physical inheritance, relations of scale and size between groups – set limits and exert pressures, but neither wholly control nor wholly predict the outcome of complex activity within or at these limits, and under or against these pressures. (1974: 130)

Garnham and Dallas Smythe, while not occupying mutually exchangeable positions, remain overly committed to economistic forms of explanation. Williams's discussion of mass communication is preferable on at least two levels. First, and most importantly, he describes the evolution of television as a complex discontinuous process. For instance, the technology of television was largely shaped by military research into new forms of communication; and the idea of public service broadcasting arose only after television had been converted into a commodity to be bought and sold in the marketplace. These two examples demonstrate how the interrelation of the state and the economy proved to be determinant in the cultural production of mass television. In other historical contexts Williams argues, with reference to America, the economy was more prominent and less fettered by state regulation. If mass communication theory were to become reoriented around tracing through the dominance of the economic, it could not very well account for the different cultural mixes of public and commercial provision in capitalist economies. Secondly – a point I trace below – Williams makes connections between the levels of political economy and cultural content. Garnham and Dallas Smythe, on the other hand, persistently downplay the ideological role of materially produced symbolic forms.

2. The hegemonic culture finds a coherence around a dominant set of norms and values. The emergent structure of feeling of the modern era is the inability to communicate, the fragmentation of cultural identity and a belief in the sovereign individual (Williams, 1989c). In keeping with other analyses of modernity (B. Anderson, 1983; Frisby, 1981; Giddens, 1990; Jameson, 1991), Williams emphasises that the modernist concern with feelings of alienation, fragmentation and exile should be reconnected to institutional dimensions. That is, according to Williams, the dispersal of modern subjectivity is due primarily to the workings of the capitalist economy and the dominance of economic forms of rationality (Williams, 1985: 262). Only through a socialist economy and the institutional recognition of the principle of self-management could a more communicative society emerge. If Williams, on this and other points, remains close to some of the germane insights of Habermas (Eagleton, 1990: 409), their conceptions of ideology are similarly flawed. Williams and Habermas overestimate the cohesive power of certain cultural norms and values. Williams implies that if artistic formations can be understood through certain value constellations, like the sovereign individual, then this reflects cultural dispositions more generally. This assumption, given the diversity of critical perspectives that exist in modern society, which are informed by structural and cultural divisions, would seem highly dubious (Abercrombie *et al.*, 1980). The concept of hegemony should not be assimilated to a discourse of an ideological cement securing the 'consensual' domination of diverse social groups. Yet, if Williams overstates the cultural power of hegemony, he does manage to offer a persuasive mix of the ideological effects of fragmentation and certain cohesive norms and values. That hegemony is able to operate through the process of social atomism as well as the institution of consenual beliefs and practices is derived from both Lukacs and Gramsci. Williams's ambivalence on this question acts as a check against other Marxists who oppose one cultural resource to the other.

3. Williams's arguments here need to be reformulated in modern social contexts. The claim of democratic realism is that institutionally underwriting the local and national media's institutional separation from the economy and the state would create a more robust communicative public sphere. While remaining sympathetic to these proposals it fails to provide an adequate ethics of communication, and remains inadequately located within modern contexts of cultural fragmentation and globalisation. Here I want to relate these issues concretely to a short discussion of the Salman Rushdie dispute.

Richard Webster (1990) argues that Western culture, since 1945, has witnessed the transference of hatred from Jews to Arabs. The representational creation of a new Other group bears a close resemblance to older forms of anti-Semitic propaganda.[4] This observation, coupled with the longer history of Western 'Orientalism' (Said, 1978), provides the cultural context that any understanding of the Salman Rushdie affair should address. According to Simon Lee (1990), liberal intellectuals saw the dispute in terms of the right to free speech of the author, rather than of British Muslims. Had the media acted in accordance with Williams's theory of democratic realism, British Muslims would have enjoyed the same rights of access to the national public domain as the establishment. The actions of the British Muslims would also have been more accurately located in a structural and historical analysis of the Muslim community in Britain and the rest of the world. News journalists involved in the symbolic construction of the event could have been drawn into gaining a greater understanding of those who evidently felt threatened by the publication of Rushdie's novel. Williams's revised public sphere would also seek to develop a more informed appreciation of how the audience might interpret media information. The media circulation of the book-burning, was, within any calculation, bound to foster a sense of cultural crisis. Indeed, one of the consequences of a more plural media could have been that the book-burning might not have taken place at all! In other words, had the initial protests of British Muslims not been either ignored or stereotyped, they might have chosen to express themselves politically in a different way. This seems particularly evident when we consider that the campaign against *The Satanic Verses* predated its public burning.

While such measures could have helped produce a community of understanding, Williams's proposals remain limited. Despite the emphasis democratic realism places upon the need to contextually locate 'other' voices, he tends to view free speech in terms of rights rather than obligations. Williams noticeably avoids such a discussion in the final part of *Communications* (1962: 135–7). This is because he conceives of a more democratic media being delivered through the rights of contributors. That Williams viewed the redrawing of the public sphere in terms of rights can probably be explained with reference to his historical context. His notion of democratic realism was constructed at a time when British culture seemed to be dominated by the market and by Reithian paternalism. Neither of these models was capable of fostering what Williams perceived to be the emergent structure of feeling. To impose obligations on cultural contributors would have meant making artistic concessions to either the normalising state or the market's need to make a profit. As it stood, these were important considerations. Yet Williams's cultural analysis remains radically under-appreciative of the multicultural nature of modern society. Thus we could have had a wider plurality of perspectives on the Rushdie dispute that simply traded insults. For Habermas (1989) participation in discussion obliges us to attend to the claims of the other, and to respond rationally. Similarly, the writing of Zygmunt Bauman (1991, 1992a) urges us to reimagine ourselves in terms of the other, and to recognise the depth of our accountability. It is only, Bauman reasons, the extent to which we are prepared to accept responsibility for the other that we can avoid perpetuating a culture without ethical content (Bauman, 1992a). The general point, however, remains that free communication is unlikely to foster relations of trust and respect unless the participants are obliged to attend respectfully to contributions and perspectives from radically different forms of human life.

On a different point, the idea of the long revolution builds a strong argument in favour of more local and national forms of cultural provision. While such a strategy could provide the backdrop for new intersubjective relations it remains insufficiently appreciative of the globalised and fragmented nature of much social life. Here Williams combines what I shall call the cultural imperialist thesis and the nationalist thesis. Both of these approaches have much to recommend them, but they remain inadequate cultural accounts of late capitalism. The cultural imperialist thesis argues that as a result of the dominance of large media conglomerates a global culture is being constituted through sameness rather than difference. The culture industry, in this perspective, produces a global Americanised culture of Madonna and McDonald's (Schiller, 1970). On the other hand, the nationalist thesis claims that it is not global but national cultures that constitute modern identities. Nation states have the capacity to organise generational experience, speak of shared memories and articulate a common destiny (Smith, 1990). My contention is that Williams often seems to want to radicalise national-local cultures to mediate the effect of an American global culture. This strategy is inadequate on at least two counts. The first is that any future radical public sphere will have to operate in the context of transnational capitalism, where the means of communication are not democratically owned and controlled. Democratic theory needs to be able to address ways in which these institutions could become subject to global social controls. Williams's concern for the local and the national encourages a regressive inwardness that turns attention away from this level. A more satisfactory theory would apply the principle of democracy at levels other than the local and the national. Indeed, many of the fragmented local cultures that would find expression in a plural media could be understood in terms of a reaction against globalisation. Eric Hobsbawm (1990) argues that the eruption of ethnic violence across Europe can be viewed in these terms. For Hobsbawm the new nationalisms are primarily a defensive fundamentalist reaction against the decline of the nation state and the continual cultural flux of modernity.[5] Hence Williams's more local media could have the unintended consequence of giving voice to a depoliticised retreat from the public.

The other consequence of the hegemony of transnational cultural production is the fragmentation of communicative relations, not cultural sameness. For example, citizens may be indifferent to the issues raised by the Salman Rushdie affair, they may prefer to read about it in right-wing tabloids, they may glance over an article concerning the event on the way to the sports page, or they may feel themselves to be too tired to absorb an hour-long programme on the relevant issues. There will of course be those who do think the issues are important, but interpret them differently from the way the contributors intended. These considerations place limits on attempts such as Williams's to construct national and local forms of solidarity and community. Of course, while a sense of limits is important, this should not distract one from the critical importance of the issues Williams raises in connection with democratic communication systems.

4. Williams's analysis of mass communication is informed by his background in Leavis's literary criticism. At a general level, Williams's cultural theory remains too concerned with artistic modes of production. It is noticeable that his discussion of hegemony offers a prominent role to 'exceptional' artistic formations. On media culture this tendency is particularly marked in his discussion of television flow and content. Notably, Williams often passes judgement on a sequence of television as if he were analysing a literary text. As with Leavis, Williams seeks through close inspection to reveal the underlying values of the text. While this can be instructive, his background in Leavisite aesthetic theory entails that he treats meaning as a stable property that emerges through attentive reading. This viewpoint not only presupposes that the audience 'reads' the mediated text in a similar fashion to literary academics, but treats meaning as fixed within the text. This is not to argue that the ideological content of *Friends* and *Fraiser*, could not be judged separately from the way situated audiences make sense of it. However, Williams's discussion of flow tends to run together his own reading of the text with that of an absent generalised audience (Laing, 1991: 164).

But these criticisms can also be overdeveloped. John Fiske (1987b) has argued, in a similar vein, that behind Williams's disdain for unstructured and random television lies the desire for a unified text with a named author. Williams is unable to appreciate how the contradictory and unresolved nature of television allows for resistant readings. While Fiske undoubtedly has a point, his own reading of Williams is too partial. Williams's writing on flow is also informed by what I have termed democratic realism. The need for more strongly authored forms of communication, as should now be clear, is directly connected to the promotion of democratic forms of community. It is perhaps the dialectic between Williams's literary disposition and his socialist humanism that any critical engagement should seek to unfold. While it is true that Williams understated the discursively open nature of popular media culture, he does link a number of important perspectives on media, democracy and community in a way which is absent from more contemporary criticism. That media cultures have an as of yet under-realised democratic function remains a crucial insight linking his reflections on cultural production and content.

Raymond Williams, in distinction to much British Marxist work on mass communication, has been able to build an analysis of political economy into a concern for hegemony and fractured forms of consciousness. No one can remain unimpressed by the theoretical range of his writing on culture, politics and ideology.

These issues will now be explored in relation to the more ideological frame occupied by the Glasgow University Media Group.

The Glasgow University Media Group and Television Bias

The Glasgow University Media Group (GUMG) produced a series of seminal studies on television news **bias** during the 1970s and early 1980s (1976a, 1976b, 1982). In what became known as the *Bad News* books they aimed through empirical and semiotic analysis to expose the systematic class bias of television news coverage. At the time, these studies had a considerable impact upon mass communication research. However the group's collective contributions have suffered something of a backlash (Fiske, 1987a; Harrison, 1985). This is due to some of their more obvious theoretical failings, a general change of emphasis on questions of epistemology and the development of audience research. My approach is to suggest that while many of the criticisms of the Glasgow group have been well founded – indeed this seems to be appreciated by some of the collective's initial members (Philo, 1990) – their studies retain a kernel of reflective insight. A critical approach to the analysis of television news remains a key component of British Marxist writing on mass communications. This said, the main weaknesses of the GUMG are the assumptions they make about the audiences' interpretative understanding, the group's confusion over questions of **objectivity** and their lack of institutional analysis.

Two Case Studies:
Bad News and Good News

First, as they might say on the *News at Ten*, the bad news. The bulk of the *Bad News* books is concerned with the biased representation of industrial conflicts during the late 1970s. Through extensive videotaped evidence they argue that the news reproduces a coherent middle-class ideology. The news, therefore, is not a neutral, objective, impartial product of disinterested reporting, but relies upon certain class-related presuppositions. For the GUMG the industrial news of the first 22 weeks of 1975 can be said to be biased on at least three counts. First, the media is biased by its misrepresentation of social 'reality'. This is not to deny that television news is not socially constructed, but to argue that some representations of the world of industrial relations are more truthful than others. In this respect, the GUMG found no consistent relationship between actually recorded work stoppages and those that were reported by television news. Instead, the picture that emerges from their research is one where certain workplaces, such as the car industry, are over-represented (GUMG, 1976a: 191). The newsworthiness of industrial disputes is seemingly decided by the perceived inconvenience of the customers of goods and services, and by those industries thought to be symbolic of Britain's poor economic performance. Next, television news can be described as biased according to the extent to which it reaffirms or leaves unquestioned the central economic relations of capitalism. The media works within a dominant ideological consensus, where strikes are never justified, and are always the fault of the workers. Television news, when it comes to reporting conflicts between capital and labour, relies upon a 'restricted code' that is overwhelmingly favourable to the status quo. For example, in reporting the problems at the British Leyland car plant in 1975, very little mention was made of evidence of low investment and bad management practice (GUMG, 1982: 20). Here the Glasgow group draw on a speech made by Harold Wilson, the then Labour Prime Minister, concerning 'unnecessary stoppages' at Leyland. They claim that the text of the original speech was considerably modified by the BBC to shift the blame squarely on to the workers. This obscures the mutual appeal to management and workers evident in Wilson's initial address. The evidence presented here can be connected to a third notion of bias, which involves the exclusion of working-class voices from the media of mass communication. One of the reasons why the television media produces such a closed ideology is that its occupational culture is dominated by people from middle-class backgrounds. Television media workers are separated both materially and symbolically from the working class. Information that contradicts the dominant middle-class world view will either be excluded or exist only in fragments. These three notions of bias combine to produce a powerful ideology that distorts reality, reaffirms dominant social relations and excludes contradictory perspectives.

Now for the good news. The GUMG (1985) follow up their research into industrial conflicts with an analysis of media coverage of the British state at war and peace. While I shall concentrate on the Falklands War, it is evident that, unlike the previous research, there is a greater concern to locate the production of media content in determinate limits. The coverage of the Falklands War was over-determined by direct forms of control imposed by the Minister of Defence, the lobby system and the journalists' own judgements of public opinion. The symbolic production of good news, necessitated by the need to cement together military, state and public concern, is highlighted in the group's discussion of task force families.

Much of the coverage of the families of those soldiers involved in the Falklands War was focused on women. According to the Glasgow group, the lives of the women only became newsworthy as a result of the absence of the men who were making the news. News journalists, in this context, represented women relatives in terms of their traditional roles as carers and emotional supports for men. This not only misrepresents the real, given the decline of traditional family patterns and women's increasing engagement in the economy, but ideologically positions women as 'vessels of emotion' (GUMG, 1985: 99). The women interviewed were unlikely to be asked to reflect critically upon state policy, and were much more likely to be asked how they felt. This discursive strategy trades upon an unspoken division between a rational male public sphere and an affective feminine private realm. Further, the heavily gendered search for good news creates the notion of family and community solidarity centred around the visible private suffering of women. The ideological positioning of women can be illustrated through a BBC news story of 26 May 1983. The item concerned the protest of 40 Navy wives over the slow delivery of information from the military. This was potentially disruptive of the way the news had framed women's experience as patriotic carers. The BBC, however, concentrated upon the Navy's assurances, thereby denying the women the opportunity to voice their complaints. The lack of access to the media provided for the women is biased in the three ways mentioned above. The dominant ideology of television news represses the diversity of women within society, reproduces a familial ideology and silences dissenting voices.

The Eye of the Beholder and Objectivity in Media Studies

In this section, I will concentrate upon one of the central confusions that debates with the Glasgow group have brought to light. The bad and good news presented in the studies both rely upon notions of objectivity and impartiality, while dismissing such claims as inherently ideological. That is, for the Glasgow group, the media's representation of the car industry and the female relatives of British servicemen is objectionable because it deforms reality. Such statements obviously rest uneasily with a repudiation of objectivity. To take another example, the value of impartiality is implicitly implicated in the argument that television news systematically excludes certain critical perspectives from the public sphere. The dismissal of this value as ideological removes the theoretical grounds for critical analysis. The GUMG would have been on more secure theoretical ground had they provided an immanent critique of the media through its own expressed values of balance, impartiality and objectivity. Because of the wide gap between those expressed values and their realisation, the tendency has been to dismiss the ideals themselves as a sham. This alternative is precisely what has been shown to be disastrous by more propagandist forms of media in authoritarian societies. The argument presented here suggests, contrary to the Glasgow group, that radicalisation of the principles of balance, objectivity and impartiality is necessary for any future democratic media. The problem is not with the ideals, but with the way in which these values are upheld in media practice.

Since the pioneering work of the Glasgow group first appeared in the late 1970s it has met with an increasingly critical response. This has been partly due to mounting scepticism about the idea of objectivity in cultural studies generally. The impact of post-structuralism, hermeneutics and psychoanalysis on cultural analysis has placed the emphasis upon the instability of meaning and the interpretative horizons of the audience. Continental theory has retreated from an analysis of the text into the subjectivity of the audience. These developments have opened up certain *repressed* questions around the themes of resistance, desire and pleasure. The focus of these studies has moved from the relatively closed discourses of broadcast news into the more discursively open field of music videos, kitsch movies and soap opera. In this work the idea of bias is often quickly dismissed as being epistemologically naive or an empiricist illusion. Here certain strands of cultural theory have argued that all social reality is linguistically constructed, and that claims to truth and objectivity are allied to the discursive practices of the power bloc (Fiske and Hartley, 1978; Fiske, 1987a; Hartley, 1992). While these studies are crucial to the continued relevance of cultural and media studies, the claim being made here is that a critical theory of media communication cannot consistently bracket off truth claims. If, claims to truth are always part of the hegemonic strategy of the power bloc, this by implication reduces subordinate groups to a politics of interruption (Laclau and Mouffe, 1985). The general drift of this form of Gramscian analysis would be to support attempts to construct a counter-hegemonic strategy even if it were irrational and untruthful (Fiske, 1992). Truth is far too important to be left to dominant social groups. While all television news involves symbolic construction, certain representations of the real are more biased than others.

To focus the analysis, these issues are addressed with reference to a study on television and the 1984 miners' strike (Cumberbatch *et al.*, 1986). This research was chosen to highlight some of the political implications of the methodological drift away from content analysis into the subjectivity of the audience. The Broadcasting Research Unit report is based upon every BBC *Nine O'clock News* and ITV *News at Ten* for the twelve months from 2 March 1984 to 5 March 1985. Cumberbatch and his colleagues argue that one of the problems with measuring bias is gaining access to a reliable account of the real that is independent of the media of mass communication. If we are faced with competing accounts of reality, as is the case with perceptions of the miners' strike, then surely, they reason, it is difficult to judge questions of bias. On this point the research team come close to the writing of Fiske and Hartley. Truth is most definitely in the eye of the beholder. In the study – the audience research reveals, not surprisingly, that those viewers who supported the miners' struggle were more likely to think that television news was biased against the strike, than those who did not. This reveals something about the way the audience reads television news. People, according to this view, when watching television news tend to assimilate new information into a pre-existing perceptual framework. It is not so much television content that interpellates the subject (Althusser, 1984), but the subject that projects meanings on to the text.[6] That this remains as inadequate as an account of the interpretative processes involved in watching television cannot be explored here. What is more our concern is the conclusion of the report, which delivers the media a fairly clean bill of health. The main finding was that the general public were largely satisfied with the 'unbiased' nature of news reporting. The one area of critique developed by the study, perceived by a wide cross-section of the audience, concerned the media's over-concentration on picket line violence. Television news' tendency to highlight the conduct of the strike rather than its causes, however, is comprehensible once one considers the event-focused nature of the news. In a nutshell, the audience-centredness of the research's content analysis neither addresses the ideological context of the miners' strike nor adequately attends to the content of television news production. As there can never be a 'value free' account of television content, the perception of bias, the researchers argue, has to involve, at some level, the interpretations of the audience.

Cumberbatch's retreat into the audience makes it impossible to make objective truth claims about television content. Following Colin Sparks (1987), I would argue that whether audiences perceive bias is a different order of analysis to whether bias exists. Judith Lichtenberg (1991) argues concurrently with this thesis that journalists cannot surrender a notion of objectivity. To doubt that there is an objective truth is to doubt we can ever get at what 'really happened' independently of our perspective. This seems to be exactly what Cumberbatch and his colleagues are seeking to argue. If this were so one could not coherently object if the media changed the sequence of events to dovetail more neatly with their perception of reality. For example, it is often claimed that the BBC misrepresented the events at the Orgreave colliery during the 1984 strike to code the miners rather than the police as violent. It is difficult to see how audience research could help to validate such a claim. The audience's knowledge of the event, unless they had alternative sources of information, would be the negotiated product of their horizons and the text produced by the BBC. Truth claims concerning media representations only make sense if they appeal to a more objective version of reality. In the case of the miners at the Orgreave colliery, the audience's distance from the 'real events' of the miners' strike means that they are hardly in a position to judge the BBC's ordering of the sequence of events. Again, to claim that their perspective, materially isolated from the conditions of cultural production, is as informed as any other obscures the question at hand. The BBC either changed the order of events or it did not. Further, if the Glasgow group are to argue, as they attempted to do above, that the media distort reality these claims are inevitably tied to a notion of objectivity. Even if it is recognised that claims to balance, impartiality and objectivity are shaped linguistically, this does not necessarily mean that they are not values worth defending. If the media gave up on these principles it would leave journalists and citizens alike with very little to appeal to in open democratic information exchange. To accept that truth is subjective, one could easily imagine how such a discussion could, to borrow Fiske's and Hartley's phrase, work in the interests of the power bloc. The argument that last night's documentary on the new social security legislation was too partial for excluding its impact on the poor could be easily dismissed. If the values of impartiality are conceived of as subjective rather than intersubjective the programme maker could retort that that is not how he sees the world. This would automatically circumvent any possibility of democratic dialogue and discussion on the public issues raised by the film. But if truth claims are seen as communicatively held intersubjective values that refer to states in the real world, this would allow for an open discussion of the issues at hand.

The debate between Harrison (1985) and members of the Glasgow group makes it difficult to judge the accuracy of the initial claims of bias. This is especially true since it has become apparent that Harrison's critique has been built upon very different source material (Philo, 1987). It seems unlikely that the GUMG's claims can be dismissed, as Harrison (1985: 59) suggests, by pointing to their self-confessed Marxist stance. If this was the case, one could never claim that television content was biased as the researcher's own prejudices would always be intimately involved in such a judgement. There is no necessary contradiction in making objective claims to truth while recognising one's own historicity. Castoriadis makes a similar point:

> The intellectual should want to be a citizen like the others; s/he also wants to be spokesperson, *de jure*, for universality and objectivity. S/he can abide in this space only by recognising the *limits* of that which his/her supposed objectivity permits of him/her; s/he should recognise, and not just through lip service, that what s/he is trying to get people to listen to is still a *doxa*, an opinion, not an *episteme*, a science. (1991:12)

Unless one is able to make truth claims in an intersubjectively defined public space, it is difficult to see how a shared public discussion could be instigated. This is a primary norm of democratic citizenship. Raymond Williams (1989b), in a critical review of a selection of writings by the Glasgow group, points out that so-called democratic institutions have failed to discursively engage with their findings. In this respect, the research of the Glasgow group can only be considered acceptable to the extent that they could gain the free rational assent of all, given certain conversational obligations. While there remains much to fault in the writing of the Glasgow group, not least their confusion on issues related to objectivity, a more democratic culture would have ensured that their findings received the public discussion they deserved.

Ideology and the Glasgow University Media Group

The concept of ideology is the issue that overwhelms the Glasgow group's writing on the mass media. They considerably overstate the cohesive power of ideology, while inadequately contextualising its production in media institutions. This is perhaps an inherent danger of content analysis. Semiotic and empirical investigation into media content – as we saw above – remains a crucial level of analysis. But any close reading of the ideologically coded nature of the text has the consequence of severing it from the material conditions of its production and reception. While this is a legitimate move, practitioners should be aware of the limits this places on their reading. Consequently the Glasgow Marxists are unable to explain how the media could be radically reformed and ignore the everyday creative labour of reading television. Let us unpack a few of these features.

The institutional location of the television media never fully occupies the intellectual foreground. The evidence of television bias, on this reading, is attributed to the dominance of media workers who were originally from middle-class back-grounds. In their writing on media reform, despite some evidence to the contrary, there is a close association between the ideological assumptions of journalists and the biased nature of television content. A more representative form of television could be promoted by including a wider cross-section of the population in media industries. The main problems of broadcasting are inaccuracy and a lack of pluralism (GUMG, 1982:153). The serious omission here is a lack of rigour in the analysis. The examination of the 'fit' between the reproduction of a professional ideology and an institutional context is seemingly ignored. Philip Schlesinger's (1978) classic investigation of the occupational culture of the BBC is interesting in this respect. Here it is the institutional anchorage of the BBC in the status quo, rather than the class background of the journalist, that is the determinant in television news production. The system of public broadcasting, according to Schlesinger, is reliant upon the norms of impartiality and objectivity in order to maintain an occupational distance from the state. Under current organisational procedures the simple inclusion of a more diverse strand of journalists would probably do little to alter the ideological content of the news. Indeed, a switch to a more adversarial style of journalism, which sought to broaden the appreciation of the plural perspectives existent in public space, would probably induce a sharp backlash from the state. Thus the national news media is biased not so much towards the status quo as towards the existent norms of parliamentary democracy. A more plural media should seek to adopt a more diverse range of journalists –

what Anne Phillips (1991: 63) calls the mirror principle – that more accurately reflects the social composition of society. But any reformulation of actual television content would need to address the structuration of television media more forcibly.

A related problem is the Glasgow group's lack of complexity in respect of the professional culture of newsmen and newswomen. To put the point crudely, for the Glasgow group, the middle-class world view ensnared in journalistic practice ensures the ideological reproduction of asymmetrical relations of power. This argument slides together a number of different analytical levels that ought to have been kept separate. First, it considerably overstates the importance of the social background of most journalists. Of greater explanatory weight are the relations of force that exist within the institution itself and its determinant relations with the steering mechanisms of money and power. Next, through the assumption that middle-class perspectives inform media culture, they fail to address the specificity of professional practice. Returning, for a moment, to Schlesinger (1978:166), the disposition of the BBC is best described as 'democratic pluralism'. The culture of public service broadcasting presumes that there are no predominant interest groups within society, enabling the BBC to provide a just balance for those who wish to carry on the conversation. This particular stance means that those who talk in terms of conflict and power are often represented as 'other'. In addition, what Schlesinger calls the 'stop watch culture' examines some of the assumptions that shape conceptions of newsworthiness. The workplace practices of news journalists value the immediacy, speed and accuracy of reporting. The event-driven nature of the news desk, rather than the coherence of certain ideological perspectives, plays a part in shaping the social composition of the news. The fact that the Glasgow group's analysis maintains a certain distance from the life-world of professional journalism oversimplifies the analysis. Finally, not only do the Glasgow group theoretically run together class presuppositions and workplace culture, but they overstate the extent to which social classes internally manufacture stable perspectives about the world. A recent point of debate in cultural theory has been the connection between social class and certain cultural beliefs (Eagleton, 1990; Hall, 1988a; Laclau and Mouffe, 1985). While there is no consensus on these issues, there is a general acceptance of Poulantzas's earlier comments on the relationship between class and culture. For Poulantzas certain ideological perspectives do not act 'as if they were political number-plates worn by social classes on their backs' (Poulantzas, 1975: 202). Ideological strategies, in this view, are only constructed in the actual process of struggle and have no *necessary* class belonging. While a number of theoretical issues are being avoided here, the Glasgow group fail to engage with the limited degree of ideological closure social classes are able to deliver. The fact that the Glasgow group explain the ideological dominance of the status quo as a result of the structural power of the middle class does not attend to ideological divisions and conflicts evident within elite groupings. For example,

Thatcherism's intellectual dominance amongst the middle classes during the 1980s did not prevent divisions between old-style 'one nation' Toryism and neo-liberalism. This is not to argue, as have some of the Post-Marxists (Laclau, 1977), that there is no relation between ideological formations and social class. However, the Glasgow group would have sharpened their analysis had they attended to the historical contingency of this relationship.

The neat alliance the Glasgow group forge between media institutions and the production of a dominant ideology does not account for television's 'contra-dictory imperatives' (Kellner, 1981: 36). Public service television is often caught between legitimising the discourse of the state and providing the institutional context for the free flow of information. Similarly, as Kellner points out, privately owned American television is caught between being run for profit and having to provide a public forum for debate. The conflictual determinant relations of television bears a relationship to television content. The Glasgow group omit to mention how the conceptions of balance and impartiality might act against the interests of the dominant bloc. The very fact that opposition leaders, trade unionists, men and women on picket lines and shop stewards are interviewed at all may allow the audience to construct alternative perspectives. In addition, television's focus on areas of social conflict may serve to give voice to certain oppositional perspectives that would otherwise have been denied wider public recognition. As other studies have shown, subjects that are viewed as threatening to parliamentary democracy such as terrorism, strikes and the peace movement, are often dealt with differently in drama and documentary contexts (Elliott et al., 1983; Williams, 1989a). This is of course not to argue that television promotes radical forms of transformation. On the other hand, the symbolic material offered by television is not so ideologically structured that it does not offer space for critical evaluation (Hall, 1980).

The main weaknesses of the Glasgow group lie in their lack of institutional analysis, confusion over themes such as objectivity, and the more often repeated criticism of their failure to engage with the processes of interpretation undertaken by the audience. Against the grain of current thinking in media studies, I have suggested that institutional forms of analysis and notions of media bias remain crucial to any genuinely critical theory of mass communication. That the Glasgow group attempted, if unsuccessfully, to link an ideology critique of television to an argument for a more plural medium is reason enough to continue to take them seriously.

Stuart Hall, Mass Communications and Hegemony

Stuart Hall is best known as a founder member of the Birmingham Centre for Cultural Studies and for his writing on Thatcherism (Harris, 1992; Turner, 1991).

Like Williams, despite belonging to a younger generation, Hall was a prominent figure in the re-emergence of the British Left in the 1960s and 1970s. His theoretical writing is closely bound up with the themes of culture, ideology and identity. While he offers a sophisticated reinterpretation of some of the central thinkers within post-structuralism, his main intellectual touchstone remains Gramsci. In mass communication research, Hall's specific contribution has been to link ideologically coded cultural forms to the decoding strategies of the audience. He has carried this through while simultaneously attending to the shifting political context of media signs and messages. For Hall the ideologically coded text remains the primary level of determination. This said, his more recent writing has displayed an increasing awareness of the discursive openness of the popular codes. Compared to the Glasgow group, Hall represents a more sophisticated level of analysis, despite their common focus on the theme of ideology. However, given that the central idea of this book is the development of a critical theory of mass communication, Hall's contribution is not without its shortcomings. His over-concentration on the theme of ideology means that other determinant levels, such as the ownership and control of the mass media, drop out of the analysis. While Williams forges a fruitful dialectic between communicative structures and democratic theory, Hall has neglected this particular dialectic.

Policing the Crisis:
The Press, Moral Panics and the Rise of the New Right

Policing the Crisis (Hall *et al.*, 1978) remains the most impressive theoretical text produced by the early founders of the Birmingham Centre for Cultural Studies. The work encompasses a complex hermeneutic that ambitiously seeks to link a press-led moral panic around mugging, the breakdown of postwar consensus politics and the growth of an authoritarian state. Hall and his colleagues discover through an empirical analysis that the press significantly over-reacted to the perceived threat of violent crime in the early 1970s. The mugging label had been imported from the United States and used by the prevailing control culture as a means of undermining the consensus politics of social democracy. Before the mugger panic had appeared in the press there had been an intensification of police mobilisation against deviant blacks. The result of this strategy was the appearance of black offenders in court which, in turn, provided the setting for the spiralling of press attention. At this point Hall, and his Birmingham-based colleagues, make the crucial distinction between primary and secondary definers. Primary definers are structurally dominant groups like the police who are able to cue in the media to a particular event. The media act as secondary definers of an event, selecting and interpreting the information received from primary definers. The definitions of the police in the resulting moral panic are given extra ideological weight in that they are able to establish a high degree of cultural closure. This would not be the case in, say, media reporting of industrial relations where the primary definers would include trade unions as well as employers. As Hall points out, by 'virtue of being criminals, they have forfeited the right to take part in the negotiation of the consensus about crime' (Hall *et al.*, 1978: 69). His remarks decentre the importance assumed by the GUMG of a middle-class journalistic culture. This argument can be added to the one I developed earlier concerning the complex historically shifting levels of analysis that should be respected by a sociology of journalism. With this in mind, and building upon Hall's contribution, Schlesinger (1990) argues that mass media research needs to develop an internalist and an externalist account of journalistic processes. That is, while *Policing the Crisis* bends the analysis too far in the direction of outside definers, a complex investigation into news gathering should aim to capture the strategies of negotiation between journalists and their sources, as well as the more frequently stated internal institutional perspectives.

The main thesis behind *Policing the Crisis* provides the political context for Hall's subsequent writing on Thatcherism in the 1980s. The widespread moral panic engendered by the press is set against a backdrop of economic and super-structural crisis. The postwar period had experienced the progressive breakdown of traditionalist ideologies through the spread of affluent lifestyles, privatised leisure and permissiveness amongst the young. The role of young people in the breakdown of a previously assumed cohesive society had already been explored by Hall (Hall and Jefferson, 1976). The displacement of older, more regulated forms of life created a considerable amount of social anxiety, so the culturally destabilising effect of the consumer boom led to a displaced reaction on to black and Asian peoples. This cultural rupture coupled with Britain's longer-term economic decline contributed to a crisis in hegemony and the search for authoritarian solutions. The loosening of traditional bonds and the need for new forms of moral and intellectual leadership were most acutely articulated by the political Right. In this strategy, politically carried through during the 1980s, the identity of the British people would be hegemonically redefined. It is with this in mind that I now turn to Hall's more substantive contributions on the media, ideology and Thatcherism.

Ideology:
The Return of the Repressed?

Hall (1982) characterises American media analysis of the 1940s and the 1950s as belonging to the 'effects' school. The aim of this research was to establish the measurable impact of the media of mass communication on human behaviour, and its conclusion was that the media is often relatively harmless, reinforcing the norms and values held by a pluralist society. The rediscovery of ideology in media studies, however, has reintroduced a notion of power and more critically addressed the construction of the real. The most important intellectual and theoretical resource in the turn to ideology is structuralism. Of particular importance here is the work of Louis Althusser, whose writing on ideology profoundly shaped the dominant form of cultural studies, although it did meet with spirited resistance in some quarters (Thompson, 1978). Althusser's influence can be traced across a wide range of cultural and political studies, including literature, film, psychoanalysis and political theory (Elliott, 1987). His critical concern is to investigate the means by which capitalist society reproduces dominant institutional relationships. The production and reproduction of ideology provides the key to this question. In his famous essay on the subject, Althusser (1984) makes the distinction between Ideological State Apparatuses (ISAs) and Repressive State Apparatuses (RSAs). Both RSAs and ISAs are social practices that have an ideological function. They are distinguishable in that RSAs (military, police) operate mainly through force, whereas the ISAs (media, education) ensure the ideological dominance of the ruling class. The production of ideology, in Althusser's formulation, has perhaps two distinctive characteristics. First, while ideology was tied to an institutional analysis, it could not be conceived of as the inversion or reflection of the real. Rather ideology, in Althusser's memorable words, represents 'the imaginary relationship of individuals to their real conditions of existence' (1984: 36). Secondly, ideology not only constitutes our symbolic relation with the real, but converts human beings into subjects. Ideology lets individuals mistakenly recognise themselves as self-determining agents, whereas in fact subjects are formed through linguistic and psychic processes. The subject *misrecognises* herself as a unique individual, rather than as an identity constructed through the social. Althusser's emphasis upon the formation of the self through ideological discourses had a formative impact on Hall.[7] For Hall, structuralism opens up two main fields of research for mass communication: (1) an analysis of dominant discourses that exclude other alternative explanations; and (2) an analysis of how the media institutions themselves serve to offer only a limited range of meanings. Let us take each of these levels of analysis in turn.

1. Hall (1977) argues that the mass media form the main ideological institution of contemporary capitalism. This can be asserted as the communication system provides the main symbolic realm through which the manufacture of the dominant consensus is forged. The media of mass communication, according to Hall, operate through the production of hegemonic codes that cement the social together. Further, the codes that represent the real are gathered from a limited field of dominant discourses drawing on a restricted range of social explanations. The preferred codes achieve their ideological effect by appearing to be natural. Following Althusser, as

language does not mirror the real one can talk of the reality effect of ideology. The experience of unmediated reality is symbolically constructed through language. Just as the subject deceives herself about the source of her identity, so the media appear to reflect reality while actually constructing it. I might think that the pictures on tonight's news of President Bush waving outside the White House simply convey reality. What I don't immediately recognise is that this is probably a well orchestrated publicity stunt designed to boost the legitimacy of the state. President Bush waving outside the White House could be a vain attempt to convey a sense of business as usual, while the nation plummets into crisis. Hall calls this the 'naturalistic illusion' (Hall, 1982: 76).

Hall's (1988b) later writing becomes increasingly aware of the charges of functionalism that have been levelled at Althusser. In Althusser's original thesis, as we saw, the ISAs transmit ideological forms of misrecognition of the real relations of domination. In this way, Althusser argues, ideology binds individuals to the social structure. Hence the mystifying effects of ideology ensure the reproduction of class society. For Hall, Althusser's emphasis on ideology as materialised in concrete practices and rituals remains a definite advance. His own analysis of Thatcherism is an investigation of the various discursive strategies employed by the popular press, television interviews and right-wing think-tanks. However, Hall's political writing on Thatcherism, while developing some of the arguments presented in *Policing the Crisis*, also seeks to redress some of the theoretical difficulties encountered by Althusser.

The New Right emerged through the breakdown of the postwar compromise between capital and labour (Hall, 1983). This was not so much a mechanical response to an economic crisis as what Gramsci describes as an 'organic crisis' – the emergence of new social forces and configurations that led to a restructuring of ideological discourses. The intensification of state control over **civil society** was coupled with an ideological manoeuvre designed to win popular consent. Hall (1988b) describes this strategy as 'authoritarian populism'. According to Hall, as there can be no general theory of the capitalist state, the theorist should seek to identify how a specifically national crisis is symbolically worked through. Thatcherism was successful because it was able to articulate the fears and anxieties of the respectable classes into a rightist consensus. This enabled the Right to speak up for 'ordinary members of the public' who were fearful of rising crime, delinquency and moral permissiveness, while the social democratic Left appeared to defend the status quo.

The argument that the structural dominance of the ruling class ensures the dominance of certain ideas is rejected by Hall. Thatcherism's genius lay in its ability to recognise that the ideological terrain was constituted through a battle over 'common sense'. One of the central lessons of structuralism can be applied here. Meaning does not depend upon how things are but more on how they are signified, so similar events can be signified in different ways. Thus the meaning of an event becomes a semiotic struggle for the mastery of discourse. In Western capitalist societies important intersubjectively held signs include 'democracy', 'freedom' and 'individualism'. These signs can be articulated by different political discourses as they have no necessary 'belongingness' to either the Right or the Left. For instance, as 'democracy' has no transhistorical meaning, its significance comes from its position within a discursive formation (Hall, 1986). Thus the mass media are best characterised as a force field in a constant state of flux. The task of political movements is to attend to the ways in which key words like democracy are currently being hegemonically defined, and to invest them with new meanings, shifting the grounds of the consensus. However, Hall recognises that to 'democracy' can be attributed a certain fixity, given its clear association with relatively durable historical meanings. This is an important qualification, in light of Laclau's and Mouffe's (1985; Laclau, 1977) more radical suggestions. Laclau and Mouffe have argued, along with Margaret Thatcher, that indeed 'there is no such thing as society'. By this they mean that the social has no underlying cause, such as an economic base, that constitutes a field of differences. Instead, they argue, hegemony is *suturing*, in that dominant discourses attempt to provide modern identities with the coherence they fundamentally lack.[8] The problem here is that Laclau and Mouffe's emphasis on the radical instability of meaning is unable to account for more durable forms of ideological closure. Hall argues, in opposition to this thesis, that while there may be no necessary correspondence between, say, democracy and parliament, historically certain connections have been forged. In Hall's terms the signifier and the signified are linked through relatively durable cultural conventions.

The focus of Hall's investigation of Thatcherism is to examine how a plurality of discourses became stitched together into a coherent web of meaning. Thatcherism was able to articulate a number of ideological threads into a coherent popular discourse. The traditional Left's belief that this was merely a case of old wine in new bottles meant they were not able to respond politically as effectively as they might.

As I indicated, Hall's analysis of Thatcherism represents a break with Althusser in three main ways. First, Althusser attributes an ideological function to certain state apparatuses (ISAs) whereas Hall reveals Thatcherism's capacity to occupy civil society. Throughout the 1980s the privately owned and controlled tabloid press was dominated by an agenda largely set by the New Right. In this way, Thatcherism was able to occupy the ideological terrain outside the domain of the state. Next, Hall argues, along with other critics of Althusser (G. Elliott, 1987; A. Elliott, 1992), that he provides an overly integrated account of the production and reception of ideology. Hall's emphasis upon the contingent and shifting nature of ideological strategies is better able to account for economic and political struggle than Althusser's own. Finally, and most crucially, Thatcherism's ability to articulate new subject positions is not adequately appreciated by the Althusserian frame. For Althusser, largely following the writing of Lacan (Fraser, 1992), the subject's entry into language requires submission to the symbolic order. The problem with Lacan and Althusser, despite their differences (Elliott, 1992), is that they do not help us to understand how already interpellated subjects can become repositioned through new discursive strategies. If as Lacan suggests, the law of culture is, by definition, the law of the father it is difficult to see how women could challenge patriarchy (Hall, 1980: 162). In more Althusserian terms, modern subjectivity is never simply the ideological effect of state apparatuses – as Althusser rather than Lacan argues – but, as Hall has made us aware, it is the result of the fracturing effects of repression and a plurality of social discourses. Althusser seemingly wants to make an over-tight theoretical fit between the reproduction of the social order and social identity. In Hall's (1991) more recent writing he has established a view of identity as always in formation, while being dependent on ideological and psychic processes of splitting and identification. This involves the recognition that the modern self is composed of a multiplicity of identities, not just one. Thatcherism skilfully articulated itself as a political strategy by appealing to a diverse range of subjects. In this way, Thatcherism, in Hall's analysis, is able to compress the divergent and culturally complex identities into a powerful hegemonic formation. In essence, the reason that Thatcherism was able to dominate politics during the 1980s was that this cultural construction was able to provide a focus for a diversity of group identities.

2. In contrast to the attention he grants to mediated messages, Hall has comparatively little to say about institutions of mass communication. In his complex consideration of Thatcherism he offers only the most limited discussion of the structurating impact of the state and capital. In fact Hall often goes so far as to suggest that what is far more significant than this relation is the limited framework of interpretations within which journalists operate (Hall, 1972a: 10). However, as we saw in relation to *Policing the Crisis*, Hall was to correct this internalist account with a structural emphasis upon journalistic sources. What is apparent is that the intersection of the cultural context of journalism and the semiotic content of media messages remains determinant for Hall (1972a, 1975; Hall *et al.* 1978). Despite Hall's more complex theory of ideological production, he shares the critical problems of the GUMG in failing to trace back cultural production to institutional levels of analysis. This aside, Hall's level of expertise is in the interpretation of media messages, which eventually leads him to open up questions of audience response neglected by Williams and the Glasgow group.

Encoding and Decoding Media Discourse

In reconceptualising the determinant role played by media messages, Hall draws from Saussure's (1974) writing on the arbitrary nature of the linguistic sign. According to this standpoint, language is a system of signs. Signs are made up of signifiers (marks on paper or sounds in the air) and a signified – the mental concept referred to. Hence the word 'newspaper' when spoken has a certain sound (signifier) and actually refers to something purchased daily, made out of paper, containing photographs and black print (signified). For Saussure the relationship between the signifier and the signified is arbitrary. By this he means that there is no necessary tie, other than convention, between the word 'newspaper' and the object signified. One of the consequences of this proposition is that meaning is an unstable property, dependent upon its articulation in discursive formations.

Roland Barthes (1973), building on the insights of Saussurean linguistics, argues that there are two levels of signification. The first level – which Barthes calls denotation – refers to the commonsense level of meaning. For instance let us take the Glasgow group's analysis of the media representation of workers' strikes in the 1970s: this would involve a description of who the media interviewed, what was said and by whom. The second characteristic of mediated messages is that of connotation. By this Barthes means the implied wider meanings that are dependent on certain cultural associations. Again, to refer to the example of striking workers, the Glasgow group make much of the significance of certain terms such as 'threat' and 'demand' when associated with labour. Their argument is that these terms, within a shared cultural framework, ideologically position workers as irrational and destructive (GUMG, 1976b) The reference of the sign, therefore, is determined by different cultural codes, with connotations adding meanings to the denoted subject. Hall (1972b) takes this further by arguing that discourses have dominant meanings that structure the meaning of the message. An ideological meaning is dependent on the fact that there is not an infinite number of readings suggested by the text. In concentrating on the ideology of the text, Hall is privileging the message in the construction of subjectivity.

Later, Hall (1973, 1980) retreats from this position to allow for resistant readings of media messages and a greater emphasis upon the polysemic nature of meaning. In the production of media messages Hall makes a basic distinction between encoders and decoders. He identifies a radical break between the frameworks of knowledge, relations of production and technical infrastructure that facilitate the encoding and decoding of meaning structures. The encoding of a media text is dependent upon certain professional norms and procedures, institutional relations and technical equipment (television cameras, videotapes, microphones, tape recorders, etc.). Once the message has been symbolically encoded it is open to the reading strategies employed by the audience. The reception of the audience is dependent upon cultural and political dispositions, their relationship to wider frameworks of power and access to mass-produced technology (radio, television, video recorder, compact disc player, etc.). There are three main ways in which a symbolically coded text can be read. A *dominant hegemonic* reading interprets the text in terms of the preferred meaning suggested by the message. If tonight's television news argues that all university lecturers should be prepared to take a pay cut and I am persuaded by this, this could be said to be a hegemonic reading. Here there is a meaningful correspondence between the practice of encoding and decoding, which is less pronounced in Hall's other two types of reading. Next, the meaning of a media text, according to Hall, could also be the result of a *negotiated code*. Here the meaning produced by the interface between the interpreter and the encoded message is subtly contested. Accepting the overall framework suggested by the dominant code the viewer/listener makes contradictory sense of the message. Here I would largely agree that certain senior members of the university should be prepared to accept a salary reduction, but believe that this should not apply to those employed on either temporary or part-time contracts. An *oppositional* reading of the same news programme could perhaps offer the interpretation that such a state-driven strategy was a means of attacking the very principles of higher education. An oppositional understanding would run against the grain of the text, making few concessions to the perspective being offered. These three forms of interpretation are offered as a means of locating texts within dominant discursive strategies, while linking them to an already coded audience.

The Over-inflation of Discourse and Other Related Critiques

We have seen that for Stuart Hall the media of mass communications is primarily constituted through discursive articulations. These strategies have to be conceptually linked to wider formations of power and hegemonic associations that articulate new and contradictory subject positions. Yet Hall's contribution to mass communication theory remains limited due to his preoccupation with discourse. Hall both overstates the incorporating power of ideological strategies and neglects to offer a substantive political economy of mass communication. In this section I shall analyse Hall's neglect of the wider structuring relations offered by the state and economy; assess the absence of a theory of democratic media production in his output; discuss his contribution towards a theory of ideology and hegemony; and debate his arguments concerning the reception of media discourse.

1. An investigation into modern media culture, Hall argues, should concentrate on the fit between the discursive construction of the message and the interpretative understanding of the audience. While Hall is correct to emphasise the importance

of this relationship, the level of determinacy, I think, lies elsewhere. Although Hall articulates a three-tiered model of mass communication, what is missing is any detailed appreciation of how the economy and the state shape cultural production. Hall's later writing tends to neglect how 'real' social relations inform the construction of media messages as well as contexts of reception. Hall's writing on institutional practices often highlights the relative importance of 'primary definers' or the media industry's occupational culture. According to Golding and Murdock (1979), Hall treats the mass media as an autonomous ideological apparatus. This is particularly evident when one considers that Hall largely ignores the growing economic interpenetration of different media sectors and the internationalisation of media conglomerates. The distribution of economic resources, argue Golding and Murdock, has a determining impact on the 'ideological' diversity of the newspaper industry. The reason that Britain has historically been dominated by a largely conservative press is the high cost of entry into the national and international market, and the lack of advertising revenue alternative publications would be able to attract (Golding and Murdock, 1979). To put this differently, the radical break between the real and the symbolic is overstated by Hall, despite some of the qualifications he makes. It is because of Hall's stress upon the arbitrary nature of the sign that he is unable to account for the more durable institutional relations that inform social discourses. Hall – if this analysis is correct – inherits the failures of much structuralist and post-structuralist thought in that he does not develop an adequate theory of reference. According to Giddens, instead of retreating into the code, social theory should seek: 'to understand the relational character of significance in the context of social practices' (Giddens, 1987b: 86). To follow the example given above, there is a definite link between *real* transnational economic relations and the *discursive* construction of media content. There is also strong evidence of a relationship between patterns of ownership and organisation, press content and the domination of right-wing political parties (Golding, 1993). What is offered by Hall is a radical critique of the idea that the structures of ownership determine media content in any straightforward manner. Yet, for all its undoubted insight, Hall's attention to discourse severs the determinate relation between material structures and symbolic forms.

To offer a current example: the Tory press has recently deserted its traditional ideological home in the Conservative party. Hall's semiotic concerns could un-doubtedly provide an interesting framework for looking at the way the hegemonic content of the press has shifted following the decline of Thatcherism. But Hall is so keen to distance himself from economic determinism that he neglects to investigate the continuing relationship between institutional formations and press content. It remains the case, that the predominantly white, male, national press retains certain perspectives that would be difficult to explain outside of an appreciation of institutional features. For instance, it is noticeable that despite the shift in public opinion Rupert Murdoch's stable of newspapers seems reluctant to embrace any national political party, except with extreme ambivalence. Even if they do so, this relationship will be contingent on their not obstructing the operation of his multi-media business empire.

2. A second and related shortcoming of Hall's account is that his pre-occupation with semiotics prevents him from opening up an analysis of how the media could be democratised. Returning to the writing of Raymond Williams, the first level such a critique would need to address is the structuration of the mass media by the economy and the state. If public service broadcasting, as Hall argues, is merely an ideological state apparatus, no good reason can be offered for its retention and reform. Here Hall follows Barthes and Althusser by arguing that the principles of neutrality and objectivity are related to the dominant ideology of the bourgeoisie. While such principles could have an ideological effect, they invite immanent forms of critique, rather than outright rejection. The democratic reformulation of the media of mass communication would be dependent on the transformation of global structural relations and the deeper embedding of demo-cratic principles. In fact, as the previous discussion of Williams sought to emphasise, the defence and revitalisation of public systems of communication has a renewed political priority given its current erosion by commercial forms of broadcasting. Hall's overtly ideological/semiotic frame of reference adds little to the issues of cultural rights, needs and obligations that ought to be imposed upon the functioning of public and private systems. If certain normative definitions of the public are to be preserved against the market's need to satisfy advertisers, then issues related to communication and citizenship take on an increased relevance.

3. Hall's discussion of ideology and hegemony has alerted us to the impor-tance of linguistic meaning and discursive formations. Thatcherism was able symbolically to reconstruct the common sense of British politics during the 1980s around an emergent hegemonic alliance. This particular interpretation, while popular during the 1980s, has also attracted its share of critics.[9] The most prominent of these remains the so-called 'two nations' thesis (Jessop *et al.*, 1984). The argument presented by Jessop and his colleagues is that Hall considerably overestimated Thatcherism's capacity to articulate new identities. Despite some of the claims made by Hall, Thatcherism did not manage to build an imaginary consensus around its political agenda. More significant than the ideological appeals of Thatcherism were the divisions within the political opposition and economic changes in the labour market. Thatcherism, according to this view, progressively abandoned the attempt to integrate the poor into universal forms of citizenship, while pragmatically appealing to those in full-time work through tax cuts and privatised services. The dominance of the New Right during the 1980s is best explained economically and politically, rather than ideologically. In short, Hall's attention to the discursive patterns of Thatcherism seems to blind him to other

levels of analysis. While providing a skilful reading of the internal markings of New Right discourse, he provides too cultural an account of hegemony and fails to consider that Thatcherism could have attracted divergent readings from different structural positions. Yet again Hall can be accused of inflating the discursive into what Perry Anderson has called the 'megalomania of the signifier' (Anderson, 1983: 45). But more to the point, and I think this is the main one, Hall overplays the hegemonic 'effectivity' of Thatcherism. That Hall severs Thatcherism from its contexts of reception, as well as economic levels of analysis, points to certain inherent limitations of semiotics.

4. The constructive side of the work of Stuart Hall lies in the tension between codes as systematically organised levels of discourse and the multi-accentuality of meaning. Ideological strategies, as Hall well understood, could only be considered effective if they made meaning stick. To argue that all meanings are as open-ended as each other would be to sever the link with questions of determination and power. Although Hall views Thatcherism as an open text, he provides a strong argument against viewing meaning in terms of 'private, individual, variant readings' (Hall, 1980: 135). For Hall the encoded text can be said to prefer certain readings within certain limits and parameters. This remains an important insight. To refer back to the Cumberbatch (1986) study, instead of understanding how meaning is projected on to television news, the researchers could have captured the way the audience constructed meaning as a form of negotiation. In Hall's terms such a study would seek to reveal the dominant discursive patterns of the miners' strike, and investigate how these messages were decoded by situated spectators. As Hall suggests, a theory of mass communication should attend to the interpretative relationship between the audience and cultural forms without collapsing either pole into a handful of dust.

However, there remain problems with these suggestions. The most important is that Hall theoretically runs together dominant meanings with what I take to be a critical conception of ideology. If ideology is taken to mean the symbolic means by which relations of dominance are either reaffirmed or left unquestioned, then it is perfectly possible for the audience to resist the dominant meanings offered by a radio show and reaffirm certain relations of power. This is easily demonstrated. I might be listening to a feminist drama in which one of the main characters declares her love for another woman to her husband. If irritation at this remark caused me to switch to another station, one could plausibly argue that my actions reaffirm the dominance of certain heterosexual practices. Such an act could hardly be described as resistant, given the current inequality between different domains of sexual activity. Hall unfortunately leaves such questions open, despite his attempts to link different levels of cultural practice. Yet despite these partial limitations Hall's contributions towards sociology of the media of mass communication are hard to overstate. Through an emphasis upon the semiotic complexity of the text and the audience, Hall has considerably broadened the economistic approach of British Marxist media analysis. His scepticism in respect of traditional Left analysis has both opened up media studies to new modes of critical inquiry, while offering a detailed analysis of media texts in place of sweeping assertion. That Hall's contribution was able to offer new opportunities to a range of critical analysis (including **feminism**, sub-cultural analysis and audience studies) while developing a substantial political analysis is reason enough to respect his considerable genius.

Summary

In the course of examining the views of Raymond Williams, the Glasgow University Media Group and Stuart Hall, I have essentially set out an argument for two main areas of inquiry. First I have argued that mass communications research should articulate a political economy of the cultural industries. Such an approach would attend to the global relationships between the economy and state formations. For this approach to be considered critical, and building on the writing of Raymond Willliams, more research needs to be done into how the principles of democracy could be applied in global settings. I have also argued that the concepts of **hegemony** and ideology remain essential for an understanding of the information age. While the writings of the GUMG and Stuart Hall are important contributions to the ideology debate, they should be reconnected with concerns related to political economy and the interpretative horizons of the audience. Common to the writings of Williams, GUMG and Hall is a certain tendency to overstate the incorporating power of ideology. The limitations of these approaches in conceptualising polymorphous media cultures will become more evident in the following chapters.

Habermas, Mass Culture and the Public Sphere

Public Cultures

Culture is an intersubjectively produced, publicly held phenomenon. It helps provide a source of identity, means of social exchange and a sense of community. In the course of the twentieth century the public cultures of social democracies are progressively becoming both commercialised and marketised. In place of the old integrative cultures of nation states there is currently emerging a fragmented global culture built upon more popular pleasures. This transnational culture is constructing new identities and undermining older versions of national solidarity. A critical notion of the public sphere helps us to view this process ambivalently. The development of new technologies and cultural forms seems to be dependent upon privatised modes of consumption rather than the principles of open debate and discussion. In opposition to these tendencies, certain writers working within socialist, communitarian and republican traditions have sought to develop new ways in which **civil society** might rediscover the ethics of solidarity and critical rationality. Whereas Marxism has proved strong on its analysis of how class domination structured cultural exchange, liberalism has pointed to the need to limit the power of the state by establishing collectively held rights. As it is conceived here, rights and *obligations* of communication are required in a civil zone free from the dominance of money and power in order to satisfy the communicative needs of citizens. This takes the emancipatory project beyond the logics of both Marxism and liberalism. The writer most clearly associated with these views – outlining one of the most important sets of issues currently facing media cultures – is Jürgen Habermas.

The contributions of Jürgen Habermas have had a substantial impact upon modern debates in social theory. His writing has cut across a variety of intellectual spheres including sociology, history, philosophy and political science to produce a substantive and complex account of modernity. Despite the growing significance of Habermas in contemporary debates, his writing on mass communication has not so far attracted the attention it deserves. The small, steadily growing body of literature that actually engages with Habermas on the public sphere often isolates these concerns from his later intellectual development and makes his contribution more media-centric than he intended. The analysis presented here will highlight some of the issues that Habermas's writing on the public sphere has opened up. This particular approach is undertaken in order to investigate the strengths and weaknesses of Habermas's defence of the public cultures in more contemporary contexts. Much recent media research has attempted to draw out the implications of contemporary processes of globalisation, diversification, conglomeration and fragmentation for modern democratic cultures. The argument of this chapter is similarly directed towards an investigation into the future of the public sphere, given the social conditions of late capitalism. Habermas's study of the emergence of the bourgeois public sphere remains germane. This is not because it provides a model that could be realised or copied; but it perhaps delivers the principles within which public cultures might best operate. The systemic organisation of media cultures could be reformulated along lines that both respect cultural diversity and impose reasonable obligations upon those who wish to engage in cultural or political dialogue. Indeed, in this respect, the failings of liberal capitalism and the collapse of scientific socialism herald new opportunities for media analysis such as those proposed by Habermas.

The Bourgeois Public Sphere

Habermas's only complete work to date on the mass media, a historical account of the rise and fall of the bourgeois public sphere, despite being completed in 1962, did not appear in English until 1989. This, as Thomas McCarthy notes in the introduction to *The Structural Transformation of the Public Sphere* (1989), is difficult to explain, given the interest in the author's other works and his well publicised commitment to the importance of human communication. The relatively late translation of this particular work is especially curious in light of the considerable amount of attention that has been focused on the early Frankfurt school and the administration of the culture industry. In order, so to speak, to redress the balance, I shall commence with an exposition of Habermas's main themes, to provide the background for the later discussion.

The bourgeois public sphere developed out of a feudal system that denied the principle of open public discussion on matters of universal interest. Although there had existed a public sphere in classical Greece, it was not until seventeenth- and eighteenth-century Europe that, along with the development of capitalism, it assumed a more distinctive form. The state, in this period, became the sphere of public authority that had a legitimate claim to the use of violence. The modern state could be clearly separated from civil society both judicially and institutionally. Civil society, as distinct from the state, comprised the domain of commodity production and exchange, as well as the 'private' family. Between the realm of public authority and civil society there emerged the critical domain of the public sphere. The purpose of the public sphere was to enable the people to reflect critically upon itself and on the practices of the state. The public sphere developed initially out of coffee houses and salons where male members of the bourgeoisie, nobles and intellectuals met to discuss works of literature. While these open-ended conversations were always based upon practices of exclusion, for Habermas at least, they retain a certain immanence. The critical potential of these ongoing conversations is maintained through three main reasons. First, the social intercourse that eventually shifted from literary to political critique opened up a social space where the authority of the better argument could be asserted against the established status quo. Secondly, areas of social debate that had been sealed off under feudalism lost the 'aura' that had been provided by the church and the court and became increasingly problematised through conversation that disregarded the status of the participants. And finally, Habermas wants to argue that the meetings that took place across Europe in salons and coffee houses, mainly between 1680 and 1730, were inclusive as well as exclusive. While the qualifications for taking an active part in dialogue remained overtly restrictive, the claim that was being made was that this activity constituted a mouthpiece for the public. Habermas argues that while the 'public' remained small, the principle of universality was beginning to be accepted: those who met the qualificatory criteria of being rational, male and propertied could avail themselves, through active participation, in the public sphere. Through the principle of publicity, he claims, it was established that the public use of reason was superior to its private utilisation. The pursuit of truth through an intersubjective dimension that reflected upon both civil society and the state, Habermas maintains, held out distinct possibilities for the reformation of asymmetrical relations of force. Thus the dominant male capitalist class maintained its hegemonic position through practices of exclusion, while simultaneously providing the cultural grounds for critique.

The tragedy of the bourgeois public sphere was that the very social forces which brought it into being would eventually lead to its decline and destruction. The institutionalised dialogue of the salons and coffee houses was to give way as communication became increasingly organised through large commercial concerns.

This transformation is best traced through the newspaper industry. The newspaper trade was originally organised as a small handicraft business, only later becoming concerned with competing viewpoints and perceptions. Habermas characterises this period as a form of literary journalism. The commercial purposes of news production receded into the background at this point, as the press was converted into what Habermas describes as the 'hobbyhorses of the money aristocracy' (Habermas, 1989: 182). But since the end of the liberal era, which Habermas dates from the early 1870s, the emergence of monopoly capitalism has brought about the commercialisation of the press. Literary forms of representation were displaced by specialised journalists who were governed by the private interests of a proprietor. The search for the exposure of political domination by the use of reason was replaced by the imposition of an ideological consensus through the mechanisms of economic and political manipulation.

The progressive institutional elimination of private communicative individuals coming into conversation in the public sphere emphasised a growing separation of public and private life. From this point on commercial culture was consumed in private, requiring no further debate or discussion. Unlike the print culture of the discursive bourgeois salons, much of the new media (television, film and radio) disallows the possibility of talking back and taking part. Just as modern **mass culture** is received in atomised contexts, so the technical development of new cultural forms has been adopted for a society based upon what Raymond Williams (1985) called 'mobile privatism'. Along with the 'privatisation' of culture, Habermas adds, there has been a corresponding trivialisation of cultural products with the aim of gaining a large share of the market. For Habermas, the operation of the market is best seen as a dual and contradictory process that has both emanicipatory and dominatory effects and implications. For example, the book market provides a small stratum of readers with access to high-quality literature. However, the lowering of entrance requirements has meant that literature has had to be accommodated to a mass leisure culture, which requires relaxation and ease of reception. These mass forms of culture have a specifically ideological function. Modern cultural forms integrate subjects into a depoliticised culture, which bypasses the public sphere where claims related to rightness could be discussed.

The cultural transformations and processes outlined above, if we follow Habermas, have led to the refeudalisation of the public sphere. Whereas once publicity meant the exposure of domination through the use of reason, the public sphere is now subsumed into a stage managed political theatre. Contemporary media cultures are characterised by the progressive privatisation of the citizenry and the trivialisation and glamorisation of questions of public concern and interest. The hijacking of communicative questions by monopolistic concerns seemingly converts citizens into consumers and politicians into media stars protected from rational questioning.

It is not fanciful to claim that there are certain parallels between Habermas, and Tom Nairn's (1988) writing on the British state. Tom Nairn, who is an advocate of what he calls 'quiet republicanism', argues that the dominant culture of Britain's ruling class is in need of reform and renewal. A specifically southern hegemonic ruling bloc has, according to his account, been cemented together primarily by the cultural dominance of the royal family. The symbolic superiority of the 'enchanted glass' has fostered a backward anti-industrialism amongst Britain's ruling class. This argument builds upon what became known, in the 1960s, as the 'Nairn-Anderson theses'. Nairn (1964) and P. Anderson (1964, 1992) proposed that the alliance between the rising bourgeoisie and the aristocracy in the seventeenth century created a sterile ideological climate. The British bourgeoisie had failed to produce, compared with the rest of Europe, either a crusading economism or a revolutionary political ideology. Further, due to the premature nature of the industrial revolution and the lack of ideas from above, the working class developed a reformist ideology. For the British working class, Marxism came too late. Nairn argues that, in more modern times, the solution to this peculiarly British disease is a form of republican redemption. The dominant national culture needs to be revived to carry through the unfinished business of a rational Enlightenment culture, which can be achieved only through a specifically northern industrial civil rights-based culture.

Both Nairn and Habermas, in their admittedly different ways, argue that the public sphere has become dominated by a depthless symbolic culture that relies upon display and ceremony, rather than open democratic decision-making procedures. They also agree that the dominant culture provides a cohesive force that addresses the people as consumers rather than citizens, ideologically binding them to specifically national forms of subordination. However, whereas Nairn and Anderson view the cultural inheritance of the bourgeoisie/aristocracy as intrinsically ideological, Habermas offers a more dialectical view in keeping with the traditions of the early Frankfurt school. As Habermas views it, the problem is not so much the delayed arrival of Marxism as the eventual hegemonic exclusion of a more informed communicative culture. Currently, the masses are not shouting for radical social reform because they are isolated from one another and alienated from the majority of media production.

Habermas, Mass Culture and the Early Frankfurt School

Habermas's writing represents an epistemological break with the early Frankfurt school. His theory of communicative rationality displaces what is usually referred to as a philosophy of consciousness, which is much in evidence in the objective and subjective forms of reason utilised by Lukacs, Benjamin, Adorno, Horkheimer and Marcuse. The idea of communicative rationality shifts from a traditional philosophy that opposes a self-sufficient subject to an object-world. Habermas's more interactive form of subjectivity suggests that selfhood can only emerge through an intersubjective language community. For Habermas (1981a, 1983a) the very fact that we are language users means that we are communicatively able to reach an understanding of one another. Habermas argues that in every act of speech we are capable of immanently raising three validity claims in connection with what is said. These three validity claims, he adds, constitute a background consensus of normal everyday language use in Western society. The three claims – that are used by agents to test the validity of speech – could be characterised as propositional truth claims, normative claims related to appropriateness, and claims connected to sincerity. While this particular dimension of Habermas's thought has been discussed in depth elsewhere (Eagleton, 1991; Thompson, 1984; White, 1988), the three pragmatic universals provide the basis for an 'ideal speech situation'. The ideal speech situation is best represented as communication with the absence of barriers. This can be satisfied only where there is an equality of opportunity to participate in communication, and where a statement is true only if it could potentially command the free consent of everyone. Hence it would only be in the context of a radical democracy, far opposed to the present, that would allow the social conditions for the people to become fully aware of their needs and interests.

In his later writing Habermas talks less of the refeudalisation of the public sphere, and more of the pulverisation of the cultural sphere by the economy and the state. Habermas describes this as the colonisation of the life-world (Habermas, 1983a). The life-world can be said to have been successfully colonised by the systemic steering mechanisms of money and power; the extent to which communicative action is bracketed off in favour of instrumental action oriented towards 'success'. By this Habermas means that the possibility of achieving rational forms of understanding are undermined by instrumental forms of reason that support an unjust social system. Habermas also claims that the defensive reactions of the ecological movement and the peace movement can be explained in these terms. The new social movements, according to this thesis, have sought to resist the expansion of the steering media, primarily by raising non-instrumental 'good life' questions. In terms of media cultures this would mean a growing emphasis upon commercial cultures that were culturally hegemonic, seeking both to maximise capital accumulation and to limit more informed criticism. The twin pressures of the economy and instituted social power, in this reading, seek to repress the critical questioning of the social through a cultural dimension.

The state of the life-world is being distorted not only by its refeudalisation and colonisation, but by what Habermas calls cultural impoverishment. Following

Weber, Habermas argues that since the eighteenth century we have witnessed the separation of three different claims related to knowledge, justice and taste. The splitting off and rationalisation of these value spheres was necessary for the emergence of an emancipatory politics, but has also contributed to a loss of meaning in the context of everyday life. Habermas attributes this phenomenon to the growing separation of expert cultures from the contexts of mundane praxis. A more emancipatory form of politics, therefore, would encompass the combined result of an institutional grounding of communicative action with an ongoing dialogue across different social spheres (Habermas, 1981b).

While Habermas does not make this particular connection, some of the arguments he develops in his later writing could be related to the development of the British press. In Curran and Seaton's (1985) seminal study they argue that the commercialisation of the press helped mould the newspaper industry into two basic formats. The quality press, in this reading, attempts to reach a small audience who are rich both in terms of the quality of information they receive and – most important for the advertisers – economically wealthy in terms of their purchasing power. The tabloid press, on the other hand, depend less on advertising and more on mass circulation for their income. Habermas's theses of colonisation and cultural impoverishment could potentially explain the much commented upon melo-dramatic content of the tabloid press (Sparks, 1992a). The commercialisation and commodification of the popular press has undermined their ability to act as rational centres of debate, and has also contributed towards a form of cultural frag-mentation, where the depoliticised masses are excluded from the central debates of our political culture. As a growing number of writers have commented, the coming of the information society has failed to create a common citizenship based upon general access to information. It is arguably only through the force of universal principles and communicative action that cultural colonisation and impoverishment could be democratically countered. Habermas is able, through the theory of communicative action, to provide the philosophical basis for the reconstitution of the public sphere, in a way that the cultural pessimism of the early Frankfurt school could not have done.

Adorno and Horkheimer's theory of the culture industry (1973; Adorno, 1991), largely developed in California during the 1940s, aimed to reveal how conglomerate capitalism dominated mass culture. Their argument was that the rationalisation of work and production was reflected in forms of instrumental reason coming to administer, control and produce superficial forms of consumer culture. The effectiveness of the culture industry was not secured through a decep-tive ideology, but by the removal from the consciousness of the masses of any alternative to capitalism. The dominant culture of late capitalism served to promote the repression of all forms of conflict, heterogeneity and particularity from the cultural sphere. This form of 'affirmative culture' both fetishises exchange over use value (where the value of a concert is secured through the cost of the ticket rather than the quality of the performance) and produces in the audience the desire for the ever same over and over again. In Adorno's thought, modern culture is a childlike and regressive desire for the repetition of certain well established cultural formulas. Here it was only modern forms of art that retained utopian moments of transcendence, as well as substantial notions of individuality, and sensuous forms of particularism. While Habermas steers clear of the high cultural pessimism of Adorno and Horkheimer, he similarly represents the production of mass culture as being subservient to the needs of capitalism. Habermas and the early Frankfurt school view commercial culture as largely absent of inherent critical potential, and dependent upon a passive audience. Although it is true that Habermas represents modern cultural forms in a more nuanced fashion than either Adorno or Horkheimer, his thought, at this stage, bears a marked resemblance to that of his intellectual forebears. Further, whereas Adorno and Horkheimer look to modernist art for a utopian critique of the dominant rationality, Habermas similarly discovers within bourgeois salon society an emancipatory and utopian logic.

The other member of the Frankfurt school, whose presence can be clearly discerned in Habermas's work on the public sphere, is Walter Benjamin. Marx was concerned with the impact of new technology (dead labour) upon labour processes (living labour), but Benjamin (1973) became preoccupied with the impact of mechanical reproduction upon works of art and their reception. Since the Gutenberg press had transformed cultural production, leading not only to the mass reproduction of print but also to photography and film, the original work of art could be said to have lost its aura. As a result of developments in techniques of production there arises a displacement of 'cultural distance' in reception processes. According to Benjamin, the decline in the mythic status of art, and its more general availability, raised the prospect of art becoming 'ordinary' and, by implication, more participatory. In the new media the authority of the original is considerably diminished by the use of sophisticated techniques of production. For instance, in photography it makes little sense to talk about an original print if all of the reproductions are of a similar quality. This more immediate form of experience allows ordinary people to become experts in popular cultural forms.

Adorno replied to Benjamin's essay with a defence of the avant-garde and a further critique of the culture industry (Jameson, 1977: 100–41). It was only the formalist work of art, inaccessible to the masses, that could resist the deformed logic of late capitalism. The destruction of 'cultural distance', which Benjamin wanted to argue had a potentially emancipatory impact, for Adorno only sought to produce 'consumers in diabolic harmony' (Adorno, 1991: 38). Despite Adorno's protests, Benjamin appreciated the decline in aura dialectically. The technical means of reproduction, particularly through the new media, held out the prospect of more democratic and mass-participatory forms of cultural production and reception.

Benjamin argued that if the development of the cultural forces of production were coupled with a transformation in social relations, this would raise the prospect of art ceasing to be the preserve of an elite. But he remained profoundly ambivalent concerning the demystification of the work of art. This was because the decline in the auratic would signal the end of a complex mode of experience. Benjamin, consistently with other members of the early Frankfurt school, thought that auratic art held forth the possibility of transcendence, which if appropriated contained the future promise of happiness. But Benjamin also argued, along with Brecht and in opposition to Adorno and Horkheimer, that Communists should seek to politicise art. This was because very deep dangers to humanity could be detected within the aestheticisation of politics evident in Fascism.

Habermas views the transformations of modern cultural processes in a similarly ambivalent manner. The commodification of culture along with the institutional separation of state and civil society led to the emergence, to use Weber's term, of a *disenchanted* public sphere. The decline of an auratic feudal society, added to the secularisation and separation of social spheres, paved the way for a potentially more 'open' society. Habermas's later writing makes particularly clear, through his utilisation of Popper (Habermas, 1981a: 70), that the rationalisation of the life-world is a necessary component in bringing forth the possibility of emancipation. Cultural traditions, for Habermas, have to be stripped of their dogmatism so that we can test the intersubjective validity of moral principles and norms of action through more symmetrical relations of power. However, according to Habermas (1983b), it is Benjamin's very attachment to myth that prevents him from producing a substantially grounded social theory. Habermas argues that Benjamin, despite his desire to politicise art, was more concerned to develop a general theory of experience than to engage in ideology critique. As Habermas explains, to engage in ideology critique requires the capacity for critical reflection and the analysis of institutional forms of structural violence. Benjamin's project can be more adequately summed up as wanting to shatter myth and aura, thereby making these elements accessible to experience. For Benjamin the cultural resources that allow human beings to invest the world with meaning were deposited in myth. Myth, in Benjamin's writing, is also wholly indifferent to and autonomous from truth claims (Menninghaus, 1991). Hence his retrieval of mythic and utopian contents from history was not so much based on a critical reflective theory as on a notion of experience. In Habermas's terms, Benjamin's attachment to the redemption of myth is indicative of a conservative cast of mind. Here Benjamin's attempt to section off parts of the cultural conversation from truth claims is forcibly dismissed by Habermas.

Habermas's formulation of the public sphere retains a certain degree of continuity with some members of the early Frankfurt school. The main point of difference is his revised philosophy of the subject, and his attempt to bring together different strands in the Frankfurt school in a fresh and challenging way. From Adorno and Horkheimer, Habermas inherits a pessimistic orientation toward the critical content of modern culture, and from Benjamin, despite important differences, he reworks the emancipatory consequences of the decline of auratic art. Having illuminated Habermas's intellectual context, I now wish to look more critically at the theme of mass culture, before reconnecting these issues to the future of the public sphere.

Problems with Mass Culture:
Habermas and the Frankfurt School

Despite the sympathetic turn of the arguments presented this far, Habermas's writing presents an inadequate account of modern culture. While he has built upon some of the more critical penetrative aspects of the earlier Frankfurt school, he has also arguably inherited some of its more culturally conservative aspects. Following some of the comments made by J.B. Thompson (1990) amongst others, Habermas's writing could be found wanting on at least four counts: (1) his over-concentration on the production and content of cultural forms; (2) the dominant ideology thesis that operates through his account of mass culture; (3) the overly pessimistic orientation of the refeudalisation of the public sphere, in a British historical context; (4) his limited grasp of more global and local public spheres.

1. The development of contemporary media and cultural studies over the past decade or so could be characterised by its closer articulation with sociology, and its expressed concern to focus upon reception contexts more explicitly. While there have been equally important trends taking place within the discipline, such as the growing analytical importance of globalisation (King, 1991) and psychoanalysis (Elliott, 1992), the discernible movement towards sociology and audience research is both important and related. In the British and German context there has been a strong link between literary forms of analysis and the development of cultural studies. What figures like Adorno and Horkheimer, along with Raymond Williams and Richard Hoggart, share is that their investigation of popular forms is deeply structured by a shared attachment to a literary culture. A 'high' form of culture was perceived by these writers to be in danger of being swamped by a cheap American culture. The invading depthless culture was understood not only as a barbarous threat to the democratic widening of a richer artistic culture, but was also assumed to be ideological to the core. Pierre Bourdieu (1990:112) has usefully described the position of the critic, who assumes that everyday agents make sense of popular cultural forms in the same way as people in academic communities, as the scholastic fallacy.

In Paul Willis's book *Common Culture* (1990), a study of the way young working-class people actively make sense of popular forms, the cultural conservatism of literary critiques of popular culture is further exposed. Without waiting for the educational benefits of a reputedly more sophisticated culture young people are seeking pleasure, autonomy and a sense of self through a commercial culture. For Willis, writers like Adorno and Horkheimer, who do not clearly distinguish between the production and the reception of modern cultural forms, are usually unable to account for the possible liberating consequences of much of modern culture. Two examples will suffice to bring out Willis's argument with more clarity. The first is Willis's own, that many young working-class people, if they are able to find paid work, are often employed in occupations that disable the worker from demonstrating very high levels of skill and autonomy. In contrast their leisure time often involves complex mediations with a diverse number of cultural forms, as Willis writes:

> work relations and the drive for efficiency now hinge upon *the suppression* of informal symbolic work in most workers, the logic of the cultural and leisure industries hinges on the opposite tendency: a form of *their enablement and release*. Whereas the ideal model for the worker is the good time kept, the disciplined and empty head, the model for the good consumer is the converse – a head full of unbounded appetites for symbolic things. (1990:19)

Willis's argument here is that any critique of commercial culture should recognise the informal and symbolic work involved in its reception.

The other example stems from Paul Gilroy's *There Ain't No Black in the Union Jack* (1987). In his account Gilroy convincingly demonstrates that black British popular culture is continually attempting to construct and reformulate traditions in black music that protest against racism. For Gilroy these popular cultural forms represent a utopian yearning for a world where race is no longer the subject of the domination of one group by another. The musical culture of young blacks is itself part of the diaspora that cuts across the internal borders of nation states. In this sense, what it means to be black is constantly reshaped through symbolic patterns and forms that have become disconnected from their initial contexts of production. According to Gilroy, young blacks are able to forge a more inclusive global political identity that challenges their exclusion from citizenship. This critical, global form of imagining is of course dependent upon the commercial culture transmitted by the culture industry. Gilroy's and Willis's arguments taken together amply demonstrate that those social groups who were meant to benefit from a revitalised political culture are already forming attachments to, and seeking meaning from, popular forms. This, as particularly Gilroy notes, has certain political consequences that need to be taken account of in any wider assessment.

So far the sociological bent of writers like Gilroy and Willis has amply demonstrated the necessity of a more investigative approach to distanciated contexts of reception. Yet there are evident dangers for cultural analysis, I would suggest, if this argument is allowed to drift into an uncritical celebration of a popular postmodern culture. Fiske's (1989a, 1989b) analysis recognises a clear break between the production of cultural forms for profit and the often subversive readings that become attached to them. Here the discursively open nature of popular texts is explored with particular reference being made to the popular refusal of the discursive practices of the power bloc. The hegemonic dominant culture, according to Fiske (1992), attempts, through appeals to impartiality and objectivity, to produce believing rather than sceptical subjects. By contrast, the lack of a unified subject position offered by tabloid newspapers and journals suggests a multiplicity of textual contradictions that require the active negotiation of a social agent. For instance, the sensational headline invites the reader, through exaggeration and excess, to question the normal and the official. While writers such as Fiske have usefully illustrated how the popular can become the site of a micro-politics of resistance, his analysis, along with others, bends the stick too far.[1]

In a nutshell, Fiske's problem is that he finds little space for the more institutional and historical understanding of mass culture offered by writers such as Habermas. Popular culture is not the mass form of deception Habermas assumes it to be, but neither, I would argue, is it the open participatory culture that some of the sociologists of reception describe. Philip Schlesinger has referred to those who overstate reception processes as the 'new revisionists' (Schlesinger, 1991: 149). Schlesinger justly argues that while the pleasure of the text is not to be under-estimated, such a concern should not be allowed to displace an analysis of institutional power. While Habermas has been criticised, correctly in my view, for ignoring the interpretative activity of audiences, he offers a political critique of forms of manipulation evident within our culture absent from writers like Fiske. For example, I may sit at home each night developing an ironic reading of political discussion programmes (Scannell, 1992: 345). Such a reading might be resistant to the programmes' intended strategy of positioning me as a political citizen with *interests* in the topics under discussion. This position would obviously count as subversive in Fiske's terms, given that I would be resisting the particular regime of truth imposed by the power-bloc. An acquaintance with Habermas's writing would alternatively allow me to develop a more political reading of a programme. One might start such an interpretative venture by pointing to the narrow range of voices that can be heard on the transmission, most of whom are selected and tightly 'scripted' by the major political parties. I might then go on to think about how the audience is allowed only a passive role in subsequent political discussion, and consider how they could be empowered within this setting. Further, I may go on to develop an institutional critique of commercial and public service television, and imaginatively reconsider ways it could be democratically reconstructed. In short, while Habermas is guilty of ignoring the interpretative horizons of the audience, cultural and media studies would seem to be surrendering a great deal if it failed to develop corresponding institutional frames of analysis.

2. The early and late Frankfurt schools assume that the media industries remove the grounds for critique, while hegemonically binding the masses to the status quo. Horkheimer's and Adorno's description of the flattening out of modern culture is paralleled in Habermas's account of a culture that cannot allow for critical forms of dialogue. This not only reduces the audience to lethargic couch potatoes, but overestimates the extent to which the media are responsible for the reproduction of asymmetrical social relations through a hegemonic discourse. For Habermas the depoliticised mass culture that requires no further comment by its audience is best represented as 'a culture of motivational integration' (Habermas, 1989: 173). Here Habermas captures a dominant theme in Western Marxism – that the reproduction of the status quo can be best explained through the ideological incorporation of subordinate social groups. This theme is also apparent in some of Habermas's other writing. His basic premiss in *Legitimation Crisis* (1976) is that the two major patterns of motivation (civil and familial vocational) are being systematically eroded. This position assumes that in order for social systems to hegemonically legitimise themselves, they are required to normatively integrate social subjects into society. Instead, as David Held (1989) argues, stability in modern societies is more likely to be produced through cultural atomism than by externally imposed consensus. Similarly, Michael Mann (1970) suggests that sociologists should distinguish between pragmatic and normative acceptance. We can argue that normative acceptance has occurred when dominant social groups have managed to mobilise consent in order to legitimise their social position. Pragmatic acceptance, on the other hand, is where persons comply to their social position because they cannot perceive a realistic alternative.

The fragmentation of modern identities can be explained economically, politically and culturally. For example, it has become commonplace within cultural studies to point to how advertisers, the music industry, newspapers, magazines, radio and television programmes explicitly target certain segments of the audience. Capitalism has become dependent upon a consuming public who are heterogeneous in their lifestyle demands. The fact that the spectre of ideological unity still lurks in cultural studies can again be partially attributed to the continued influence of Western Marxism. The dominant ideology thesis has proved incapable of explaining either the diversity of modern cultural patterns, or the complex processes of psychic identification that are induced through reception. Having said this, I would like to keep open at least the possibility of hegemonic forms of analysis. It remains the case that the public is a more ideologically unstable construction than Habermas allows, although if this argument is pushed too far the impact of mass communications on questions of cultural power becomes negligible. That the mass media have a significant ideological role to play in modernity should not be underestimated. The media may not have been able to bind the public together culturally in the way Habermas suggests, but certain hegemonic capabilities are certainly retained by the media. Here it is important to stress that mass communication research does not have to make a choice between ideological unity or cultural fragmentation. Media cultures, given certain structural conditions, are capable of producing either effect. A more nuanced approach would seek to highlight the tensions within unity and fragmentation, and institute a dialogue between hegemonic incorporation and social atomism.

3. Habermas's notion of the refeudalisation of the public sphere, while maintaining a certain critical purchase, remains far too sweeping to adequately capture the operation of modern mediated cultures. Habermas's contention that the *society of the spectacle* has replaced a rational public sphere oriented towards claims to rightness considerably overstates the case. There are two distinct arguments I want to make against Habermas in this respect. The first is that, once Habermas has introduced the idea of the public sphere, he seems to jettison any specific historical framework. What he is unable to account for is the historically constituted institutional tension that exists within modern society between the economy, the state and broadcasting. My other argument is that while Habermas, correctly in my view, stresses the importance of an officially sanctioned national public arena, he cannot readily account for the emergence of both more international and local public spheres.

Let's take an example from the history of British broadcasting. Paddy Scannell (1986, 1990, 1992) has recently argued, in a robust defence of public communication systems, that since its inception public service broadcasting has been based upon the principle of universal access and the supply of mixed programming. National service broadcasting, through the recontextualisation of private life into a public arena, and vice versa, has considerably broadened the range of what can legitimately be discussed in the public domain. But, as Raymond Williams (1962) and others have pointed out, the BBC has traditionally maintained a paternal relation with its audience and has been too deferential to the British establishment. According to Scannell, however, this cultural pattern was to encounter a transformation in the late 1950s. With the introduction of rival competition from the ITV network, the public broadcasting system was forced to adopt a more democratic stance in its dealing with those in positions of authority. The emergence of a more populist and open style of presentation sought to make the state answerable to the public. The ability of news journalists to retain a certain degree of 'independence', from outside attempts to control the content of news production, is obviously reliant upon specific institutional contexts. While this raises the question of public broadcasting's relation with outside 'definers' like the state, police and trade unions, there remains considerable evidence that they have historically carved out a relatively autonomous set of social practices.

To give an example. Historically the British state has consistently interfered with the making of documentary, news and drama programmes about Northern Ireland. According to Elliott, Murdock and Schlesinger (1983) the constant threat of state intervention has realised within the BBC an internal form of self-censorship, which acted as a deterrent to the production of critical perspectives on Northern Ireland. In addition, the then Home Secretary Douglas Hurd's announcement on 19 October 1988 that the government was to prohibit the direct broadcast of named terrorist groups sought to further muffle criticism of the British state. We could argue that this is a good example of how the modern state has attempted to 'bracket off' and manage certain areas of public debate, but it has not been completely successful in this venture. The very fact that the state has overridden claims to free speech in this area has made it the object of criticism. The ban did not disable more independent film makers like Ken Loach or certain sections of the 'quality press' from opening up discussion on the subject. Further, public broadcasting institutions continued to transmit a small number of film documentaries on Northern Ireland, some of which have been sharply critical of the British state.[2]

Arguably, if the British state were unable to completely control the flow of information to its citizens on Northern Ireland, we must be justifiably sceptical of the extent to which the media can be said to have been refeudalised. This is not intended to imply that 'Others', who are perceived as a threat to a specifically imagined national community, are not often portrayed in terms of a conflict between good and evil. Here Habermas's writing would retain a critical force as such cultural representations bypass Enlightenment claims to truth and rational questioning. But if Habermas's arguments are to have more than a general validity, he would have to account for the relatively decommodified and discursively open spaces that have resisted or been ignored by colonisation strategies.

4. Habermas's writing on the public sphere is explicitly connected to the nation state. This remains an inadequate conceptual framework for an understanding of the public sphere. The modern state is constantly being permeated from above by the operation of transnational institutions, while having to face new demands for autonomy from below. The international readership of certain business or quality newspapers signifies that there is an emergent global public sphere for certain elite groupings (Sparks, 1992b). This can be connected to other globalising processes which serve to point to what Gilroy (1987) called earlier a specifically black diaspora, or what Benedict Anderson (1992) has named long-distance nationalism. Further, we might follow John Keane (1996) and offer a spatially differentiated account of the public sphere. The public sphere is comprised of: '*micropublic spheres* in which there are dozens, hundreds or thousands of disputants interacting at the sub-nation-state level; *mesopublic spheres* which

normally comprise millions of people interacting at the level of the nation-state framework; and the *macropublic spheres* which normally encompass hundreds of millions and even billions of people enmeshed in disputes at the supranational and global levels of power'. (Keane 1996: 169)

We can point to the micro-public spheres evident within locally defined media most often found within newspapers and radio, but might also include small-scale radical publications or even homemade videos made for personal, professional or political purposes. The national public sphere comprises the majority of the 'big' media including national television networks, radio and the press. Here local and international issues are filtered through a national optic and are considered along with matters of national importance. Finally, a global public sphere informs individuals of events taking places in contexts far removed from their own. These might be news reports of war zones, documentaries concerning human-rights abuse, or dramas based in global cities such as New York and Tokyo. Issues related to self-identity and citizenship then cannot always be understood in terms of specific national cultures. A recognition of these transformations could lead to an abandonment of the attempt to preserve national cultures against 'alien' forms of erosion, and address issues of cultural diversity in terms of its implications for modern bundles of rights and obligations (Parekh, 1991; Barbook, 1992). Through the new social movements one can also discern the emergence of a more local fragmented public sphere, where small groups have met to openly discuss a host of themes from nuclear disarmament to sexuality (Phillips, 1991). These groupings have been the source of small-scale and independently distributed press and information networks. That Habermas ignores these dual cultural processes serves to weaken his defence of the importance of the public sphere to a radical democracy.

But Habermas's desire to generate procedural norms could be applied to a more spatially sensitive notion of the public sphere. The most important development in this context has been the arrival of transfrontier broadcasting via satellite and cable systems. Currently many of these commercial services escape the duties and obligations that apply to public service media (Negrine, 1994). Such systems, currently evade requirements of balance, impartiality and quality. The application of universal norms of obligation are seemingly crucial in this context if certain citizenry requirements are to be met and unfair competition restrained. Some of these questions and their relation to public service broadcasting are explored in the next section.

The Public Sphere and Public Broadcasting

Most of the literature that has taken up Habermas's arguments on the public sphere has sought to utilise his work in terms of a defence of public systems of broadcasting. The argument presented by a number of authors is that the deregulation and commercialisation of national public services is a threat to democratic citizenship, in that it delivers control of our information into the hands of international conglomerates. According to this scenario, this will lead to the erosion of 'quality' forms of debate, the abandonment of special interest programming that cannot secure the backing of advertisers, and the conversion of citizens into consumers. The rise of neo-liberalism has made it necessary to intellectually restate the need for a democratic public sphere. Neo-liberals have denounced state-organised broadcasting because it is high-cost, prevents the free flow of information by restricting advertising and disallows choice.

Public broadcasting, according to those who wish to preserve a notion of the public sphere, remains important for three main reasons: (1) historically it has occupied an institutional space that has some independence from both the economy and the state; (2) public broadcasting potentially provides a national arena for a diversity of social groups to communicate with one another; (3) it addresses the public as citizens rather than consumers.

1. Habermas's original outline of the public sphere stresses that the intellectual space for critical debate was opened up through its institutional differentiation from the state and civil society. This allowed for the emergence of the principle of publicity, where the public use of reason is privileged over its private use. The mechanism of the licence fee has traditionally been used to insulate the BBC from commercial pressures and the government of the day. However, as J.B. Thompson (1990) and Nicholas Garnham (1990) have pointed out, the so-called neutrality of the BBC has often been compromised in practice. This can be partially explained as a result of the concentration of power in a bureaucratic elite who sit at the apex of the BBC's organisational structure. This distinctive elite has traditionally been drawn from those with privileged social backgrounds, whose definition of the 'public interest' has tended to bear a close resemblance to that of the government of the day. This particular argument is often traced back to Reith's famous remarks defending the government during the General Strike in 1926. I would, however, maintain that the 'independence' of the BBC adds up to more than an ideological form of misrecognition. Paddy Scannell (1986) through his research on the popular national radio programme of the 1930s, *Time to Spare*, has demonstrated that early forms of public broadcasting retained a certain degree of autonomy from state control. The programme originally sought both to encourage voluntary attempts to alleviate mass unemployment and to provide a 'public' space for the experiences of unemployed people. Despite much cynicism on the part of the Left, the self-descriptions of the working class that emerged through a nationally defined public sphere served to open up debates on the issue of unemployment amongst members of parliament. Once the exchanges within the House of Commons had

been picked up by the press, Ramsay MacDonald's government sought to silence the radio series, and with it the growing 'public' awareness of issues related to poverty and unemployment. Reith, in the face of considerable government pressure, refused to discontinue the series. He asserted that if the government banned the programme he would replace the scheduled transmission with twenty minutes of silence. At this MacDonald decided to give way.

Despite my defence of public broadcasting against those who would want to assimilate its operation to a dominant ideology, there remains, as Raymond Williams (1962, 1974, 1985) suggested, a strong argument for its democratisation and more formal separation from the state. The provision of a universal service committed to the delivery of high-quality forms of information remains a key component of modern forms of citizenship. This argument has been further demonstrated by Henry A. Giroux (1999). In the American context there is considerable concern that large media conglomerates will progressively undermine civic and democratic values. American culture is becoming a corporate culture. The preservation and extension of democratic and civic sensibilities actively requires the development of state-supported and non-commercial television. In other words, critical debate and open public deliberation requires the curbing of the power of big media, and the public spaces that enable citizens to become active cultural producers of a range of media material.

2. A reformulated public sphere, according to Curran (1991) and Garnham (1990), could provide the opportunity for different groups and classes to take part in a common public dialogue. Public service broadcasting could, on this model, provide a shared domain for a pluralistic group of individuals to explore whether or not they have interests in common. Unfortunately this argument does not treat seriously enough the earlier stated questions of cultural fragmentation, and ignores the proliferation of information available in modern post-industrial society. Peter Golding (1990) has plausibly pointed out, despite some of the more utopian expectations, that access to modern forms of information is structured by the practices of the state, as well as social divisions of class, race and sex. Audiences are not only fragmented by their particular cultural dispositions (Bourdieu, 1984), but are also divided through their differential access to new forms of information technology. One does not have to be a 'brute' materialist to be persuaded that the move towards deregulated cable communication systems will mean increased choice for those with large disposable incomes and comparatively less for those who have not. Even if the state were to commit itself to the expansion of public service communications, it would be unlikely, given the developments in new technology, to be able to secure the close attention of a national community.

This problem is exaggerated if we consider the extraordinary amount of information that is currently made available to citizens within modernity. Modern societies, as many post-industrial thinkers such as Baudrillard (1988a) and Melucci

(1989) have recognised, cannot be characterised by lack of information, but by what might be called information overload. The world market of late capitalism, through the financing of cable television, videos, books, popular magazines and newspapers, has filled the world with information. Such is the proliferation of modern culture that no one person would ordinarily be capable of digesting all the information offered in a single newspaper in a single day. While Baudrillard, like other writers, has interpreted the growth of information in a politically conservative fashion, he does pose difficult questions for any attempt to reformulate the public sphere.

These considerations place limits on attempts such as Curran's, Garnham's and Giroux's to construct new national forms of solidarity and community through cultural institutions. It was the profound belief of the old New Left that emergent forms of community and understanding could be promoted through the democ- ratisation of mass forms of communication. This strain can also be discerned in Habermas's writing. Habermas's account seems to presuppose that by putting people into conversation the end result will be the emergence of common versions of the good, and increased social solidarity. While such a strategy could provide the backdrop for new intersubjective relations, it remains insufficiently appreciative of the globalised and fragmented nature of much of social life. Hence any attempt to reinvest in a pluralised public sphere would do well to except the constraints imposed upon it by global and information-overloaded information cultures. The compression of time and space evident in global media cultures both undermines and supports the possibility of moral universalism. Keith Tester (1999) suggests that the conversion of mass suffering evident within televised famines and disasters into a spectacle can produce disengagement and indifference on the part of the audience. Enhanced visibility does not guarantee social solidarity.

3. Due to the public service model's insulation from the market, it has, according to its supporters, traditionally addressed the people as citizens rather than consumers. For Habermas and Garnham the citizen can be defined as inhabiting a political realm where, through public rights of debate, communally agreed rules can be collectively discussed. Within the public sphere, then, the con- sensual generation of general norms of action becomes paramount. The legitimacy of certain political traditions, within the modern world, now rests upon their imaginative and creative appropriation rather than on a timeless mythic dominance. Alternatively, within the economic realm, subjects are addressed as either producers or consumers who have essentially private rather than public interests. The problem with the stifling of public broadcasting is that individuals are increasingly treated as consumers rather than as active citizens with rights and obligations. For instance, consumers are not democratically consulted as to the investment and marketing strategy of conglomerates. It has been one of the more successful ideological strategies of the neo-liberalism to muddy the distinction between citizenship and

consumerism. Once we theoretically run together these two spheres, Garnham (1990) objects, there is no foreseeable reason why in neo-liberal discourse, voting rights should not become dependent upon purchasing power.

If instead we accept that the values of consumerism should be separated from those of political citizenship, then this seriously questions the legitimacy of the exclusive private ownership of the symbolic means by which events are made public. The privatisation of modern culture can also be discerned in the sorts of appeals made by politicians to voters. In modern liberal democracies it is common for politicians to address the voting public as 'taxpayers' or 'ratepayers', rather than as reflexive members of the public concerned for the common good. This tendency, it is argued, would be exaggerated if our culture became dominated even further by deregulated forms of transnational cultural production. A commitment to public service broadcasting should be rethought less as a means of preserving a 'peculiar' national culture, and more in terms of universal norms of citizenship (Barbook, 1992; Thompson, 1978).

The problem remains that the information required by citizens within a global culture cannot be generated internally within an isolated nation state. While there is certainly a strong case for separating the different value spheres of consumption and citizenship, the public and the private, these distinctions need to be redrawn internationally. In thinking about the future of public broadcasting, we need to develop policies that address the international as well as the national arenas. A more internationally based public sphere would aim to exchange information across the boundaries of the nation state, challenge national stereotypes, and focus on the global implications of the policies of nation states. A reemerged public sphere, relevant to the modern world, would necessarily be dependent upon more global forms of public collaboration than we have witnessed thus far (Murdock, 1992).

There are, however, major problems facing the welcome attempts to apply Habermas's writing to current issues in mass communications research. These difficulties lie both with those who have sought to apply notions of the public sphere and with Habermas himself. In practice, media theorists have tended to abstract Habermas's concern with the public sphere from his wider emphasis on the institutional realisation of a radical democracy. The most cursory glance at Habermas's work reveals that the application of democratic norms to mass media cultures occupies only a small part of the citizenship claims he brings to the fore. Habermas's arguments have inadvertently been made media-centric. A wider analysis of the culture of late capitalism would have to engage with certain material and cultural constraints that prevent the citizenry from fully participating in democratic decision-making. The social practices of media cultures provide only a partial explanation of this situation. The other problem, which I indicated above, lies with Habermas's status as a philosopher. It is clearly left to others to apply the universal norms of the bourgeois public sphere to current situations. While I would defend the intellectual credibility of such an enterprise, the way in which these values are *fitted* into empirical contexts requires special attention. It should be obvious that Habermas's concern with communicative rationality is the product of a print rather than an electronic culture.[3] This of course does not make such ideals redundant, but it does mean that closer investigations into the structuring power of electronic cultures is required. The main problem these cultures pose for the reformation of the public sphere lies in their speeded-up and fragmented nature. This perspective argues that modern cultures have witnessed the disappearance of private space and the decline of historicity. My own view is that these trans-formations make the case for public rather than commercial systems stronger rather than weaker. But there is a case to be answered. How could a revitalised public sphere provide a sense of continuity and dialogue concerning the crucial issues of the day? What measures could be taken to ensure a pluralistic public debate is inclusive rather than exclusive? These and other questions remain crucial to the application of Habermas's normative programme.

There also remain other areas of media experience that Habermas's inter-pretative concern with the mass media poorly articulates. How, for instance, could we apply the ideal speech situation to a visit to the cinema? Seemingly, in Habermas's theory, it would only have relevance if we engage in a wider form of communal reflection on the film in question and the institutional relations of image production. The problem with this line is that it fails to connect with much of contemporary cultural experience. For instance, it is noticeable that Habermas, unlike the early Frankfurt school, has very little to contribute on aesthetic questions. This is mainly due to his desire to rescue communicative reason from the members of the school who pit an aesthetic sensibility against instrumental forms of reason. Again, in more contemporary contexts, I have much sympathy with Habermas's wish to combat avant-gardism on the Left and cultural conservatism on the Right. His argument, much like that of Williams, is not that artists should give up experimen-tation, but that they should seek to create a dialogue between the aesthetic and the political realm. This would entail that artistic expression should respect certain social obligations without seeking to falsely unify the domains of art and politics. However, such sentiments, while worthy, fail to connect with more common forms of aesthetic enjoyment.

The popular engagement of fans with music, television and film cultures belies a feature which is not easily recognised within hermeneutic concerns. Susan Sontag (1994) has famously argued that a concern for interpretation often neglects to analyse the sensory experience of the work of art. This argument, placed in the context of popular media cultures, has a certain explanatory value. For example, my enthusiasm for the opening ceremony of the Olympic Games is only partially related to the meanings that can be attributed to it. More likely such viewing practices are an engagement with the excessive display of colour and the overall sense of spectacle. Returning to film, we commonly hear of productions that have to be seen in the cinema. The technical and aesthetic context of the cinema, along with the relative isolation of the audience, provides image presentation with a certain dramatic effect. The opening sequence of Jane Campion's film *The Piano* displays the arrival of a young woman and her daughter in New Zealand. The vastness of the landscape and the smallness of the travellers is borne out well by the big screen. This sense, as almost everyone who has seen the film will tell you, would be inadequately captured by television. The impression created is determined by an aesthetic appreciation of the cultural form, which is distinct from the interpretation of linguistic meaning. It is unlikely that Habermas would seek to deny this phenomenon, and I might agree with him that it does not have the 'political' importance that can be connected to the regeneration of public cultures. Yet his analytic distance from reception contexts means that he supplies only a partial view of contemporary media culture.

Habermas, the Public Sphere and Citizenship

In Habermas's written response to the revolutions of 1989, he imaginatively rethinks what an alternative political project might look like in a post-Marxist Europe (Habermas, 1990a). Habermas represents the key task of the Left as being the assertion of universal interests in an attempt to remoralise public conflicts. In conditions of late capitalism, the idea that the Left can unproblematically seek to socialise the steering mechanisms of money and power should be dismissed as an anachronism. The extent to which certain needs and values emerging in the life-world can put limits on the operation of money and power remains for Habermas an empirical question. The principles of communicative action should be applied to public forms of administration, without seeking to completely subordinate them to its logic. Habermas adds that while a critical theory should not attempt to be too prescriptive in its recommendations, the regeneration of a rationally based public sphere remains a necessary political project. He does not take the argument any further in this context. I might add, however, that unless we are able to collectively realise a sense of community and attend to the needs, fears and concerns of others, the end result will be more destructive forms of social atomism. For this agenda to emerge, as I hope I have indicated, citizens will be dependent upon the provision of 'quality' forms of information and democratic forums for discussion.

The development of a more communicative culture that seeks, in Arendt's (1958) phrase, to 'enlarge thought', is only possible in modern contexts through the radical democratisation of the culture industry. The presentation of a plurality of voices, particularly of those that are not immediately present in day-to-day encounters, is especially necessary in a globalised and fragmented culture. A source of hope, I would argue, remains ordinary people's continued capacity to feel a sense of solidarity with others in contexts far removed from their own. Public service programmes that sought to emphasise these affective feelings would need to show the subjects under discussion as being worthy of equal respect, while seeking to strengthen an emotional intersubjective web of empathetic concern. This 'ethic of compassion' (Habermas, 1990b) grows out of the process of mutual recognition evident within personal relations and early socialisation processes (Benjamin, 1988). That empathetic relations are still possible in a mass mediated commercial culture is best demonstrated by the global concern expressed for human suffering by Live Aid in 1986. The imagined connectedness with others expressed by this event is not to be underestimated. However, as I have emphasised, while these ethical demands remain at the heart of any attempt to reformulate a more internationally based public sphere, we should, given the material and symbolic relations of global culture, remain cautious in the light of their possible effects.

Throughout this chapter I have argued that Habermas's writing on the public sphere, despite its short-comings, retains considerable strength through the emphasis placed upon communication and participation (Rustin, 1992). This is a major contribution to the current political and sociological debate on citizenship. Following on from T.H. Marshall (1992) modern forms of citizenship have often been rather passively conceived in respect of the rights and obligations that are granted social subjects (Giddens, 1985, Turner 1993a, Turner 1994). The central thrust of Habermas's critique is that current attempts to reimagine new forms of social solidarity through a discourse on citizenship is dependent upon the establishment of the material conditions that allow for popular democratic engagement by an enlarged group of the citizenry. Here I shall briefly sketch out a number of related problems with Habermas's theoretical attempt to reconsider notions of citizenship in relation to the public sphere. In this, the final section, I claim that there at least three problems with Habermas's approach to contemporary citizenship. Here, I want to argue that Habermas's writing on the public sphere and participatory forms of democracy needs (1) more definitely to recognise that communicative action could be subject to certain limits; (2) to become more specific as regards the relation between direct and representative democracy; and (3) theoretically to revise its universalistic orientation in order to account for difference.

1. Perry Anderson has perceptively remarked that behind Habermas's thoughts there lie the 'earnest ideals and serious optimism of the German Enlightenment' (Anderson, 1983: 65). Despite Habermas's intention to provide a structural analysis of contemporary social forces, his thought maintains a considerable distance from the current political crisis of late capitalism. The philosophical bent of Habermas's thinking, while providing a number of key insights, often remains far removed from

an analysis of contemporary social structures. According to Anderson this has produced an excessive formalism in his writing and a pedagogic disposition towards politics.

The weakness of Habermas's ethical minimalism becomes apparent once one asks for justification. The problem remains, as Charles Taylor (1989, 1991) has argued, that Habermas cannot tell me why I should wish to live rationally, or seek to reach an understanding with others. Castoriadis (1991), who follows a similar line of argument to Taylor, argues that ultimately Habermas, in seeking to answer this question, grounds his reply in a mythic biological foundation. Habermas's contention that human beings are intersubjective language users whose everyday practice presupposes their emancipation, cannot readily inform us why we should strive for freedom. All that Habermas tells us is that more emancipated forms of life are made possible through the application of universal validity claims. He does not, nor can he through an overly minimal ethics, offer strongly evaluated reasons as to why I should prefer more enabling discursive democratic frameworks. As Taylor (1991: 32) says, 'the fact that we should prefer rational understanding to norm-free steering mechanisms is closely bound up with our understandings of human dignity'. To take another example; the reason that the peace movement opposed the Gulf War, had less to do with a breakdown in communication, crucial as this was, than with the impending prospect of mass forms of human suffering. If Habermas is unable to offer modern citizens more strongly evaluative reasons as to why conversations should aim to produce a consensus, then a 'free' conversation is just as likely to produce further entrenched versions of hatred and misunderstanding.

Unless Habermas can substantially redraw the line between questions of justice and the good life, he will not be able to answer some of the fundamental issues his work undoubtedly raises. Seyla Benhabib (1992) has argued that for a commitment to a conversational ethics to be morally convincing, its dependence upon certain substantive presuppositions should be recognised. Benhabib proposes that within symmetrical forms of communication we treat others with equal respect, and recognise that all persons within the conversation have equal rights. These ethical prerequisites to egalitarian forms of communication are of course open to question but, she suggests, their normative foundations cannot be generated by human speech. All we can say is that if they are violated then force has taken the place of persuasion. In the light of these objections, a more ethically 'thick' attempt to secure the principles of communicative action is to be welcomed. Such a move would seek to open up questions of culture in relation to human needs. Yet it is currently unclear whether Habermas's discourse ethics is best suited to this task. As J.B.Thompson (1995) has argued it is no longer clear what practical relevance discourse ethics has for global media cultures. Practically, discourse ethics applies to those who share a common social location and who are able to dialogue directly with one another. But under global conditions where the media is able to recontextualise imagery into local contexts, what would an all-inclusive conversation look like? How could the millions of spatially diverse people whose lives are affected by issues from poverty to pollution and from AIDS to the proliferation of nuclear weapons make their voices heard? These concerns do not necessarily automatically cancel the questions raised by discourse ethics, however, they do ask that greater consideration is given to the social contexts within which they operate.

2. Habermas has recently argued that it is not the role of the philosopher to be prescriptive as to how the principles of democracy may be applied (Dews, 1986). Habermas, similarly to Marx, argues that he is unwilling to supply a blueprint for change as this would further pre-empt the future result of a democratically forged consensus. But while this argument has a certain coherence, it is open to a number of objections. In particular, and given Habermas's defence of participatory forms of democracy, it does seem odd that he has not attempted to be more prescriptive on the themes of direct and representative democracy, the form most compatible with communicative action being direct democracy. Direct democracy and 'ideal' forms of speech allow for a rationally formed consensus only after a period of argumentation amongst all interested parties. But Habermas would certainly accept that direct forms of democracy can only be allowed limited expression in a large complex society (Bobbio, 1987; Held, 1989). While Habermas has consistently argued that the limits of communicative action can only be tested empirically, it is not clear how a minimal ethics could be readily applied. while not intending to diminish the importance of communicative ethics, contemporary democratic practice is best characterised as the application of power from below, and the redistribution of power as opposed to its concentration. Following Norberto Bobbio (1987), the argument is less how to apply the rules of communicative action than how a distinctive mix between representative and direct democracy could find expression. To argue, as Habermas seems to, that the partial socialisation of society's steering mechanisms is dependent upon the application of a minimal ethics misses this point.

The current global concentration of the ownership and control of media systems means that economic power is often translated into political and cultural power. In Europe, the impact of media conglomerates should make us aware of the need to ensure that the press, radio and television are not controlled by monopolies. Such a demand could only inadequately, as Habermas well understands, be formulated as a demand for direct participation. The need for agents of political authority to oversee the distribution of ownership and impose communicative obligations at all levels of representative democracies remains important. Further, a case could also be made for making public systems of communication at local, national and global levels democratically accountable. Such proposals deserve more considered treatment than is available here. Yet what is evident is that these concerns are more effectively articulated in terms of Bobbio's definition of representative democracy than in terms of Habermas's concern with discourse ethics.

3. Habermas emphasises universal forms of citizenship as a means of reintroducing the themes of solidarity and community into contemporary political debate. These values were meant, as we saw, to operate as a corrective against the individualistic tone of neo-liberalism. However, within the debates around citizenship there has been a growing awareness that universal theories tend to neglect the fundamentally diverse and specific nature of human needs (Parekh, 1991). This issue has found its deepest point of resonance amongst feminist writers (Benhabib, 1992; Lister, 1991; Pateman, 1989; Phillips, 1991). A theory of 'citizenship', according to these writers, should recognise universal needs and interests while closely attending to forms of difference that do not violate generalised needs and obligations. It is a specific feature of Kantian theories, like those developed by Habermas, that they retain a certain blindness to structural and cultural difference. The imposition of universal norms, as T.H. Marshall (1992) well understood, is often weighted in favour of certain groups rather than others. As both Lister (1991) and Pateman (1989) make particularly clear, the assumption of sameness seems to have an inbuilt tendency to be insensitive to the needs of women. But they also add that 'difference' **feminism** could equally serve to entrap women in positions of dependence and subordination. What is required is forms of citizenship that attempt both to reform the practices of the state – carving out spheres of autonomy – and to restructure a more egalitarian form of **civil society** (Held, 1989).

That Habermas's writing retains problems with regard to contemporary feminism is undeniable. While it is true that any theory of a public sphere pre-supposes a distinction between the public and the private, the problem feminist writers have made us aware of is that the traditional mode of drawing this distinction legitimises the oppression of women. In this respect, Carole Pateman comments:

> In popular (and academic) consciousness the duality of the female and the male often serves to encapsulate or represent the series (or circle) of liberal separations and oppositions: female, or – nature, personal, emotional, love, private, intuition, morality, ascription, particular, subjective; male, or – cultural, political, reason, justice, public, philosophy, power, achievement, universal, freedom. (Pateman, 1982: 109)

Rosi Braidotti (1986) has provocatively argued that the exclusion of women from an independently male public sphere led to the dominance of a masculine form of reasoning. Seemingly, building upon other writers such as Jessica Benjamin (1988) and Nancy Chodorow (1978), she argues that through the male child's renunciation of his primary identification with the mother, he is able to establish firm boundaries and an independent self. The masculine dissociation from the feminine reproduces a public world that upholds detached forms of reasoning. In Habermas's rationalistic account of the public sphere the idea of femininity is reproduced as the 'other'. For Braidotti, thinkers like Habermas reproduce a binary opposition between the feminine and reason. This is perhaps most marked in Habermas's ideal speech situation, where the triumph of the better argument seems to depend upon the exclusion of emotion and affect. Further, the divide in Habermas's conception of the public sphere between 'serious' discussion and pleasure, and between public discourse and consumerism maps onto a distinction between masculinity and feminity. As Joke Hermes (1997) argues this represents the politics of citizenship and the politics of pleasure as belonging to separate planets. Here the assumption seems to be not only is popular entertainment devoid of political content, but that it connects with a gendered understanding of popular culture and the feminine. These points against Habermas's divorce between reason and desire are well taken, but also, I would argue, they rest upon a form of argument that potentially removes the grounds for critique.

As Kate Soper (1990) has argued, to propose that the male public sphere represents an affect-free zone is to collude with masculine forms of subjective misrecognition. For Soper, the male-defined public sphere is anything but impartial, and this can be demonstrated with reference to the opinions of certain male judges in recently publicised rape trials. The forms of moral reasoning apparent in these cases would appear to be anything but detached and impartial. Further, if rationality and impartiality are seen as inherently masculine forms of reason, feminists are not in a position to coherently oppose male forms of domination. Part of the feminist case against the public (male) and private (female) split has been that it is unjust. Women's exclusion from the public sphere has not only robbed them of the possibility of equal forms of public participation, but has prevented men from actively engaging in child-rearing. The political reordering of these spheres is dependent upon the universal application of the principle of equality that is sensitive to difference. The dismissal of such arguments as inherently masculine denies their inherently emancipatory logic and consigns women to the realm of the irrational. The argument that needs to be pursued here then is the rejoining of reason and emotion in a less patriarchally dominated society. The beginnings of such a move would be the recognition that talk shows, news broadcasts, soap operas, celebrity interviews and sports programmes are all capable of raising questions which are of concern to modern citizens. Yet while Habermas can be criticised for neglecting the so-called other side of reason, his emphasis upon a rational public sphere has not been adequately refuted by his critics. Indeed, we could equally argue that communicative forms of reason would allow for a greater reflexivity in terms of our emotional needs. The relations between reason and emotion could become redrawn, allowing citizens opportunities to take up certain rights of participation and forge empathetic relations with others. Again, communicative rationality, given the cultural complexity of modernity and the operation of unconscious feelings, would not allow social subjects to become self-transparent, but it could certainly provide the framework of rights and obligations that would allow for the emergence of new, less instrumental subject positions.

On the other hand, Nancy Fraser (1994) has pointed out that Habermas's analysis of the public sphere remains oblivious to the ways in which money and power reinforce masculine forms of domination in the private sphere. She argues that Habermas's colonisation thesis tends to focus upon the way in which these two 'media' reshape public rather than private institutions. For our purposes this remains a crucial dimension in mass communication studies. As the following chapter will show, masculine power in the household often means that male-headed nuclear families reproduce relations of power in everyday interaction with communication technologies. Further, feminist-led research has sought to highlight the ways in which subordinate family members (women and children) have developed resistant strategies by drawing upon hegemonically ambiguous semiotic cultures.

Summary

Habermas's analysis of the emergence of the public sphere has proved to be an important resource in the struggle to preserve public systems of communication. The principle of publicity holds that culture is intersubjectively produced and should be opened up to rational questioning. Communicative action also has implications for the rights and obligations of modern citizenship, although these universal norms need to be skilfully applied with due respect to difference and the impact of electronic cultures. Habermas's theory was also found to contain a number of blind spots with respect to popular aesthetics, reception contexts, the history of communications, the spatial dimensions of the public sphere and masculine power. These aside, Habermas's projections provide an essential contribution to mass communication studies and should continue to inform critical research in this area.

Critical Perspectives within Audience Research

Problems in Interpretation, Agency, Structure and Ideology

The Emergence of Critical Audience Studies

Basically two kinds of audience research are currently being undertaken. The first and most widely circulated form of knowledge about the audience is gathered by large-scale communication institutions. This form of investigation is made necessary as television, radio, cinema and print production need to attract viewers, listeners and readers. In order to capture an audience modern institutions require knowledge about the 'public's' habits, tastes and dispositions. This enables media corporations to target certain audience segments with a programme or textual strategy. The desire to know who is in the audience at any one time provides useful knowledge that attracts advertisers, and gives broadcasters certain impressions of who they are addressing.

Some critics have suggested that the new cable technology will be able to calculate how many people in a particular area of the city watched last night's Hollywood blockbuster. This increasingly individualised knowledge base dispenses with the problem of existing networks of communication where the majority of advertisements might be watched by an underclass too poor to purchase the goods on offer. Yet the belief that new technology will deliver a streamlined consumer-hungry audience to advertisers sounds like an advanced form of capitalist wish fulfilment. This might be the strategy behind a number of investments in new communications technologies, but its realisation is a different matter. Audiences have devised ways of avoiding semiotic capitalism's attempts to make them sit through obligatory periods of advertising. This is achieved by watching another channel, making a cup of tea during the commercial break, or pressing the fast-forward button on the video. In response, commercial culture has sought to integrate advertising into the programmes themselves. Although this makes some form of engagement with consumer products unavoidable, the audience has not been rendered passive. During the 1994 World Cup, American viewers keen to avoid a variety of commercial strategies that had been integrated into the commentary switched to Spanish-language cable television stations. These provided better coverage, as the advertising was not as intrusive, although it is unlikely that many of the viewers would have understood the linguistic framing of the event. This example points to a situation where the capitalisation and proliferation of different networks make it easier for the audience to escape 'particular' media strategies for their attention. The channel-hopping viewing patterns fostered by these conditions will again make it more difficult to calculate audience share.

But, as Ien Ang (1991) has argued, the practice of making the audience statistically knowable has the consequence of reifying its actual social practices. We may know that 20 per cent of women health workers watched last night's episode of *Ally McBeal*, but this actually tells us very little about their viewing context, or indeed the meaning that was constructed from the programme by the women. The form of quantifiable knowledge required by commercial and state institutions is continually disrupted by the everyday practice of the audience. For Ang, and others, the members of the audience remain slightly anarchistic. Our health worker settling down to watch *Ally McBeal* might also be zapping over to another channel to watch the new Prince video, or indeed she could be interrupted by a work-related telephone call. In such a context it would be difficult to decide what actually counts as 'watching'. It is the so-called ordinary practices and pleasures of viewing, listening and reading that constitute the second paradigm of mass communication research. This strand of audience watching has been developed by interpretative approaches to sociology and media studies. Against the more instrumental concerns of commercial organisations these studies have sought to address the life – world contexts of media audiences. Here the concerns of audience research are focused on offered interpretations and the social relations of reception.

Contemporary interest in the interpretative activity of the audience usually contains a strong critique of the cultural pessimism of certain members of the early Frankfurt school, and an indebtedness to the so-called uses and gratifications approach. As we saw earlier, certain members of the Frankfurt school tended to view popular culture through a specific attachment to modernist art. This particular cultural disposition meant that they did not problematise the reading activities of a socially situated audience. It is a disposition evident in literary approaches to the media, like that of Raymond Williams, and Fredric Jameson, whose readings of culture are intended to both mirror and replace those of absent social subjects. Uses and gratifications research, on the other hand, sought to substitute the idea of what measurable 'effects' the media have on the audience with an analysis of the ways in which people use the media. This research, mostly pioneered by post-war social psychology, brought to the fore the notion that the audience's perceptions of messages could be radically different from the meanings intended by their producer(s). While there remains some dispute as to the debt current audience research owes to this perspective, it is not our concern here (Curran, 1990; Morley, 1992). Instead, a word or two needs to be said, by way of an introduction, on the intellectual roots of the renewed concern with the audience. The strands of cultural theory I want to address have all grown out of the questioning of the assumption that the meaning of an action can simply be taken for granted. That is, the subjectivity of the audience is constructed through its interaction with certain material conditions of existence and a variety of symbolic forms. These concerns are usually connected with a symbolic conception of culture.

The writing of the anthropologist Clifford Geertz (1973) has been particularly vital in helping shape a *symbolic* approach to cultural studies. Geertz argues that what we call culture is the web of signification that has been spun by meaningful actions, objects and expressions. In this sense, culture is neither objective nor subjective. The empiricist claim that the production of hard objective data (such as that produced by viewing figures) can provide a secure anchoring for the social sciences is dismissed by this approach. Such objectivistic claims seem to hold out the possibility of breaking out of the circle of interpretation altogether. Geertz's stress on the symbolic nature of culture retains an openness to further interpretations by the lay actors themselves or the investigative sociologists. Here there is a need to distinguish between first- and second-order interpretations: a separation needs to be made between the intersubjective meanings produced by the agents themselves, and the sense social scientists make of these interpretations. Cultural expressions are meaningful for social agents as well as for the researchers that study them. Further, if we can agree that meaning is a public and intersubjective property, this entails that it is not somehow held inside people's heads. In short, a good interpretation of a particular linguistic community is not governed by the author's cleverness, but by his or her ability to take the reader to the 'heart' of the symbolically produced common meanings.

James Carey (1989), commenting on the recent 'interpretative turn' within media sociology, argues that there has been a corresponding move away from functional approaches. By functional analysis he means research that concentrates upon whether or not the mass media confirm or disrupt the status quo. A more symbolic approach to cultural forms, he suggests, would seek to examine the interaction of symbolic meanings within communication. And yet while this is a legitimate area of inquiry, there remains a fundamental difficulty with this kind of approach to mass communication studies. To put it bluntly, some of the studies that have utilised this particular understanding of culture remain under-appreciative of the operation of power and social structure in the production and reception of symbolic forms. Following on from the previous two chapters, I shall argue that the production of meaning should be related to the operation of institutions and power. Further, that the symbolic celebration of the interpretative capacity of the audience, in certain instances, has been allowed to replace a more critical and normative social theory. However, within such an analysis, we need to be particularly careful that notions of power apply to both public and private domains, and that we recognise that audience studies is a key development within the study of media and culture.

Though there are many approaches to audience research that might have been examined, I shall focus on three main areas of debate, defined as follows: (1) building upon Stuart Hall's encoding and decoding essay, David Morley has offered a provocative analysis of the interpretative capacity and viewing contexts of the television audience; (2) John Fiske's writing has drawn upon a range of cultural theory to argue that the guerrilla activity of the audience offers a means of resistance to the dominant power bloc; (3) feminist theory has made its main contribution through an analysis of women's pleasurable and potentially utopian reading of popular romances and soap operas. While providing a critical commentary on each of these perspectives, I shall also seek to suggest how these contributions might be both improved and extended.

David Morley and the Television Audience:
Encoding/Decoding Revisited

Like Stuart Hall, David Morley's specific contribution to cultural and media studies has grown out of the Centre for Contemporary Cultural Studies at the University of Birmingham. Between 1975 and 1979, while still at the Centre, Morley applied Hall's (1980) famous encoding/decoding essay to the study of the popular current affairs programme *Nationwide* (Morley, 1980, 1992). To quickly recap, Hall's essay argues that there is a basic distinction between the social processes that encode and decode media texts. Cultural forms can be said to be encoded through a specific historical mix of institutional relations, professional norms and technical equipment. The decoding strategies employed by the audience are similarly dependent upon social structural relations, political and cultural dispositions and access to the relevant technology. While Hall's essay states the dual nature of textual production, it is most often remembered for the emphasis it places on three forms (preferred, negotiated and oppositional) of audience reading strategy. This model forms the backdrop to Morley's *Nationwide* study and subsequent studies in audience research.

Semiotics, Sociology and the Television Audience

In this section I aim to trace through the shifting contours of David Morley's concern to provide a theoretical perspective adequate to capture the cultural practices of the television audience. Let me begin by briefly outlining the main concerns of his *Nationwide* study, before moving on to his later contributions. Following Hall, the process of meaning generation, Morley argues, is dependent upon the internal structure of the television message (semiotics) and the cultural background of the viewer (sociology). The 'meaning' of *Nationwide* is the product of the preferred reading offered by the text and the cultural dispositions of the audience. At the level of the encoded text, one needs to address both the explicit content and the 'invisible', taken-for-granted meanings. The popular discourse of *Nationwide* was concerned with the arena of home, leisure and consumption while rendering silent the more public world of work. In order to understand how the horizons of the text are able to connect with the cultural presuppositions of the audience, Morley seeks to make explicit the text's mode of address. *Nationwide* addressed the audience as individual citizens who live in a specifically national political community. This is different, say, from the mode of address employed by game shows that usually 'speak to us' as though we are members of happy nuclear families. That is, any ideological analysis should seek to reveal the way in which popular texts produce certain subject positions. But it is central to Morley's argument that through different decoding strategies the preferred meaning of the text can be resisted by the culturally coded reading strategies of the audience. Thus *Nationwide* does not have a causal 'effect' on the audience but must be interpreted. This does not mean, however, that the audience is able to read any meaning into the text. The text acts as a structured polysemy that while never achieving 'total' ideological closure can open up certain meanings while closing down others. In this sense, Morley is sharply critical of those modes of cultural theory that reduce meaning either to the subject positions inscribed within the text, or to the subjective prejudices of the audience.

In his more recent writing, Morley (1992: 60) has again returned to the writing of Stuart Hall. Here, following Hall's critique of Lacan and Althusser, he has argued that any theory of interpretation needs to attend to the space between constituted subjects and specific discourses.[1] A theory of interpretation would have to encounter the constant interruption by discourses other than those embedded within the text. Hence, as we saw in the discussion of Hall and Laclau, modern identities are the heterogeneous construction of a multitude of discursive practices.

For example, a white, male, working-class trade unionist would be capable, depending on the context, of offering either dominant hegemonic, negotiated or oppositional readings. To put the point more concretely, our trade unionist may be a Labour voter, a sexist and a racist all at once. The problem with Morley's *Nationwide* study, as he later realised, is that the audience's reading strategies are mainly understood through a class paradigm (Morley, 1981, 1992).

In the *Nationwide* study, Morley and his colleagues showed two editions of the programme to a culturally diverse number of groups. Then they decided to interview the subjects in clusters in order to investigate how talk became collectively constructed through discussion. In conversation with the various groupings, Morley was able to further refine the encoding/decoding model. The bank managers' conversations, he discovered, hardly commented on the content of the programme as it seemed relatively uncontroversial. This meant that the subjectivity of the bank managers was closely aligned with the dominant reading position offered by the text, rendering the constructed nature of the text invisible. This reading sharply contrasts with a group of trade unionists who were able to render the ideological construction of the programme visible by identifying it as in the interests of middle management. But Morley also found that oppositional readings were not confined to subordinate groups. Print management trainees produced an oppositional reading based upon a rightist perspective. On the other hand, where the disjuncture between the audience and the text was too wide, the subjects often fell silent. This was the case with further education students drawn from inner city areas. Here there seemed to be little actual point of identification between the subjective prejudices of the group and the semiotically constructed text. These observations, for Morley, suggest certain problems with the original encoding/decoding model derived from Hall's writing. The difficulties experienced with this approach are defined as follows: (1) the idea of the preferred reading invokes the notion that the message content is governed by the conscious intentionality of the message sender; (2) the encoding/decoding metaphor invokes a 'conveyor belt' of meaning, rather than the possibility of radical discontinuity between these levels; (3) decoding suggests that the audience attends to the text and produces meaning, whereas if the text has little resonance for the reader it could in fact be ignored; (4) preferred meanings are easier to detect within texts that have a single closed narrative. Other more open texts, such as soap operas, that rely upon a plurality of narratives and relatively unfixed subject positions, may resist a dominant hegemonic reading by the theorist. These criticisms provide a useful backdrop for an analysis of Morley's family television project (Morley, 1988).

The research on family television represents an advance on the *Nationwide* study in three main ways. First, Morley decided to conduct the interviews inside the subjects' homes, since one of the problems with the earlier research was that it was conducted in rather 'artificial' settings isolated from the normal viewing context. The oppositional reading of *Nationwide* produced by the male trade unionists, reasons Morley, would probably lose much of its intensity in a more familial context. Next, Morley argues that the *Nationwide* study left too little room for contradictory decodings. Here he begins to develop a more critical appreciation of the debate I mentioned earlier between Laclau and Hall. Morley accepts that the *Nationwide* study overly compressed the interpretations of the audience around a class paradigm. Here Laclau's writing is valuable in that the subject is represented as being constructed by a matrix of discourses. But Laclau, according to Morley, retains a tendency to reduce the subject to an 'effect' of discourse.[2] Although Morley does not develop the point in any great depth, he argues that discourses provide the cultural resources within which the interpretative subject makes its readings (Morley, 1988: 43). Resisting the Althusserian strain of Laclau's writing, Morley argues that it is difficult to predict the readings subjects will make by attending to the ways in which they have been constructed in discourse. Instead, as many writers critical of post-structuralism have claimed, the subject has the capacity for critical forms of reflexive thinking. To argue that the audience is more than the 'effect' of social practices and discourses is not to argue for the narcissistic return of the omnipotent subject. The fact that the subject remains decentred through social and unconscious processes, while being capable of acting creatively in the social world, is an important feature of the study. Thirdly, and most decisively, Morley's attention to the sociological setting places a greater emphasis upon the ways in which television is actually used in family contexts. This is indicative of his move away from semiotics to a more sociological concern with the power relations that shape viewing practices. This change of emphasis, according to Morley, highlights the way in which the activity of watching television is primarily a 'privatised' activity constituted through family relations. Despite this shift in Morley's concerns, he wisely in my view, aims to keep open the possibility that the preferred meaning is capable of reworking the subjective prejudices of the audience.

The family television project was based upon 18 white families (two adults with two or more children) who were interviewed in 1985. While Morley pays close attention to the viewing context (he interviews unemployed, working-class and middle-class families), his research finds a new focus in the importance of gender for television viewing. The gendered nature of social activity centred around television is evident in all the households and cuts across social class. Morley writes that 'investigating television viewing in the home is by definition investigating something which men are better placed to do wholeheartedly, and which women seem only able to do distractedly and guiltily, because of their continuing sense of their domestic responsibilities' (Morley, 1988: 147).

In most of the families interviewed it was the adult male of the household who had control over the viewing patterns of the other family members. The prominence of male dominance in the household extends to the operation of the television and the video recorder. Masculine control, however, is never absolute and is constantly being challenged by other family members. To offer a few examples. A member of the third family of the study (an unemployed father) describes his relationship to television as 'addicted – it's like a dope to me' (Morley, 1988: 68). Morley notes that within this household the television is rarely switched off and the father exhibits a masculine obsession with watching the television in uninterrupted silence. This was characteristic of men's preferred style of viewing generally, whereas women were much more likely to be involved in at least one other social activity. It was also recognised, by both men and women, that men watched far more television than women. Again this is accounted for by Morley in terms of the gendered division of the household. For men, the home is experienced as a site of relaxation, but for women of all social classes the desire to enjoy television always has to be traded off against feelings of guilt and obligation. When the women were able to negotiate some space, usually when the husband was absent, they tended to watch entertaining programmes which were negatively valued, especially by their husbands, who stated a preference for more factual output. Indeed, such was men's control of the domestic setting that the unemployed father mentioned above exhibited a strong resistance towards attending events outside the household. As these activities were often free, Morley interprets the father's reluctance to go out as a means of fending off the potential loss of 'total power' (Morley, 1988: 70).

The mother of the tenth family of the study (working-class) displays an acute awareness of the role that soap operas often play in women's lives. Women's relative isolation from the public sphere means that they often have three main topics of conversation (children, housework and television) that provide the social 'glue' for community life. Morley notes that, according to his study, while it is men who consume the predominant amount of television, women, on the whole, are more likely to admit that they engage in talk about it. In Morley's (1992) later writing he interprets men's attachment to realist and factual programming as a mode of defence against getting involved in fantasy or emotion. Alternatively women's need to be 'doing something', while watching television, can be associated with the way 'in which gendered identities are constructed in patriarchal society. The reason that watching television remains a guilty pleasure in modern nuclear families is that women's gender role demands that they constantly subordinate their own needs, desires and pleasures to those of their male partners'.

Ann Gray (1992) has followed up some of Morley's research with an investigation into women's relationship with domestic video technology. Like Morley, Gray argues that the 'effects' tradition in communications research denied the cultural competence of the subject. She adopts an approach which neatly complements that of Morley, in that she stresses the importance of the sociocultural context of women's interactions with video and video recorders. Her research highlights gender as the main determinant of the specific use of domestic technology. Gray found that most women, irrespective of social class, were in general not proficient in the operation of the video, and had particular difficulty with the time recorder function. Gray discounts the idea that women's lack of accomplishment in this area is connected to a general fear of technology. According to Gray, and deeply characteristic of the domestic division of labour, women show a mastery of kitchen technology that is absent in most men. But adult women, when compared to other members of the household, were at a distinct disadvantage when it came to organising their viewing via the video recorder. She found that the storing of visual information on videotapes was usually a male-defined activity. This said, the women interviewed in the study had a marked preference for viewing a particular production once only, as opposed to some of the men who displayed a tendency to view the same films over and over again. Here again, Gray shares with Morley the necessity of placing private domestic pleasures within a sociological context where gender relations are determinant.

Class, Power and Ideology in Domestic Leisure

The observations made by Morley on the sociological and semiotic nature of television viewing open up important perspectives in media research. The discussions in the previous chapters have concentrated upon the specifically public nature of modern mass communication systems. Morley, particularly in the family television project, moves against this trend by arguing that the gendered operation of power within 'ordinary' domestic settings is the crucial determinant of viewing patterns. These insights, by no means peculiar to Morley, share much with feminist schools of thought. The theoretical splitting of public and private contexts is characteristic of both liberal and Marxist approaches to the media of mass communications. In this context, the contributions of Williams and Habermas, amongst others, remain overly orientated around a masculinely defined public sphere. While an analysis of the public institutional settings of the operation of mass communication networks remains crucial, this should not be allowed to overshadow the importance of the private sphere. The unequal relations within familial settings has, according to Morley and Gray, a decisive impact on the decoding strategies adopted by the audience.

The problem remains, however, that research such as Morley's reproduces some of the gendered divisions between public and private outlined above. Morley's rather exclusive focus on family settings tends to isolate them from the way in which they are continually permeated by the operation of more public forms of money and power. As a consequence the structural importance of gender divisions retains a significance for public and private life. This omission is probably a consequence of certain shortcomings with the encoding/decoding model borrowed from Stuart Hall. As I indicated in Chapter 1, Hall's concern with meaning and semiotics distances the analysis from more material institutional frameworks of power. Notably, Morley has specifically developed the decoding rather than the encoding dimension of this model. While his later writing has gone some way towards correcting this bias, I believe his research to be inadequately reconstructed in this respect. My main difficulties with Morley's work on mass communication theory include the following:

1. Morley (1992: 275) has sought to defend himself against the charge that he neglects to analyse the intersection of macro and micro contexts. He claims to recognise that any study of the meanings and practices of the audience should involve both an analysis of the interconnection between symbolic and material resources, and the recognition that the audience is not completely 'powerless' despite its isolation from control over institutional processes. Morley argues that he treads a judicious path between the structuralist tradition that reduces the practices and interpretations of the audience to an effect of the text, and the uses and gratification approach, where the emphasis is placed upon certain atomised psychological responses, rather than an historical and sociological account of audience actions. In this respect, he argues, his research has much in common with Anthony Giddens's (1984) theory of structuration:

> It is not a question, finally, of understanding simply television's ideological (or representational) role, or simply its ritual (or socially organising) function, or the process of its domestic (and more broadly social) consumption. It is a question of how to understand all these issues (or dimensions) in relation to each other. (Morley, 1992: 276)

Anthony Giddens's theory of structuration is designed to avoid the sort of polarisation Morley detects in opposing uses and gratifications research and structuralism. Giddens refuses to see action and structure as separate terms of analysis; instead he represents them theoretically in terms of what he calls a 'duality'. Agency is normally thought of as the capacity to do otherwise to that which one has done. What social theorists themselves need to do is to forgo the temptation of opposing this sense of agency to determining structures. Instead, as the term 'duality' suggests, agency and structure are best thought of as interdependent theoretical categories. Giddens writes:

> Understood as rules and resources implicated in the 'form' of collectivities of social systems, reproduced across space and time, structure is the very medium of the 'human' element of human agency. At the same time, agency is the medium of structure, which individuals reproduce in the course of their activities. (Giddens, 1987a: 220–1)

Giddens, for me at least, best illustrates his theory of structuration through a discussion of language use. The rules of language (*langue*) are drawn upon in the actual production of speech (*parole*). Hence one of the unintended consequences of language use is the reproduction of certain generative rules. These rules of language may of course also change, as a result of actual practice. Language, as a set of rules and resources, cannot be thought of as produced by or for any one agent; instead *langue* pre-exists *parole* and is a precondition of language use, not a direct product of it. Thus social structures can be conceptualised as sets of rules and resources, at once enabling and constraining action. At the same time, human agents, as a matter of routine, reflexively monitor their conduct and are able to provide reasons for their actions. This observation does not imply that agents will always be aware of the consequences of their actions, nor will they be equipped with a complete understanding of the conditions of their actions. Leaving aside the various criticisms that have been made of structuration theory, I would argue that Morley's writing on the media can only be superficially associated with Giddens's theoretical writing.

Giddens argues that the structuration of human activity takes place within institutional settings. Morley, in this context, barely mentions the unequal distribution of material and symbolic resources that are dependent upon class as well as gender. This can be illustrated by returning to the unemployed father of the family television project. Here the father's obsessive television viewing is explained as illustrating masculine forms of control evident within domestic contexts. This seems to be especially evident in the father's reluctance to attend cultural events outside the home, in that this would undermine his control over the household's cultural pursuits. Morley's interpretation ignores Golding's (1990) argument that a person's position within the class system will structure an agent's access to certain cultural goods. That is, just because the family has received free theatre tickets does not mean they will have access to the appropriate clothes, transport, or money for the childminder. In addition, as much of Bourdieu's (1984) research has shown, the cultural competencies necessary for the enjoyment of certain kinds of theatre are determined by family background and education. Thus through the operation of power certain dominant social groups restrict the range of material and symbolic options open to agents within public and private settings. Giddens would argue that while this power is never absolute, it does place restrictions on the autonomy of even the most patriarchal father. Yet again, while Morley (1992) has gone some way towards acknowledging these points, they are absent from both the *Nationwide* and family television projects.

Secondly, cultural goods are mostly produced by commercial institutions to be bought and sold in the market-place. As Marxist social theory has argued the *success* of a cultural commodity within a capitalist culture is determined by its ability to make a profit. In the earlier discussion of Raymond Williams's specific contribution to mass communication research, it was made clear that the need to return a profit seriously restricts the variety of cultural products that are made available. Consumers, following Giddens's model, are not passive in this process as they can refuse to buy specific products, but they do not have direct forms of control over the cultural forms that are made available. Hence the capitalist division of labour is a relatively durable set of rules and resources that 'bounds' consumer choices. Again, Morley's emphasis upon more microsocial contexts bypasses this important point.

2. Any analysis that involves the unequal distribution of power inevitably leads us to the terrain of ideology. The study of ideology can be usefully defined as 'the ways in which meaning (signification) serves to sustain relations of domination' (Thompson, 1984: 13~1). Such a concern presupposes an examination of the ways in which structures of domination are mystified, simultaneously reaffirming and obscuring relations of force. To address the mobilisation of meaning in the context of relations of domination, as Morley well understands, is to attend to the ways in which meaning is interpreted in everyday settings. Morley, despite his more focused attention on domestic contexts, wants to keep open the possibility that preferred readings of texts can reinforce certain dominant norms and values. Further, as the *Nationwide* study made clear, programmes that criticise power structures can also be resisted by the more openly ideological perspectives of the viewer. While there remain a number of problems with the way Morley formulates the problem of ideology, here I want to concentrate on the issues opened up by Greg Philo (1990).

The 1984 miners' strike was a long and bitter dispute that dominated British news coverage for its duration. Philo wants to argue that hegemonic operation of power and authority was able to manipulate the public's understanding of the strike. He demonstrates this by asking a wide cross-section of the audience to assemble from a series of photographs a news story representative of the strike. The aim of this exercise was to discover whether a photograph of a gun would be associated with the police, the working miners, or the striking miners. He found that the gun was overwhelmingly connected with the striking miners, even amongst those who were sympathetic to the aims of the strike. Philo interprets this as significant and relates it to the dominant ideological frames of news production that were present during the strike: that the picket lines were violent and that the main responsibility for this state of affairs lay with the striking miners. Yet Philo's research also reveals that, regardless of political perspective, those who had either been directly or indirectly involved with picket lines during the strike were less likely to believe they were mostly violent places. So those with 'personal experience' of picket lines did not readily accept the dominant perspectives offered by the media. The other major reason offered for doubting the television news was access to alternative perspectives, primarily through the quality press, and the local press and radio. The effective criminalisation of the strike by the state and the national broadcast media had the effect of minimising more public forms of solidarity with the miners. The state's manipulation of news reporting was most evident in the attention paid to the 'big return' at the end of the strike. Here the underlying theme of national news reporting became the number of people returning to work (the figures being supplied by the state-owned Coal Board) rather than the number who stayed out on strike. The ideological 'effect' of this discursive strategy was again to limit the solidarity of the strike by isolating those miners who had withdrawn their labour.

Philo's main concern with more 'micro' studies like Morley's is that they are unable to show the social processes by which certain meanings are generated by dominant social groups, and made to stick. This is a powerful charge. Although Philo's research comes close to stressing a modified version of the dominant ideology thesis, he does demonstrate the necessity of linking certain consciously held perspectives to the dominant social order. Interestingly, while Morley's later work wants to keep open the possibility of the preferred reading, he is unable to provide many examples of this process working through. Philo's more macro approach has the advantage of being able to demonstrate how the state and national media were able to provide the ideological framework within which debates about the miners' strike took place. Yet Morley's more specifically located writing, given the points made above, offers a corrective to Philo's grand ambitions. The blind spot of Philo's perspective, as Morley discovered in the *Nationwide* study, is that occupational group discussions artificially divorce meaning from context. Philo does not really address the ways in which linguistic meaning is dependent upon the socially situated interpretations of lay actors. Indeed he retains the Glasgow group's emphasis upon the ways in which a dominant ideology transmitted by the news media helps shape the legitimate discursive arena of political debate. For instance, the miners' strike could have been attributed different meanings at different periods of the strike (the interviews took place a year after the strike was over), and the strike could have been divergently interpreted depending on whether it was read in public or domestic settings. This argument could be taken further if we remember that the year-long miners' strike was an exceptional political event. As Morley's *Nationwide* study showed, the readings attributed to television content are more likely to produce a complex and divergent range of meanings than to hegemonically secure social consensus.

3. The communications media are often felt to be a powerful source for the distribution of ideas and concepts about the social world. Critical studies, particularly within the Western Marxist tradition, have tended to concentrate upon the ways media content has shaped conscious beliefs and practices. The traditional criticism of this perspective is that it overstates the cohesiveness of the messages transmitted by the media, and neglects to analyse the way differentially situated

social agents interpret a range of information. Morley has further criticised this paradigm by arguing that notions of ideology should be expanded to look at how the media contribute to the temporal organisation of the day. Broadcasters are continually making assumptions about the way that audiences organise their day and, more importantly, who is watching. We regularly talk about *morning* newspapers, *breakfast* television and Radio 4's book at *bedtime*. The shared ritual of engaging with these cultural forms can be as important as the informational content.

These are important developments, as they demonstrate ways in which the media structure social life that go beyond actual consciously held beliefs. But Morley (and Philo for that matter) could still be criticised for mainly concentrating upon the way that ideology leaves its trace on conscious perspectives. Terry Eagleton (1991) has argued that the most politically important thing about spending large amounts of time watching television is not the ideological effect it has on the viewer. What is probably most crucial is that while people are watching television they are not engaging in more serious political activity. In Eagleton's terms 'television is more a form of social control than an ideological apparatus' (Eagleton, 1991: 35). This is an important point that has not been lost on repressive regimes that have sought to keep the populace entertained on a diet of cheap commercial television, which can be purchased on the world market. In contemporary Western societies the importance of television can be associated with the privatisation of leisure activities in the home (Phillips and Tomlinson, 1992). The ideological consequences of a more homecentred leisure culture is perhaps to be found in the atomisation of leisure practices and social forms of isolation from wider collectives. Indeed, as Lefebvre (1992) once argued, leisure time is expected to be a form of relaxation and therefore a break from the world of work. Thus the ideology of leisure is not to be found in the content of television news broadcasts, or the ways that citizens interpret them, but in the fact that it is meant to be a passive and not particularly intellectually demanding activity. This is not to suggest that media studies should return to the early Frankfurt school's notion of the passive consumer of **mass culture**, but it is to argue that for most of the audience, most of the time, modern culture is engaged with as a form of escape. Moreover, although Morley's more sociological emphasis pays close attention to the domestic context, his semiotic leanings overstate the ideological importance of the interpretative capacity of the audience. Yet when we come to explore more explicitly actual contexts they are more complex than these speculations allow. For example, James Lull's (1991) study of the mass introduction of television into Chinese society during the 1980s both induced more individualised patterns of leisure, while exposing ordinary people to an increased diversity of semiotic material. Despite the fact that Chinese television remains heavily regulated by the state the shift towards 'home centeredness' could also be linked to an enhanced form of ideological pluralism.

In this short section we have seen that Morley's research on the television audience opened up a semiotic and sociological analysis of audience activity. These arguments were considered to be of particular importance in light of recent feminist critiques of a masculine obsession with the public rather than the private sphere. Morley's analysis bears out that the particular 'use' the audience makes of media technology and cultural forms is decided through the human archaeology of domestic settings. But Morley's writing, despite some of the qualifications he makes, remains distant from wider structural contexts of money and power. This was evident in relation to the structuration of domestic contexts through more macro frameworks of power, the absence of a theory of ideology that incorporated these very structures of domination, and in the fact that the functioning of certain cultural activities as forms of social control may be more important than their semiotic richness. These matters will continue to be of concern in the following sections.

John Fiske and the Pleasure of Popular Culture

John Fiske, like David Morley, has sought to articulate a theory of popular culture that builds upon Hall's original encoding/decoding essay. Running through most of his writing on popular culture is the distinction between instrumental streamlined forms of production that characterise capitalism, and the creative meanings invested in these products by the consumers. There is a radical break between the interests of the economic institutions that produce cultural forms and the interpretative concerns of the audience. Fiske expresses this distinction as an opposition between the 'power bloc' (the dominant cultural, political and social order) and the 'people' (sets of felt social allegiances cut across by class, gender, race, age, etc.). The 'power bloc' produces uniform mass-produced products which are then transformed into practices of resistance by the 'people'. As Fiske argues, 'popular culture is made by the people, not produced by the culture industry' (Fiske, 1989a: 24). To be considered popular, therefore, commodities have to be able to be mass produced for economic return, and be potentially open to the subversive readings of the people. For Fiske, once I have purchased the new Madonna compact disc from the local music store, the product has become detached from the strategies of capitalism. The music of Madonna is not simply a standardised product that can be purchased through the institutions of global capitalism, but is a cultural resource of everyday life. The act of consumption always entails the production of meaning.

The circulation of meaning requires us to study three levels of textuality while teasing out the specific relations between them. First there are the cultural forms that are produced along with the new Madonna album to create the idea of a media event. These can include concerts, books, posters and videos. At the next level, there is a variety of media talk in popular magazines and newspapers, television pop programmes and radio shows all offering a variety of critical commentary upon Madonna. The final level of textuality, the one that Fiske claims to be most attentive to, involves the ways in which Madonna becomes part of our everyday life. According to Fiske (1987a, 1989b), Madonna's career was launched by a rock video of an early song called 'Lucky Star'. She became established in 1985 as a cultural icon through a series of successful LPs and singles, the film *Desperately Seeking Susan*, nude shots that appeared in *Penthouse* and *Playboy*, as well as the successful marketing of a certain 'look'. Fiske argues that Madonna symbolically plays with traditional male-dominated stereotypes of the virgin and the whore in order to subtly subvert patriarchal meanings. That is, the textuality of Madonna ideologically destabilises traditional representations of women. Fiske accounts for Madonna's success by arguing that she is an open or writerly text rather than a closed readerly one. In this way, Madonna is able to challenge her fans to reinvent their own sexual identities out of the cultural resources that she and patriarchal capitalism provides. Hence Madonna as a text is polysemic, patriarchal and sceptical. In the final analysis, Madonna is not popular because she is promoted by the culture industry, but because her attempts to forge her own identity within a male-defined culture have a certain relevance for her fans.

While Fiske draws from a range of cultural theory, most notably semiotics and post-structuralism, the work of Michel de Certeau (1984) has a particular resonance for his approach. For de Certeau, popular culture is best defined as the operations performed upon texts, rather than the actual domains of the texts themselves. Everyday life has to operate within the instrumental spaces that have been carved out by the powerful. To read a fashion magazine, listen to a punk album, put on a soccer supporter's scarf, or pin up a picture of David Bowie, is to discover a way of using common culture that is not strictly proscribed by its makers. The act of consumption is part of the 'tactics' of the weak that while occupying the spaces of the strong converts disciplinary and instrumental time into that which is free and creative. The specific tactics that evade instrumental modes of domination, or what de Certeau sometimes calls cultural poaching, in practice never become reified as they are constantly shifting and thereby evade detection. In this vein, de Certeau describes as 'la perruque' those artful practices that are able to trick order. For instance, the practice of writing a love letter while at work is a means of stealing time from an instrumental activity and diverting it into a more sensuous pursuit. Thus while the practices of the powerful dominate the production of cultural forms and regulate the spaces of their reception, the reading processes of the weak elude strategies of direct control. To take another example derived from de Certeau; while Spanish colonisers were 'successful' in imposing their own culture on indigenous Indians, the dominated were able to make of this imposed culture something different from that which the conquerors intended. This was not achieved through revolutionary struggle, but by accepting the culture of the Spanish and subtly transforming it for their own ends.

Following de Certeau, Fiske dispenses with the notion of the 'preferred reading' evident within the original encoding/decoding model. Both Fiske and de Certeau are keen to distance themselves from cultural theories, like those proposed by the early Frankfurt school, which assume that the consumer becomes more like the product, rather than the notion that consumers make the product more like themselves. More conservative cultural accounts, for de Certeau, stem from the Enlightenment belief that certain authorised forms of knowledge were capable of transforming the habits of the people. This particular disposition establishes a definite hierarchy between those professional intellectuals who construct the text and those who are meant to passively assimilate it. The 'power bloc', in this reading, attempts to close down the potential meanings of the text by hierarchically fixing certain interpretations over others. The modern world, however, has witnessed a decline in the power of tradition in general, and intellectuals in particular, to proscribe meanings in this way. De Certeau writes:

> Just as the aeroplane makes possible a growing independence with respect to the constraints imposed by geographical organisation, the techniques of speed reading obtain, through the rarefaction of the eye's stopping points, an acceleration of its movements across the page, an autonomy in relation to the determinants of the text and a multiplication of the spaces covered. Emancipated from places, the reading body is freer in its movements. (De Certeau, 1984:176)

Indeed, for de Certeau, the need to write flows from a psychic desire to master and order the world. The emergence of the novel, therefore, was an attempt to recapture some of the cosmological language that had previously defined one's place in the world within traditional society. In the modern age of atomised individualism there has been a further decline in the commitment to certain beliefs. Further, as those institutions, such as religious and political organisations, lose their capacity to engender belief, the people take refuge in media and leisure activities. We now live in a 'recited' society that constantly circulates narratives and stories through the medium of mass communication. In the post-truth world, the people are saturated by a plurality of discourses that are struggling for the consent of the audience, the difference being that the explosion of messages that characterises modernity is no longer stamped with the 'authority' of their authors. De Certeau aptly describes the way in which old religious forms of authority have been supplanted by a plurality of narratives that empower the reader, rather than the writer. Similarly, Fiske argues that the shift from national to global capitalism has meant that the system of production has become more distant, leaving the necessary space for oppositional tactics. The central paradox of modernity identified by Fiske and de Certeau is that the more information that is produced by the power bloc, the less it is able to govern the various interpretations made of it by socially situated subjects. To illustrate this point, Fiske (1987b) draws upon the seminal research of Hodge and Tripp (1986) into children's relationship with television.

Hodge and Tripp aim to refute the joint myths that television is necessarily educationally bad for children and that parents and children read television in the same way. This concern is particularly evident in their attempt to unravel the reasons for the popularity of the soap opera *Prisoner Cell Block H* amongst Australian schoolchildren. Hodge and Tripp found that the schoolchildren identified with the women prisoners of the television series. The authors explain this phenomenon through the structural similarities of the position of the children within the school and those of the fictional prisoners. Schoolchildren and the prisoners live under a single authority, are treated alike in a tightly scheduled order imposed from above, and have their activities co-ordinated by the rational planning of the institution. The schoolchildren also articulated a number of points of similarity, between the school and the prison, in terms of the way they are often shut in, separated from friends, have no rights, wouldn't be there unless they had to be, and are made to suffer rules they see little point in keeping. The pupils' own self-perceptions resembled those represented by the prisoners, who were also reduced to 'childlike' roles within the programmes. Similarly, the teachers and the prison warders, as figures of authority, were often positioned together. Hence the popularity of *Prisoner Cell Block H* is the result of the children's understanding that schools are like prisons. To return to Fiske's arguments, as Hodge and Tripp amply demonstrate, the 'popular' is an open, fluid and shifting culture that is realised through the symbolic tactics of the weak. The symbolic practices of the schoolchildren can only be made sense of if their various interpretations are understood in terms of the asymmetrical relations of power that exist between adults and children. If Fiske's conclusions are accepted, research into children and television should be concerned less with the ideological corrupting influences of television than with the way it is used as a form of resistance.

Life's More Fun with the Popular Press

In a reprinted interview, Fiske describes his own theoretical output as being concerned to articulate 'a socialist theory of pleasure' (Fiske, 1989b). These irreverent forms of *jouissance* that erupt from below are opposed to the disciplinary techniques utilised by the power bloc. Here there is a double pleasure involved in the audience's reading of popular texts. The first is the enjoyment involved in the symbolic production of meanings that oppose those of the power bloc, and the second concerns the actual activity of being productive. These practices are particularly important within modern settings, as not unlike his colleague John Hartley (1992), Fiske argues that modern bureaucratic politics is controlled by a small, powerful minority. The 'distance' of parliamentary democracy from the fabric of people's everyday lives means that participation in the political comes through the creative use of popular products. In this scenario, the market, unlike the declining high culture of the powerful, brings certain cultural products within the critical horizons of the people. The problem with much of the cultural production of the power bloc is that it remains insufficiently polysemic and too concerned with the discovery of objective truth. The search for a final universal truth, which this position implies, is totalitarian rather than democratic. The result is the closing down of the plurality of truths that should be allowed expression under a democratic order. Arguments that the news should be more accurate and objective are actually supportive of the discursive practices of the power bloc. A more democratic form of electronic journalism would seek to ironise truth claims by seeking to reveal the ways in which they are socially and historically produced. To claim that there is one truth, therefore, is to capitulate to the dominant regime of truth, and deny the potentially liberatory pleasure of the text. But once the production of information has given up 'the tone of the author-god' (Fiske, 1989b: 193) this should encourage viewers to become more actively involved in making sense of the world. While citizens are excluded from direct forms of involvement in the decision-making processes of modern representative democracies, they could be allowed more micro forms of participation in a semiotic democracy.

Fiske (1992) has recently sought to make these theoretical points more concrete through a discussion of the press. Here he outlines three different forms of news production: quality, alternative and popular. As we saw above, the cultural production of the 'power bloc' ideologically disguises the interested nature of its production by appeals to universal values. In this way, the quality press, through the production of objective facts actually gears its output towards producing belief rather than scepticism amongst its readers. The eighteenth-century public sphere, defended in Habermas's (1989) account, was not so much about communicatively opening up certain repressed questions, as it was a strategy of domination. It was the power bloc rather than the citizens who decided to circulate certain forms of information that did not require the active engagement of the weak. Next, the transmission of more radical perspectives is sustained by the alternative press, which is dependent upon the practice of radical journalists and is mainly consumed by the educated middle class. This form of news is more critical of the practices of the dominant than the quality press, but its readers and writers are usually made up of more marginal representatives of the power bloc itself. The tabloid or popular press, unlike the quality or alternative press, deconstructs the opposition between news and entertainment. This is a necessary move as entertainment is just as much a discursive product as so-called 'hard' news, and for the news to become more popular it needs to be able to pleasurably engage the audience. Fiske also claims that while the quality press produces a believing subject the tabloids encourage more critical forms of cultural production amongst their readers. Through the production of open texts the tabloid press produces:

> sceptical laughter which offers the pleasures of disbelief, the pleasures of not being taken in. This popular pleasure of 'seeing through' them (whoever constitutes the powerful them of the moment) is the historical result of centuries of subordination which the people have not allowed to develop into subjection. (Fiske, 1992: 49)

What is important about the tabloid press is not whether the articles and features it runs are actually true, but its oppositional stance to official regimes of truth. Fiske illustrates this argument by referring to a story concerning aliens landing from outer space, which he claims to be a recurrent one within tabloid journalism. The point about such stories is that they subversively blur the distinction between facts and fiction, thereby disrupting the dominant language game disseminated by the power bloc. Further, while official news attempts to ideologically mask the contradictions evident within its discourse, the tabloid press deliberately seeks to exaggerate certain norms, hereby *abnormalising* them. Fiske's argument here is that the sensation-alised stories characteristic of the tabloids produce a writerly text in that they openly invite the interpretative participation of their readers. The tabloids, like other popular texts such as Madonna and soap operas, maintain their popularity by informing people about the world in a way that is open to the tactics of the weak. In this reading, the various forms of depoliticisation evident within Western democracies are attributable more to the quality than to the popular press. On the other hand, Fiske claims to be aware that the popular press is rarely orchestrated towards politically progressive ends. But the cultural and stylistic form of the popular press could, according to Fiske, be turned against the interests of the powerful. A Left political strategy should steer clear of 'preachiness' (Fiske, 1989a: 178) and advocate pleasurable texts that refuse the temptation of imposing certain socially correct meanings. This would hold open the possibility of a genuinely left-wing paper that did not seek rigidly to control the meanings produced by its readers.

Pointless Populism or Resistant Pleasures?

The main strength of John Fiske's approach to the study of media and culture is the emphasis he places upon the creative work undertaken by the audience in the production of negotiated and oppositional readings. The study of popular culture is not about the macro issues of political economy, ideology or the public sphere, but about the evasive tactics of the weak. This view offers an important corrective to those who continue to ignore the capacity of the audience to involve themselves in semiotic insurgence. Fiske's work has proved to be important to those who wish to respect the ambivalent pleasures of popular culture providing a close reading of different textual and audience strategies. Fiske's work has allowed for the study of fan communities, pleasurable forms of identification and interpretive moments that have read cultural forms against the grain. But I want to argue that the writing of John Fiske has a number of flaws. Here I shall offer five main reasons for this claim: (1) his account pays insufficient attention to the institutions that structurate the reception of symbolic forms; (2) his arguments foreclose the possibility of a theory of ideology; (3) his view of the popular press excludes any concrete investigation of its actual content; (4) he lacks a critical conception of the political importance of the fragmentation of the public sphere; and (5) he consistently substitutes his own reading of popular forms for those of the audience.

1. Fiske's socialist theory of pleasure is dependent on a view of the market democratising the people's access to cultural goods. This assumption can only be maintained if mass forms of culture are compared with so called 'high culture'. As Bourdieu (1984) has argued, access to the relevant cultural disposition for the enjoyment of the 'official arts' is dependent upon the subject's family and educational background. This disposition, or what Bourdieu refers to as the dominant aesthetic, is a learnt bodily sense that emphasises the primacy of detachment and contemplation over active forms of involvement. The habitus of the dominant class can be discerned in the ideology of natural charisma, as well as the notion that 'taste' is a gift from nature. The dominant lifestyle is historically born out of a division within the dominant class between the industrial bourgeoisie and the intelligentsia. The intelligentsia's separation from material necessity has meant that they have traditionally misrecognised their own cultural production as disinterested. Bourdieu's aim is to treat apparently neutral practices, such as those involved in cultural production, as a strategic means of gaining money and power. The intelligentsia's aesthetic disposition naturalises their specific production and reception of certain types of symbolic goods. In opposition, the popular aesthetic, the product of the cultural disposition of the working class, expresses a desire for participation and immediate forms of gratification. This would explain the popularity of soccer as a spectator sport amongst working-class males, given the opportunities for participation through fashion, chanting and singing. The range of cultural practices that are embodied in the popular aesthetic are distinct from those generated by the dominant aesthetic. Hence the social space generated for audience participation within the dominant aesthetic is more tightly regulated. To gain pleasure from the less spontaneous atmosphere of an art gallery or museum, according to Bourdieu, presupposes that one has access to the appropriate social codes and dispositions.

To return to Fiske, we can see that his and Bourdieu's accounts retain a similarity in relation to the popular need for a strong sense of involvement in cultural practices. Whether these practices are the result of the excess of the tabloids, the writerly texts of soap operas or the more immediate pleasures of soccer spectatorship, they can be defined in opposition to both the instrumental production of the power bloc and the aesthetic disposition of the bourgeoisie. There does indeed seem to be some justification in the argument that the popular culture of the marketplace is more inclusive than that of the educated bourgeoisie or the power bloc. But neither Fiske, nor Bourdieu, in their admittedly distinct analyses, pay any sustained attention to the institutions of the culture industry (Garnham, 1986b). For instance, the commercial institutions of late capitalism are geared towards targeting certain audience segments. Dick Hebdige has described the post-Fordist move away from mass to more flexible forms of production as the 'sociology of aspiration' (Hebdige, 1989: 53). By this he means that commercial forms of culture are symbolically arranged to connect with the lifestyles and the future desires of consumer groups. What is not clear is that the oppositional readings of target groups actually constitute forms of resistance that subvert the economic structures of late capitalism, or that commercial forms of culture are as materially accessible as Fiske implies.

Computer games, for example, are sold to a young teenage audience through television advertising, trade magazines, television programmes, radio shows and the popular press. Fiske could argue that some game formats constitute relatively open texts, which leaves them open to semiotic forms of resistance. The problem with this argument is that it is difficult to see how the structures of late capitalism are threatened by this activity. Indeed, as with other cultural forms, computer games are likely to have a certain semiotic openness deliberately built into them. As I argued in Chapter 2, structures of domination are just as likely to be maintained through social atomism as by ideological consensus. A society whose imaginary is constituted through difference and diversity rather than sameness provides a plurality of markets for capitalist accumulation strategies. Of course this does not mean, as Fiske demonstrates, that certain readings critical of the dominant social order cannot be opened up through an engagement with the popular. What I am arguing instead is that a fragmented culture may undermine the social cohesion necessary to produce relations of solidarity with those not immediately present in time and space. This situation is likely to destabilise political attempts to symbolically create alliances amongst the weak against the power bloc. Indeed, one could argue that the culturally fractured nature of the audience works in the interests of the culture industry, as it provides new markets and promotes an individualistic culture.

If this argument is followed, then a more effective means of resisting the capitalist computer game industry would be by the use of decommodification strategies. Such practices could include the setting up of public lending libraries for computer games and the production of new games by co-operatives. That such projects are unlikely to occur is surely due to the fact that investment is controlled by large transnational corporations, which in turn are progressively privatising public forms of culture. This problem is completely bypassed by Fiske. In fact, he even suggests, at one point, that new forms of solidarity evident on the dance floor, in fan culture and other popular practices could provide the basis for a more socially just society (Fiske, 1989a: 176). A more institutional frame of reference could have more adequately contextualised the creative responses of the audience by linking them to socially reproducible structures of domination. In this interpretation semiotic playfulness and the dominance of the status quo could be more closely related than Fiske is aware.

Similarly, the absence of an institutional perspective blinds Fiske to material rather than symbolic distinctions amongst the audience. As Peter Golding (1990) has argued, the Western capitalist nations exhibit massive inequalities in terms of their access to cultural goods. This situation is mainly determined by the much publicised ever-widening gap between rich and poor. Fiske seems to assume that the capitalist market has a democratising effect in that it makes widely available a whole range of pleasurable texts. This argument, as we have seen, has some validity, if one compares genuinely popular cultural forms to those that require the application of scarce symbolic resources. Yet if we return to the analysis of computer games presented above, what should be obvious is that it neglects to mention the unequal distribution of the necessary computer technology. In 1986, 32.1 per cent of those whose household income was over £550 a week owned a home computer, compared to 1.3 per cent of those surviving on £45 or less (Golding, 1990). By 1998 these dimensions had remained remarkably stable with 8 per cent of the poorest 20 per cent owning a home computer compared to 57 per cent of the top 20 per cent (Golding, 2000). Class structure then erects certain material, in addition to symbolic, barriers to cultural forms of participation, that are neglected by Fiske's concern with signs and symbols.

2. A critical theory of ideology is dependent upon the notion that certain linguistic signs symbolically reinforce or leave unquestioned material relations of domination. Fiske, I would argue, forecloses the possibility of a theory of ideology by always reading the popular as a form of resistance. Returning to Bourdieu, it is apparent that Fiske lacks a theory of cultural domination as such. Bourdieu refers to the dominant aesthetic as arbitrary, since there is no intrinsic reason why certain upper-class accents and tastes should be indicative of a high culture. Culture is a tool of class domination. The bourgeoisie misrecognise their lifestyle and cultural forms of production as being ahistorical and disinterested. The education system, for example, reproduces the dominance of the bourgeoisie through the recognised superiority of the dominant aesthetic. Bourdieu and Passeron (1977) argue that education institutions impose the dominant form of life on the working classes.

The dominant habitus does not socialise subjects into the cultural patterns required by the education system, but results in the self-exclusion of the dominated classes. Through a process that Bourdieu calls symbolic violence, the working class recognises that the dominant habitus is superior to its own. For Bourdieu (1991) language does not serve as a pure instrument of communication but expresses the social position of the speaker. It is not, in other words, the complexity of the bour-geoisie's vocabulary that ensures its superiority. Instead the symbolic dominance of the bourgeoisie is maintained by its ability to censor the legitimacy of other modes of expression. Working-class lifestyles, on this reading, are culturally domi-nated and evaluated from the perspective of the dominant cultural style. Thus even those who enjoy the robust activities of supporting a soccer team are likely to view higher forms of cultural practice (such as visiting the opera) as having greater worth. Alternatively, Fiske views the popular as the site of resistance rather than domination. He discounts the possibility, which admittedly Bourdieu overstates, the people would view their own cultural practices as being less impor-tant than those of the power bloc. What Bourdieu's analysis reveals is that certain cultural styles and dispositions are able to impress themselves upon others due to relations of authority that exist outside of language.

On a different subject, Michael Schudson (1993) shares Fiske's doubts concerning the extent to which advertising directly affects consumer choices. This is because advertising competes with other forms of information (press reviews, peer assessment, brand loyalty) and is also the subject of popular disbelief. In some respects, however, advertising can be a powerful medium for persuading more *vulnerable* consumers of the merits of a particular product. One such group are young children, who necessarily have access to more restricted sources of infor-mation when compared to adults. While they are able to make sense of television advertisements, they are unable to decipher much of the output of the print media and are relatively inexperienced cultural consumers. Fiske, in response, would undoubtedly object that Hodge and Tripp's study argues that children and adults read television in very different ways. While this may be true, Fiske is unable to account for the reasons why children seem to be such easy prey for advertisers. Jim McGuigan (1992) adds that not only are advertisements geared towards creating material desires amongst a young audience, but television programmes and films are often specifically produced in order to sell a range of products from expensive toys to T-shirts. That is, children may decode symbolic forms differently from the ways the producers of the image intended, while becoming convinced of the desirability of a particular product. Thus, in so far as Fiske is hostile to a critical concept of ideology, it would seem that he is able to appreciate only a narrow range of cultural practices.

3. What immediately strikes the reader of Fiske's analysis of popular culture is the inadequacy of his perceptions of its content. Although Fiske's (1982)

background in semiotics means that he was fully equipped to probe the internal structures of popular texts, he gives them a decidedly one-dimensional reading. There are, in fact, few sustained analyses of popular texts in his work. This leads one to doubt some of the claims he makes on behalf of popular culture. At the heart of his view of the popular press is the assumption that discursive modes of exaggeration produce a certain scepticism within the reading subject. For Fiske, stories about aliens landing from outer space subvert the language game of the power bloc. One of the problems with this argument is that Fiske offers very little by the way of evidence to support his argument concerning the widespread nature of such stories. Indeed, much more evidence is available for arguing that the actual content of the tabloid press is overtly ideological. For instance, the systematic content studies of Van Dijk (1991), have demonstrated the racist nature of much of press content. In a study of the British and Dutch press during the 1980s he uncovers the extent to which press coverage ideologically reproduces a system that sustains white group dominance. While these issues cannot be explored here, it could be argued, in terms of actual content, that the popular press is more readily characterised by the racist nature of its content, than by the sort of bizarre stories Fiske discovers. Rather than abnormalising commonly held norms, the popular press is more often involved in symbolically creating certain out-groups. The white national press consistently ignores those subjects that are of most concern to ethnic minorities (housing, work, health) while representing them as a social problem (riots, crime, immigration). There is a case for arguing – and this point is forcibly made by Van Dijk – that by representing ethnic minorities in such a way the press is helping to sustain white dominance. This is not to argue that such stories would necessarily be uncritically accepted by their readers, but I would want to at least hold open such a possibility. That Fiske largely ignores such arguments compromises his more impressionistic view of the content of popular culture.

4. In dealing with the alternative press, Fiske argues that it has a tendency to be authoritarian and overly prescriptive. Similarly, in his view the culture of the power bloc concentrates upon the 'official' activities of the rich and powerful in a way that is distant from the lives of so-called ordinary people. These very practices constitute the major reason, offered by Fiske, for the 'culture gap' that has opened up within Western democracies between elected politicians and the populace. In place of the quality and alternative press, Fiske advocates a more politically diverse range of popular texts. This argument contrasts with the perspectives of Williams and Habermas offered in previous chapters.[3] Williams and Habermas suggest that modernity has witnessed the growing differentiation of high- and low-quality forms of information. This and other processes, including the privatisation of knowledge, social atomism, economic stagnation and the restricted nature of democracy, has contributed to the progressive depoliticisation of the public sphere. In turn, this has created a social vacuum which the tabloids fill with their particular brand of

scandal and sensation. Fiske, on the other hand, uncovers some of the discursive strategies that have been incorporated by popular news, and reminds us that the audience is capable of making plural meanings. However, Fiske's argument that a pluralist, participatory culture can only be sustained once the quality press has become more like the tabloids is perhaps mistaken. Colin Sparks (1992a) has argued that the popular press tends to represent the world in terms of an individualised conflict between good and evil. The quality press, regardless of its political content, is much more concerned with relating 'events' to the public context of social and political relations. Sparks justifiably argues that an informed public debate necessarily rests on the discussion of institutional processes and practices opened up by the quality press. I would add that Fiske misunderstands the original notion of the public sphere that has been developed by Williams and Habermas. Despite the limitations of their approaches, both writers stress the need for a communicative sphere protected from the operation of money and power. Thus the culture of the power bloc should be less about producing belief, and more concerned with the process of argument and discussion. That the actually existing public sphere often employs ideological strategies to legitimise the dominance of ruling elites is undeniable. But, as Williams and Habermas argue, a more democratic society and culture can be ensured only by the production of diverse forms of knowledge, and the social and political structures that encourage democratic forms of participation. John Keane (1991) argues in this vein that informed debate amongst the citizens of modern democracies, especially within globalised settings, is dependent upon high-quality forms of information. In his terms, and similar to Sparks, good investigative journalism depends upon the patient processes of investigation that seek to keep a watchful eye over those in power. However, Fiske's arguments point to the possibility that 'new formats' such as talk shows, infotainment and fan magazines have something to teach so-called 'serious' political discussion. It is indeed possible that less hierarchical and rigid formats operationalised by these cultural forms can lead to the mixing of critical knowledge and pleasure. As I have argued, the fear of these formats on the part of cultural commentators, can often be read as a fear of the feminine (Gray 1999). As we shall see, it has been feminist media scholarship that has best developed our understanding of the subversive value of the popular. Yet these qualifications aside, Fiske's analysis remains blind to many of the ideological and material strategies that continue to constitute the popular.

5. Fiske's central claim is that the fluid practices of consumers constitute a form of resistance against the dominant instrumental society. While I have questioned some of his assumptions concerning the notion of semiotic resistance, Fiske has been accredited with opening up the theoretical space for the investigation of the audience. The problem here is that, similar to de Certeau, Fiske often substitutes his own experience of the text for that of the audience. John Frow (1991)

argues that de Certeau's semiotic categories lead him to implant his own voice, where we should expect to find those of the users of popular culture. Fiske offers very little by way of empirical evidence to support his claims concerning the vibrant activities of the audience. This is due to his own enthusiasm for popular texts and his intellectual background in semiotic forms of content analysis.[4] His analysis of the intertextual nature of Madonna is largely based on his own skilful reading, and only briefly engages with the perspectives of her 'fans' through the letters page of a teenage magazine. Similarly, Fiske's argument that the tabloid press is open to the subversive tactics of the weak remains at the level of the text. He is unable to offer any empirical support for his argument. Admittedly, while television and film studies are beginning to open up perspectives on the audience, there has, as yet, been little research of a comparable quality on newspaper culture.

One of the few examples of such research is offered by Mark Pursehouse (1987) in an ethnographic account of the reading practices of tabloid consumers. Pursehouse accurately describes the mode of address of the *Sun* newspaper as 'heterosexual, male, white, conservative, capitalist, nationalist' (1987: 2). His study represents the interview subjects as artfully negotiating with the way in which the newspaper is symbolically constructed. This was particularly evident amongst the women readers who viewed the page three pin-ups and the sports sections as off limits. Pursehouse also reveals that many of the readers viewed the paper as a source of fun and relaxation to be enjoyed as a 'break' from work routines. Yet the newspaper is commonly interpreted as a working-class paper, unlike the qualities, which are presumed to have a more middle-class readership. The *Sun*, for these readers, is defined by the personal use it has in ordinary contexts. We can interpret this reading as a form of ideological masking or dissimulation. As J.B. Thompson (1990) has put it, dissimulation is established when certain social relations are linguistically concealed. When the newspaper is read as a form of private entertainment it becomes detached from the axes of power and politics. The identification of the newspaper as working-class, I would suggest, denies its political and institutional location. As is well known, the *Sun* is owned by the global media empire of Rupert Murdoch, and throughout the 1980s it helped construct the authoritarian populist politics of the far Right. That Pursehouse's readers are unable to give the newspaper a more political reading is probably the result of its being seen as a means of private pleasure rather than public concern. Fiske's lack of hermeneutic sensitivity to the horizons of the audience, despite his claims to the contrary, slides his own reading of tabloid newspapers into that of the audience. More interpretatively sensitive investigations should both open out the space for the responses of the audience, while positioning them within unequal social relations. This is precisely what Fiske fails to do.

Feminism and Soap Opera:
Reading into Pleasure

In feminist research into popular media cultures the emphasis has been placed upon rescuing women's pleasures from overtly masculine frameworks and definitions. These studies have stressed the importance of commercial cultures in providing a space for utopian readings and transgressive identities. Again I will argue that although studies which underline the ambivalent nature of popular cultures are important, they neglect a wider range of political interests with which feminism is concerned.

The recent changing paradigms within feminist theory have had a marked impact on culture and media studies. Both perspectives, in recent times, have witnessed a move away from a concern over constraining social structures towards an investigation of the social construction of identity. Michelle Barrett and Ann Phillips (1992) offer some interesting reflections on the theoretical shifts in feminist attempts to 'destabilise' previously secure masculine frameworks. In particular, Barrett draws some comparisons between contemporary and 1970s feminism. Seventies feminism, she claims, can be roughly characterised by the belief that it was possible to locate the cause of women's oppression. Most feminists argued, according to Barrett, that the essence of male domination could be located within the social and family structure. This trend was expressed in media studies through attempts to objectively identify the exclusion of women from the employment structures of the media, as well as the ways in which patriarchy was supported in sexually stereotyped images and representations (Tuchman, 1978). The picture being presented here is one of progressive feminist aims being subordinated by a male-dominated media. It was widely assumed, amongst old-style feminists, that the process of change could be accelerated by presenting more positive images of women. This perspective reproduced a simple binary opposition between the excluded voices of progressive feminists and the dominant ideological culture. But, according to Barrett, this consensus has now been broken by the impact of post-structuralism and the opening up of issues around sexual difference. Feminists, along with others concerned with identity issues, seek to establish gendered selves as discursively unstable constructions. The aim is to fruitfully deconstruct simple polarities between men and women, straights and gays, lesbians and gays, and unravel the complex ways in which identities are actually constructed. Likewise, the emphasis on identity in cultural studies has opened up a less moralising examination of popular culture and the public sphere. In the study of popular texts academics have lost a certain lofty and objectifying aura. This less regimented atmosphere of discussion has allowed media researchers to own up to their own enjoyment of the popular while throwing light on the contradictory pleasures of the audience. Through studies of women's interpretative relationship to popular culture, cultural studies has addressed previously repressed issues of pleasure and identity. Thus groups within feminism and cultural studies have jointly sought to map out the ways in which the self is fashioned out of contemporary cultural forms. The merging of the concerns of feminism and cultural studies, I would argue, is marked in the study of romantic fiction, soap opera and women's magazines.

Feminism, Mass Culture and Watching *Dallas*

The classic study of women's relationship to soap opera remains Ien Ang's (1985) study of the American serial *Dallas*. While Ang was compiling her study, *Dallas* was being shown in 90 countries and had become part of a global culture. Indeed, according to Ang, in her own country the Netherlands, during the spring of 1982, *Dallas* was being watched by just over half the population. The programme itself, for those who have never seen it, concerns the personal relations of a family made rich by Texan oil. Ang's book is an attempt to account for the popularity of the series through an interpretative understanding of the pleasures of the audience and her own evident enjoyment of the programme. At the time, the main reason that was being offered by the Dutch media for the success of *Dallas* was the **cultural imperialism** thesis. By this Ang means an account that represents a synthetic global American culture that is repressing more authentic national cultures. For Ang the implication of this argument would be to restrict the free trade in commercial culture to enable national forms of cultural production. Such a perspective, on her account, is flawed in that it would probably lead to cheap attempts by nation states to imitate *Dallas's* glossy production, but more importantly, such a view fails to account for the reasons why the audience tune in each week. The related argument that the arrival of *Dallas* is explained as resulting from media hype and the dominance of the culture industry is similarly dismissed, since by implication it reduces the audience to cultural dopes. Along with Morley and Fiske, the guiding theme of the research is to take a hermeneutics of trivial pleasures seriously.

Ang got in touch with fellow *Dallas* watchers by placing a small advertisement in a Dutch women's magazine:

> I like to watch the TV serial *Dallas*, but often get odd reactions to it. Would anyone like to write and tell me why you like watching it too, or dislike it? I should like to assimilate these reactions in my university thesis. (Ang, 1985:10)

She argues that popular pleasure is defined by immediate and sensual forms of enjoyment. As both Fiske and Bourdieu point out, the enjoyment of the popular is usually associated with a more relaxed bodily attitude in that the notion of being entertained offers a release from the usual demands of society. But even these suggestive remarks offer comparatively little in terms of addressing the specific pleasures of the audience. By offering an interpretation of the respondents' own self-interpretations, Ang claims that the avid watchers of *Dallas* find it *emotionally realistic*. This might, at first, seem like an odd claim to make on behalf of a programme whose context is far removed from the daily lives of the vast majority of the audience. Indeed, Ang notes that it was *Dallas's* perceived lack of realism that was the most common complaint amongst the programme's detractors. This argument, which Ang partially blames on the cultural circulation of the media imperialism thesis, misunderstands the complexity of popular reactions.

First, to complain that a work of fiction is unrealistic is to misunderstand the nature of symbolic production. The text, Ang reasons, does not reflect the world but in fact produces it. The realism identified by *Dallas* fans is not empirical but psychological. The 'reality effect' of *Dallas* is not produced through its correspondence with the world outside, but through the feelings of direct involvement that it forms within the audience. The fascination with the world of J.R. and Sue Ellen, Pamela and Bobby Ewing is the result of the audience's identification with 'more general living experiences: rows, intrigues, problems, happiness and misery' (Ang, 1985: 44–5). Like other soap operas, *Dallas* provides a plurality of narratives that symbolically invents a notion of community around the family. As a melodrama, however, *Dallas* embodies what Ang calls a tragic structure of feeling, in its construction of family life. By this Ang means that family life is not so much romanticised as 'constantly shattered' (Ang, 1985: 69). The characters within *Dallas*, in keeping with the tragic structure of feeling, exhibit little self-reflection and lack control over their own lives. This connects with a realisation amongst the viewers that suffering and pain are the everyday fare of personal relationships. The world of *Dallas* was felt to be realistic by certain sections of the audience because it took for granted the workings of patriarchal society. The tragic structure of feeling not only symbolically opened up a world where the celebration of happiness is always short lived, but represented those with power as most often being men.

Other than the tragic structure of feeling, Ang discovers other ways of relating to *Dallas*. She found that many of the viewers had developed an ironic disposition towards the programme. This is a form of viewing that partakes in the pleasures of *Dallas*, but in a way that utilises humour as a means of creating a form of social distance between the reader and the text. Ang views this reaction as a defensive means of preserving the pleasure of the text against the normalising discourse of the cultural imperialism thesis. The notion of cultural imperialism, on this reading, not only represses the cultural productivity of the audience, but acts as a means of symbolic violence against popular tastes. Ang, however, wants to defend the ordinary pleasures offered by *Dallas* by linking these concerns to a utopian feminist politics.

Feminism is utopian to the extent to which it bases an imaginary politics on the future possibility of living in a world where men no longer dominate women. The dialogic involvement of the mostly female audience points to a basic contradiction in the text between the different subject positions offered by Sue Ellen and Pamela. While Ang recognises that both Sue Ellen and Pamela are trapped in patriarchal structures of domination, they embody culturally distinct ways of subjectively expressing this relationship. Sue Ellen, in tune with the tragic structure of feeling, displays a cynical recognition of the inevitability of male dominance, while Pamela holds forth the utopian possibility of equal forms of sustaining love between men and women. That both characters eventually share the same miserable fate should not distract feminists from seeking to unravel the ways in which the process of reading mass culture opens up new forms of political identity. It is not that Ang is unaware that those imaginary positions that we take up in fantasy are not necessarily allowed to reflect critically on the real. She does, however, close the study with a call for feminists to examine more closely the ways in which the spheres of actual lived social relations and psychic identification may cut into one another. In doing so, she indicates a critical path between the lumping of women's private pleasures into the ideological prison house (Modleski, 1988) and the populist celebration of the resistant housewife (Fiske, 1987b).

Psychoanalysis, Identity and Utopia

Other feminists have sought to develop the themes outlined by Ang. Looking back, Ang's study is perhaps most marked by her lack of concern to develop a psycho-analytic understanding of gender construction, and neglect of the social context of the audience. In this respect, Janice Radway's (1987) slightly earlier study has proved to be seminal for a number of feminist writers seeking to develop the themes of identity, mass culture and utopia (Geraghty, 1991). Like Ang, Radway maintains a utopian politics by considering the reading practices of women consumers of popular culture. But she takes these issues further by seeking to link a more complex notion of gendered subjectivity to a psychic process of identification. In addition, Radway crucially relates the pleasures of reading romantic fiction to women's subordinate position within patriarchal households.

Running through Radway's study is a concerted emphasis on the ideological complexity of romance reading. Her fieldwork focuses on a small group of avid romance readers from a Midwestern town called Smithton in the United States. In a later article she claims that the romance study presents the reader's world as a 'collaboratively produced patchwork quilt, where small, separately (but also collectively) worked patterns are stitched together over time by a variety of seam-stresses' (Radway, 1987: 109). As with Morley and Fiske, Radway provides a critique of a theory of meaning that commences with the individual reader. Her argument is that the social meaning of the romance is a product of the interrelation between the cultural life-worlds of the readers, ideology and relations of power.

The identifications of the women readers are largely unknown to the producers of the romance fantasies. This disjuncture between the encoders and the decoders was mediated by a trusted selector from whom the women purchased their romance novels. The selector, in this sense, was able to narrow the distance between the capitalist production of the novels and the expressed needs and desires of the women. Hence the role of the mediator was far more important than the advertising strategies employed by the romance producers in determining which books the women actually read. A similar gatekeeper role also informs other cultural activities such as the music press's reviews of new releases, a friend's recommendation of a novel, and the video store's enthusiasm for certain titles. This aside, what was evident from an investigation into the interpretative understandings of the women was that many of the readers read the romances as symbolic of female triumph. This was because the most popular novels offered a narrative of transformation where cold, distant, isolated men became on the story's conclusion caring, nurturing and feminised. It was the ability of the romance to articulate a deep form of human understanding between the hero and the heroine that accounted for its success. The novels that deviated from this predictable pattern often left the reader unsatisfied. In the case of disappointing narratives, the mediator would either recommend avoidance to other readers, or the women themselves wouldn't bother to read the text once they realised that the novel didn't end happily.

The practice of novel reading seems important for the women because it enables them to negotiate a certain amount of social space for their own leisure pursuits, and opens up a limited critique of patriarchy. Radway notes, along with others (Gray, 1992), that the women's enjoyment of the romance novels can only be accomplished once they have successfully negotiated the cultural derision of their husbands, as well as their own sense of guilt. The guilty pleasures involved in romance reading are emotionally sustaining in a male-dominated social order that seeks to discipline women into subordinating their own needs to those of significant others. Their reading operates in a compensatory way, offering them, via the text, the emotional support they are denied in their personal relations with men. The romantic escape, however, is also dependent upon a form of utopian receptiveness where the reader has the feeling that her own needs are being met in a caring and receptive way. Paradoxically, the romance both ideologically helps sustain the women in patriarchal relations and holds forth the possibility of more nurturing human relationships.

At this point, Radway draws on the psychoanalytic writing of Chodorow (1978). Chodorow argues that the masculine subject establishes his identity through a process of disidentification with the mother. The repudiation of his first love object is necessary for the psychic establishment of the self as an 'independent' person. The boy's identification with the father leads him to value autonomy over dependence and separation over connection. Thus, while the young male is able to recognise the other as separate from the self, he often has difficulties in experiencing empathetic relations with others. The need for the establishment of firm boundaries between self and other is also coupled with a fear of being reabsorbed by the mother. This, Benjamin (1988) argues, following Chodorow, holds the key to understanding men's desire to dominate women. Male anxiety concerning the maternal body leads to the wish to have power over it and, ultimately, to denigrate it. This perhaps partially explains masculine aversion to popular texts that champion feeling, affect and emotion. Conversely, the girl's more intense form of identification with the mother does not allow her to express her own *separate* desires. Mothers, Chodorow argues, tend to experience their daughters as more like themselves than their sons. As a result girls are not encouraged to separate themselves off and more readily develop psychically through their interrelations with others. Romantic fiction occupies the fold between patriarchy's denial of the women's own needs and the psychic desire for more relational and emotionally sustaining human relationships. But, as Radway well understands, the utopian wishfulfilment experienced by the women is only able to question the women's most intimate relations. The relational world of the text remains ideologically separate from the masculinely defined public world.

The difficulty with Radway's reliance upon Chodorow is that she cannot very well explain the women's desire, however guilty this may be, for a separate social space in which to enjoy the novels. As Elliott (1994), Sayers (1986) and Flax (1990) have argued, Chodorow's argument does not account for the psychic emergence amongst feminists for more autonomous social relations. In Radway's own study, the women express some of the difficulties they encounter in seeking to negotiate the isolation necessary for reading. This space was desired not only so that they could encounter a more nurturing form of masculinity, but so that they could widen their own horizons by engaging with the differing historical and geographical locations mapped out in the novels. Thus there is a desire for separation that enables the fulfilment of more emotionally sustaining forms of identification. Radway's reliance upon Chodorow means that the desire for separation amongst women remains under-theorised. As both Radway and Gray have pointed out, although subordinate, women s own demand that they enjoy a form of pleasure, often belittled by men, leads them into conflictual negotiations with their male partners. Again, while one of the strengths of Radway's study is that it raises some difficult questions related to identity that have been ignored by discourse analysis and main stream media studies, there remain a number of unanswered questions in this respect. However, the argument that audience theory should form a closer relationship with psychoanalytic perspectives is one of the main achievements of Radway's book.

Reading Magazine Cultures

Finally, I want to look at some of the latest developments in audience research in respect of the consumption of magazines. This has been particularly significant for myself as I have been involved in this research, which has, not surprisingly, prompted some rethinking on my part on the significance of audience studies more generally. As we shall see, questions of gender have been particularly prominent within this area and have largely grown out of earlier waves of feminist research into the media of mass communication.

Much of the early research on women's magazines, informed by the work of the Centre for Contemporary Cultural Studies in Birmingham, was cast within an encoding/decoding perspective, with an emphasis on 'decoding' the text through various theoretical manoeuvres rather than through more direct encounters with actual readers. Angela McRobbie's study of the 'romantic individualism' encoded within *Jackie* (originally published as a CCCS Stencilled Paper in 1978) is a classic example of this genre. The essay is described by McRobbie as offering 'a systematic critique of *Jackie* as a system of messages, a signifying system and a bearer of a certain ideology . . . which deals with the construction of teenage femininity' (1991: 81–82). According to McRobbie, magazines like *Jackie* served to introduce girls to adolsecence. Their ideological work represented 'a concerted effort . . . to win and shape the consent of the readers to a particular set of values' (1991: 82). The magazine in McRobbie's terms retains a role as a powerful ideological force despite identifying processes of decoding. McRobbie was therefore openly hostile to the magazine for its portrayal of a 'cloyingly claustrophobic environment' characterised by 'monotonous regularity', 'narrowness' and 'repetition' (1991: 117–18). With only one paragraph on how readers actually looked at *Jackie*, her method was semiological, privileging her own reading of the magazine over more formal content analysis and without any direct involvement from readers. Four sub-codes were identified and relentlessly pursued: romance, personal/domestic life, fashion and beauty, and pop music. Yet in the concluding section McRobbie admits that 'this does not mean that its readers swallow its axioms without question' and that we need to know more about how girls read *Jackie* and how they encounter its ideological force.

McRobbie addresses the 'one-sidedness' of her earlier analysis in a subsequent essay which aims 'not to denounce . . . but to understand' the popular appeal of the magazines (1991: 184). This later essay traces the changes in magazine content and in academic practice between the 1970s and 1980s, including 'the spaces these magazines offer for contestation and challenge' (1991: 186). McRobbie documents the decline in romance and the ascendancy of the commercial culture associated with pop music and fashion epitomised in the shift from *Jackie* to *Just Seventeen* as the best-selling magazine for teenage girls. Acknowledging that feminists such as Janice Radway (1987) and Janice Winship (1987) had shifted their attention 'away from texts and meanings, to the readers and their different and complex readings' (1991: 137), she opens her analysis a little more to the pleasures of the text. Drawing particularly on Winship's work, for example, McRobbie contrasts a negative view of the internal logic of the 'problem page' (characterised by an unsisterly individualism) with a more positive assessment of its external logic (how the magazines are read and giggled over collectively). While McRobbie acknowledges this move away from 'the text in all its ideological glory' (1991: 138), actual readers fail to make an appearance in her analysis.

We have already seen the important role played by Radway in helping to shape feminist approaches to popular media cultures. This role is of particular significance in respect of the analysis of magazines. Radway's work signals an important break with text-centred approaches, emphasising the agency of 'ordinary readers' as well as the internal contradictions of the text. Radway's work grapples with the tension that her readers feel between the pleasures of the text and the uneasy sense that reading romantic fiction reinforces patriarchal ideology with its fantasies of male chivalry, female subordination and the all-encompassing world of romantic love. Radway argues that reading romantic fiction is 'a collectively elaborated female ritual through which women explore the consequences of their common social condition' (1987: 212), emphasizing how readers construct their reading as a 'declaration of independence' from their socially determined domestic responsibilities. Rather than insisting that romantic fiction is fundamentally conservative or incipiently oppositional, Radway explores the ambiguities of the genre. She also demonstrates that women's readings are embedded in their social lives and that their media use is 'multiply determined and internally contradictory' (1987: 7–8). Radway attempts to isolate a variety of patterns or regularities among the diversity of readings she uncovers (including notions of fantasy, guilt, luxury, self-indulgence, 'reading for instruction' and compensation). Among this diversity of readings, Radway suggests, 'similarly located readers learn a similar set of reading strategies and interpretive codes which they bring to bear upon the texts they encounter' (1987: 81).

A comparable approach is adopted by Elizabeth Frazer (1992: 195) who uses a concept of 'discursive register' ('an institutionally, situationally specific, culturally familiar, public way of talking') to argue that teenage readers of *Jackie* engage in frequent and dramatic shifts in register without those registers being necessarily contradictory. Based on a series of group discussions with 13–17 year-old girls, she demonstrates that readers are rarely 'victims' of the text. Notions of ambiguity and contradiction are therefore increasingly prevalent in recent approaches to magazine reading. Thus Hermes (1996: 3) writes of a mixture of pleasure and guilt, while Ballaster *et al.* (1991) reject the stark choice between 'bearer of pleasure' and 'purveyor of oppressive ideologies'. They assert that:

> the identification of 'contradiction' . . . fails to embarass either editors, writers
> or readers . . . The success of the women's magazine is no doubt connected
> with its ability to encompass glaring contradiction coherently in its pages.
> (1991: 7)

If McRobbie's early work was characterised by an emphasis on the text to the
exclusion of actual readers, the most recent research on women's magazines
is characterised by the opposite tendency: an emphasis on readers to the neglect
of the magazines' actual content. For example, Joke Hermes's (1995) work focuses
on readers as the producers of meaning with almost no attempt to distinguish
between the various magazines they read. Criticising the over-emphasis of earlier
studies on the text, she identifies what she calls 'the fallacy of meaningfulness'
(1995: 16): the assumption that all forms of popular media carry significant
meanings. In contrast, Hermes insists on the everyday and mundane character of
magazine reading for the majority of her readers (accessed via 80 in-depth
interviews). Magazines are 'leafed through' during gaps in their readers' everyday
routines; they are 'easily put down' rather than invested with any deeper significance. In this account, magazine reading emerges as 'a low-priority means of
spending leisure time or unoccupied minutes' (1995: 20) rather than having any
greater cultural or political significance. Rather than offering a single 'academic'
reading of the text, her approach involved an identification of the interpretive
repertoires through which different women made sense of the magazines.

Compared to the richness of feminist work on women's magazines, previous
work on men's magazines has been much more limited. There was a brief flurry
of work associated with media debates about the 'new man', following the launch
of *GQ* in the late 1980s (Moore, 1989; Chapman, 1989) and a variety of accounts
in the 1990s examining the 'new visual codings' of masculinity in the style press
and early men's lifestyle press (Mort, 1996; Nixon, 1993, 1996, 1997; Edwards,
1997). Some of these accounts were hostile to the emergence of new forms of
masculinity, seeing them as a pretence or as a strictly commercial development:

> consumption is being redefined as an activity that is suitable for men – rather
> than simply a passive and feminised activity – so that new markets can be
> penetrated. More products are being aimed at young men and shopping is
> no longer a means to an end but has acquired a meaning in itself. (Moore,
> 1989: 179)

Others were more concerned to explore the the circuits of meaning fostered by the
magazines. Both Mort and Nixon focused on the cultural significance of recent
changes in men's fashion photography and the style press (Mort, 1996; Nixon,
1996, 1997). Their work concentrates on the emergence of 'softer' forms of
masculinity and the blurring of sexual scripts. Tim Edwards (1997) places a similar

emphasis on the way that men are being encouraged to look at themselves and at each other as objects of desire. Yet while these studies have made an important contribution, these authors have little to contribute about the emergence in the 1990s of more 'laddish' forms of masculinity and their associated commercial cultures. Here I want to tentatively introduce some of my own research (conducted with Peter Jackson and Kate Brooks) into men's lifestyle magazines. This research aimed to explore the different circuits of information involved in the production and consumption of men's magazines including interviews with editors, exploration of magazine content and focus group interviews with mostly young men (Jackson *et al.*, 2001). Focusing on a range of titles from *GQ* to *Loaded* and from *FHM* to *Attitude* we sought to examine the ways in which the magazines and their consumption could be related to wider questions of masculinity and sociological changes in respect of men's changing position within society.

In particular, we explored the different discourses and fantasies that the magazines make available to their readers. In general, the magazines address the reader as a 'mate'. The magazines attempt to become the 'reader's friend' by offering handy hints, pointing out obvious pitfalls and providing useful advice, all in the language of 'common sense', with irony being used as a warning against taking anything that is said too seriously. In this sense, the magazines are careful to avoid talking down to their readers. Further, drawing on focus group discussions with a wide range of men (and a smaller number of women) we sought to understand the magazines in the context of men's changing identities and gender relations. In particular, we explored how our focus group participants attempt to 'make sense' of recent changes in masculinity and consumer culture through their reactions to the magazines, including their coverage of previously neglected topics such as fashion, health and relationships. Though our analysis focuses on 'men's talk', the inclusion of some mixed-gender focus groups and one all-women group provided additional insights into contemporary constructions of masculinity and gender relations. Indeed, the group that was most openly hostile to the magazines and critical of the resurgence of 'laddish' forms of masculinity was the only all-female group. However given the magazines are mostly aimed at men it is men's voices we sought to capture in the focus groups. At the end of this process, we identified a range of discursive repertoires through which our respondents attempted to 'make sense' of the magazines. We identified a range of discourses from 'naturalness' to 'honesty' which, with a considerable degree of ambivalence, largely affirmed the culture of the magazines. Media constructions of 'laddishness' had come to seem so 'natural' that for many respondents there was no need to defend them or to consider alternative forms of masculinity. While some participants were critical of the magazines' celebration of 'laddish' masculinities, many more revelled in the lack of restraint implied by what they construed as a return to more 'natural' expressions of masculinity, including, for example, the opportunity to look at pictures of 'sexy' women in an unselfconscious and relatively guilt-free way. However, returning to a more 'honest' or 'natural' expression of men's 'true selves' is partly contradicted by some of the magazines' encouragement of a greater sense of 'openness' to new forms of masculinity. The men we interviewed also identified the role the magazines' played in unfixing the male subject, and generally broadening the different scripted ways there are of being a man. Magazines like *Men's Health*, for example, encourage men to be more 'open' about themselves (to talk about their feelings, for example), while bringing out into the open certain (previously repressed) aspects of masculinity, including more public discussion of men's relationships, fashion and health. However, the magazines constantly monitor this process, using humour and other devices to help 'distance' their readers from any embarrassment that they might feel at being seen to take these issues 'too seriously'.

In terms of masculinity, the more 'certain' world of patriarchal relations is not only part of a wider nostalgia for a social order that protected men's material interests, but the reaction against a new world of economic changes, the questioning of sexuality by lesbian and gay groups, the undermining of traditional notions of public and private, and the political role played by feminism, which have all served to destabilise modern masculine identities. Hence, in a situation where certainties and tradition are being progressively undermined, they have (somewhat paradoxically) to be 'constructed'. The construction of certitude in cultural forms need not, however, be read simply as a 'backlash' against feminism. Instead, we suggest that, while such formations have political implications, they may be understood as a more complex response to changing gender relations. Arguably, the construction of certitude gives both men and women a sense that the social world is more stable than it actually is. That is, images of phallic masculinity promote a cultural 'comfort zone' giving the self (however temporarily) a sense of fixity and psychic security. How, then, might this analysis be applied to our understanding of men's lifestyle magazines? It is most apparent in the profusion of 'how to' sections that are carried in many of the magazines, offering advice (often in a semi-ironic tone) so that readers can brush up on a variety of techniques from the monitoring of sexual performance to changing a car tyre. Similarly our interviews with the groups of 'young' men moved between the naturalisation of masculinity and **reflexivity**. In this sense contemporary consumer culture positions male subjects in terms of a number of different and contradictory locations. It is the magazines capacity to be able to accommodate both more 'open' and reflexive aspects of modernity along with the certitude of traditional features that explains their appeal. This enables male consumers to 'open up and close down, to move into and withdraw from the flow of messages' (Melucci, 1996: 51). Hence the magazines represent the commodification of contemporary gender anxieties. That is, they are sources of cultural power in respect of the speed at which network capitalism simulate new markets and help inform the changing definition of contemporary masculinity. In this analysis, therefore, we are not forced into making a choice between viewing the magazines as either forms of flexible accumulation or a largely conservative gender politics. That is, as with women's magazines, it is seemingly the ambivalences within the text and the ways in which they are read which account for the magazines' commercial success.

The development of research into magazine content and audiences, then, has further impressed upon media researcher's the importance of increased reflexivity within the research process. This has lead to the 'opening' of questions which involve the relations between interviewer and interviewee, the instability and shifting nature of the audience, the intertextual nature of meaningfulness, and finally that media scholars and the audience are always already constituted through certain discourses (Alasuutari, 1999). These questions have developed earlier waves of theorising, seriously questioning the extent to which audience studies can be said to 'naturalistically' capture the horizons of the audience. That is audience studies have progressively become aware of the complex levels of social and cultural construction that are involved in making claims about ordinary patterns of media consumption. The development of the study of magazine cultures has further emphasised the importance of gender in seeking to understand the interpretative practices of audiences. That gender is currently the most important category within sociological and cultural studies of media audiences also underlines its comparative neglect by other traditions of media studies.

Feminism and Critical Theory

One of the most controversial issues for feminist media theorists has been the formation of the gendered subject. This issue is complex, and it involves a number of related issues and questions. Yet, I shall argue, the emerging paradigm that seeks to unfold feminine (and of course masculine) forms of *jouissance* should be reintegrated into a wider media sociology. In terms of the development of feminism and media studies this would suggest a critical re-engagement with earlier strands of research that articulated more institutional frameworks. While feminist researchers have been uncovering women's previously neglected readings of popular culture, there has occurred the widely reported deregulation of public service broadcasting and the corresponding globalisation of the media of mass communication. These structural changes should not be thought of in isolation from the viewing, reading and listening practices of the audience. My focus in the following discussion will be on reconnecting feminist concerns with the need for a reformulated public sphere. Hopefully, such a discussion will contribute to a more substantial utopian feminism, that goes beyond a concern with soaps and paperback romances, important as this undoubtedly is.

Melodramas such as *Dallas* have long been part of a genuinely popular cultural tradition. Since the 1790s, melodrama's rhetoric of excess, sense of the spectacle and championing of the sentimental in the battle between good and evil has been delighting the people, while offending more refined tastes (Barbero, 1993; Brooks, 1976). As Barbero points out, the cultural form of the melodrama can be traced back further to the bawdy seventeenth-century literature produced for the popular classes. The Spanish *cordel* and the French literature of *colportage* offer a combination of high and low culture that draws upon the language of the people. These popular texts ironised high culture while relaying heroic tales of bandits and criminals. It is then these popular styles and idioms, in Fiske's terms, that are now hegemonically incorporated by the power bloc and disseminated for popular enjoyment. It seems that if we historically retrace the shifting hegemonic alliances of the melodrama, the idea of popular pleasure as a subversive articulation of the people is never far away. To return to Ang's study of *Dallas*, the tragic structure of feeling was expressive of the ordinary everyday concerns of the women embedded within a patriarchal society. Ang, as we saw, even suggested that 'the language of the personal', mediated by *Dallas*, offered a feminist-inspired utopian politics. Those theorists, Ang assures us, who concern themselves with issues such as cultural imperialism are actually aligning themselves with national elites who are seeking to preserve declining national cultures.

Ang's argument against the media imperialism thesis is that *Dallas* is a polysemic text whose construction is dependent upon the social and discursive context of the viewer. Similarly, Katz and Liebes (1985), like Ang, are generally dubious that *Dallas* imprints the values of Western consumer capitalism on to the consciousness of its global audience. Their study reveals that different ethnic groups bring their own identities to a judgement of the programme's content. In general, they found, in accordance with Ang, that it was the melodramatic nature of the narrative, rather than the glitter of consumerism, that captured the attention of the audience. Katz, Liebes and Ang all argue that if the social meanings of American capitalism are subverted by the audience's interpretations then this disproves the media imperialism thesis. Soaps such as *Dallas* affirm and validate the importance of the immediate and the everyday, rather than the interests of global capital.

The argument that the media imperialism thesis ignores the cultural complexity of the audience is of course correct. Yet there remains the reverse problem that a concern with the ambivalences of subjectivity, identity and the discursive construction of the audience cancels a concern for the political economy of media production. Yet here I should like to distance myself from those such as Curran (1990) and Evans (1990), who have argued that politically the semiotic concern with diverse meanings constitutes an uncritical pluralism. The values of the audience researchers are more adequately characterised as respectful attention to the sorts of popular practice that historically have been marginalised by the academy. This *new* history from below reveals the 'art of making' our 'space within their place' (Fiske, 1993: 70). Hence politically audience studies is better thought of in relation to the recovery of difference and otherness than the bland celebration of plurality. As many have commented there seems to be a gendered division within academic circles in terms of this particular dispute (Hermes, 1997; Gray, 1999). While male theorists are mostly concerned with the public power of media cultures, feminist scholarship has tended to concentrate upon the sphere of consumption. This in effect has meant that feminist media analysis has neglected questions of public cultures, whereas the 'malestream' dismisses audience studies as being less important than the study of the official public sphere (Geraghty, 1997).[5]

The recognition of the gendered division of research should hardly surprise anyone who has read this far. However, I want to argue that a feminist inspired critical theory of media cultures needs to think of ways of deconstructing these divisions. That is while researchers will undoubtedly continue to retain their own particular points of departure, we need to ask what critical resources are available for developing more systematic research agendas. These agendas (in light of what I have already said) would need to proceed in such a way that deconstructed gendered assumptions, while respecting the domains of political economy and the diverse subjectivities of the audience. Feminists, for instance, surely want to achieve a public culture where issues such as male violence are discussed in an informed, democratic manner.

According to Soothill and Walby (1990), the British press consistently isolates issues related to sex crime from those of power and masculinity. The press is more likely to represent rape through sensational accounts of deviant outsiders (usually described as being animal-like, i.e. 'The Fox' or 'The Panther') in such a way as to ideologically abnormalise the offenders. Such a strategy displaces a concern for male power, while assuring heterosexual men and women that rape is the product of evil. That the readers of these stories could resist the ways in which rape is publicly portrayed is not in doubt. Indeed, recent evidence suggests that while viewing fictional rapes, women with no experience of male violence were much more likely to blame the victim, than those who had (Schlesinger *et al.*, 1992). This, as Schlesinger and his colleagues cautiously argue, cannot be considered a direct effect of the media. But surely a more informed media discussion of the issue of male violence could pose certain questions, challenge stereotypes, provoke critical thinking, allow a more plural range of perspectives and treat the matter with the public respect it undoubtedly deserves. A democratically reformulated public space would discuss the legal procedures for dealing with male violence, the funding of victim support units, the protection of the victim's identity, rehabilitation and punishment of offenders, safer forms of public space and the social construction of masculinity. Such a discussion would involve men's and women's identities as critical and reflexive members of a regenerated public sphere. This conversation could not only be predicated upon certain rights of access, but would also involve the obligation to attend respectfully to the perspectives of others, with due regard to the power relationships evident between men and women. That is, a critical media culture inspired by a feminist analysis would seek to reformulate still powerful conservative gender ideologies and the more problematic aspects of hegemonic masculinity. Hence without arguing for a return to the feminist cultural politics of the 1970s there is an evident need to rejoin the analysis of political economy with the semiotic complexity of the audience in such a way that deconstructs gendered oppositions. As I argued at the end of the previous chapter, this would involve a view of mediated citizenship which critically cuts across the domains of public and private. That feminist analysis has brought us closer to the emergence of such an agenda is not to be underestimated. In this we have to be careful that a progressive media politics is mutually concerned with the liberation of the subject from conservative gender ideologies and the critical questioning of wider cultural frameworks. That is, feminist inspired media studies needs to be able to offer more normative judgements as well as alternative institutional arrangements (Fraser, 1995). A transformative feminist media politics then would need to be able to link (where possible) the critical potential within the audience to the necessity of redesigning and reworking how 'public space' becomes constituted and defined through a range of discourses and practices.

Summary

The interpretative concerns of David Morley, John Fiske and feminist audience theory have sought to produce a hermeneutics of audience activity. These debates, especially when the semiotic articulation of meaning becomes intermeshed with a sociological concern for domestic power relations, have made a crucial contribution to media theory. While respecting the specific differences of these approaches, however, it should be stressed that these strands of audience theory share certain common problems. Much audience theory remains over-concerned with the microscopic worldview of socially dispersed viewers, readers and listeners. It was noted that the structuration of reception practices in economic, political and cultural institutions was often displaced by more local concerns. The semiotic focus upon the production of meaning (encoding and decoding practices) was inadequately appreciative of the social function of consumer leisure activities within late capitalism. This said, particularly in respect of David Morley and feminist audience theory, such approaches have considerably broadened the political implications of media theory. At this point, audience theory has introduced a politics that aims to criticise attempts to normalise difference. It has only been able to do so to the extent to which it is alive to the complexity of contemporary gender relations, the discursive construction of the subject, and the power relations that continue to shape our most intimate connections with others. That this agenda now needs to be rejoined to questions of public and private power has been sustained throughout. While such attempts are dependent upon scholars from future generations they should be grateful that they already have such intellectually germane traditions upon which to build.

Marshall McLuhan and the Cultural Medium

Space, Time and Implosion in the Global Village

Technical Media

The modern dissemination of cultural forms has radically restructured the parameters of time and space. From the production of daily newspapers to the electronic transmission of the latest racing results, the technical forms of mass communication are altering the experiential content of everyday life. Technical media are currently capable of relocating symbolic impressions globally and at an ever-quickening rate. The globe is straddled by competing international news agencies that are capable of cueing in local and national information networks. Some of these 'news events' are transmitted in so-called real time. This both recontextualises information across the permeable borders of nation states and gives the appearance of instantaneous communication. The split-second transmission of stories, regardless of their actual content, has made the world a smaller place while correspondingly shrinking human conceptions of time. And yet the mass media's impact upon the construction of horizontal spatial relations and the temporal dimensions of social life remains chronically under-researched. Theoretical problems of this order remain at least analytically separate from the issues related to cultural content that have dominated certain schools of mass communication. Today, given the growing pervasiveness and globalisation of electronic forms of media, such concerns demand further investigation.

The radical impact of new forms of communication upon the dimensions of space, time and human perception are the dominant motifs of Marshall McLuhan.

His work was, initially at least, widely recognised as articulating some of the most profound changes that the new media technologies were ushering in. But although McLuhan made an initial impact in the early 1960s (for a short time becoming something of a media celebrity himself) he currently has few followers or admirers. This undoubtedly has had as much to do with his erratic writing style as it has with the substantive content of his ideas. In cultural and media studies, his ideas were at first warmly welcomed as making a major breakthrough in articulating some of the dimensions of the emergent electric culture. But the bubble of enthusiasm was soon to burst, and McLuhan's propositions were widely dismissed as exhibiting a form of technological determinism. Such has been culturalism's concern to distance itself from technical explanations that it has neglected to analyse the difference cultural media make. It presumably makes a difference to modern cultures whether they receive most of their information from global television networks, or from a national press printed only once a week. The other problem is that certain versions of postmodernism, such as that offered by Baudrillard, have reworked some of McLuhan's main propositions. What is defended by Baudrillard is the descriptive relevance of McLuhan and the emphasis upon technological determinism, refuted by an earlier wave of cultural critics. While I shall return to problems of interpretation, here I aim to move against the grain of his most vocal detractors and forcibly suggest that his work be critically re-evaluated by students of the media. I will defend a version of McLuhan's writing that does not rest well with culturalism or postmodernism: that McLuhan's emphasis on technical media is important for distinguishing between different modes of cultural transmission (oral, literate, electric) and that these media structurate intersubjective social relations. There are nevertheless problems with McLuhan's approach, which I will raise while opening out the importance of the questions he asked.

Before outlining McLuhan's contribution to a social theory of mass communication, it is necessary to take a short detour through the writing of fellow Canadian, Harold A. Innis. This is particularly pressing in that McLuhan and Innis share a similar intellectual context and make the study of mass communication central to the shaping of modernity itself. Here the technical apparatus of the mass media are considered to be constitutive rather than merely incidental to the shaping of contemporary social relations. This perspective, despite the evident differences between McLuhan and Innis, is markedly different from the approaches we have encountered so far in this book.

Innis, McLuhan and Canadian Social Theory

Innis (1950, 1951) was an economic historian who in the last 10 years of his life produced two works on human communication. For Innis, communication networks are important in terms of the information that they carry and the wider impact they have upon social forms of organisation. Any given medium of communication, as opposed to the message, is biased in terms of either time or space. Media such as parchment, clay and stone that were dominant in the pre-printing era of human history were time rather than space biased: they were very difficult to transport through space, but proved to be a hardy medium that weathered the passage of time. As time-biased media can be strongly associated with the physical presence of particular places, they are relatively stable social phenomena that bind past, present and future. Conversely, media that are light and less durable (such as printed paper) are spatially biased in that they can be more easily relocated. Transportable media favoured the growth of administrative relations across space, thereby facilitating the decentralised growth of secular and political authority. Media that are time biased, on the other hand, helped sustain centralised religious forms of tradition. As James W. Carey (1969: 275) argues 'in cultural terms, time meant the sacred, the moral, the historical; space the present and the future, the technical and the secular'.

Innis attempts to extend the relevance of his distinction between time- and space-biased media through a comparison between oral and literate societies. The principal medium of communication in oral societies is speech, although, as Innis recognises, this is not the only means. Reliance upon speech as the means of communication encourages a strong temporal bias within oral societies. This is because speech can only travel short distances and is not a particularly efficient medium for the storage of information. According to Walter Ong (1977) this partially explains the conservative nature of the institutional arrangements evident in most oral societies. Without written forms of communication, tradition has to be carefully preserved in repeatable and formulaic rituals and practices. Both Ong and Innis recognise that the absence of writing encourages human societies that have strong temporal biases. Written traditions, for Innis, are more likely to be space binding in that they tend to privilege the future over the past. The invention of writing not only crystallises the oral tradition, making it an 'object' for the investigation of future societies, but also allows different traditions and cultures to escape the spatial limitations of the village. According to Innis, time and space are perhaps best viewed as a dialectic where the progressive elimination of one pole leads to the dominance of the other. Carey (1989) has suggested that Innis's approach could also have a more contemporary relevance. Thus one could argue that the press enables extension through space rather than time. The event-driven nature of the press often means that yesterday's headlines are quickly forgotten, whereas the identity of the press is more likely to be appreciated in spatial terms (local, national or international). The press, as a modern transportable medium, is best conceptualised in Innis's terms as space rather than time biased.

Though I believe Innis is right that the medium of communication has implications for issues related to space and time, I think he goes astray when he presents time and space as necessarily having a bias towards one pole to the partial exclusion of the other. To me this is unsatisfactory. For instance, it is arguable that nationalism is both temporally and spatially biased. Nationalism is usually thought of as articulating a historical bond between past and present members of the nation state, while also providing a sense of spatial connection through certain rituals and traditions. This argument is further complicated if we consider that the transmission of national sentiment and culture has historically been dependent upon a variety of media including the cinema, magazines, newspapers, radio and of course television. This indicates the limitations of Innis's 'technological determinism', although this point has been somewhat overplayed by certain schools of cultural studies. Nevertheless, Innis is right to call our attention to the fact that the technical media of communication have a definite impact upon the social organisation of culture, but his conceptualisation of the interface between technical media, space and time would have to be radically rethought to account for more contemporary processes. That the dominant mediums of communication influence the development of historical societies is further elaborated by Marshall McLuhan.

The Medium is the Message

Marshall McLuhan is best known for the provocative thesis that the most important aspect of media is not to be located within issues connected to cultural content, but in the technical medium of communication. The medium, declares McLuhan, is the message. According to him, to attend to the ideological or semiotic construction of, say, an article in today's newspaper is to miss the point. McLuhan insists, again and again, that the study of the way technical forms of media shape human perception constitutes the most important theoretical issue facing media studies today. The best example he supplies of this process involves the importance of electric light in recontextualising social relations (McLuhan, 1994: 52). The electric light I switch on in my office each morning carries no message, but transforms relations of space and time. For example, it allows me to work late in the evening or early in the morning. This affects the way I structure my public and private life. Of course the electric light has wider consequences in that shopping centres, leisure facilities and workplaces can be operable 24 hours a day. Again, it is electric light's capacity to restructure social relations and perceptions that is given analytic priority.

McLuhan, however, was not always of this particular cast of mind. In his first major work *The Mechanical Bride* (1951), he was very critical of the opportunities for manipulation and control opened up by emergent forms of media. Although many of the themes that were to propel McLuhan into wider forms of public recognition were already apparent at this juncture, his writing has much in common with the literary sensibilities of Raymond Williams and the early Frankfurt school.[1] Consumer society, he argues, echoing more familiar approaches to mass media, imposes a form of passivity upon those subjects who live on an insubstantial diet of canned music and packaged news programmes. Here McLuhan criticises contemporary culture for only offering the illusion of diversity, producing mass uniformity, and eroding the social base of good literature. Predating later developments in postmodernism and semiotics (a theme I shall return to) he argues that 'in America, low, middle, high are consumer ratings, and nothing more' (McLuhan, 1951: 59). Advertising both produces social distinctions in order to ideologically mask commercial practices of buying and selling, and has a dehumanising effect on those caught up in the process. The commercialisation of the most intimate human relations reduces the expression of sexuality to 'a problem in mechanics and hygiene' (McLuhan, 1951: 99). The mechanical reproduction of representations of the human body both abstracts from the sensuous nature of human experience and provides a breeding ground for sadistic desires and fantasies. Thus the alienating effect of modern forms of communication both produces pathological side effects and acts as a means of domination. But in McLuhan's subsequent writing he abandoned what might be termed a critical-literary disposition towards consumer culture in favour of a more celebrative mode.

The bulk of McLuhan's later writing is concerned to develop a theory of media that reverses many of his earlier reflections. In the first place, McLuhan no longer takes cultural content as his primary point of concern. In the main, this is due to his attention to the technologies of cultural dissemination. Here modern technologies are no longer viewed as alienating. This is because they are best represented as extensions of the body or, as McLuhan occasionally remarks, the human nervous system. By this he means that the wheel is an extension of the foot and clothing is the technical projection of skin. As a further illustration, and perhaps more importantly in terms of McLuhan's thesis on the media, the book is conceptualised as an outgrowth of the eye, while radio is represented as the technological expression of the ear.

Crucial to an understanding of these processes is the dominance of print culture after the appearance of Gutenberg's bible in early modern Europe (McLuhan, 1962). Following Innis, McLuhan argues that the portable medium of print enabled ideas and perspectives to be circulated across space. In terms of time, the dominance of a writing culture had shortened human memories, because information could now be stored in the durable medium of the book. However, the portability of the book, as B. Anderson (1983) also shows, allows for the cultural expression of nationalism outside of the control of established forms of religious authority. Anderson argues that the period between 1500 and 1550 combined print capitalism's need to find new markets, the technological advances of the printing press, and the expression of languages other than Latin in print.

These factors created new languages of power that helped foster forms of national legitimacy undermining the central authority of the feudal church. While McLuhan makes a similar point, his main emphasis lies elsewhere. The fixing of language into print is important not only because it creates a spatial bias, but because it fosters a bias within human perception. McLuhan argues that 'The invention of the alphabet, like the invention of the wheel, was the translation or reduction of a complex, organic interplay of spaces into a single space. The phonetic alphabet reduced the use of all the senses at once, which is oral speech, to a merely visual code' (McLuhan 1962: 45).

In the medieval period, manuscripts were firmly located in physical space, rarely used punctuation, and were mostly read aloud. Medieval scholarship, in McLuhan's terms, was more for the ear than the eye. With the move towards a predominantly print culture the human senses had become increasingly compartmentalised and specialised. Whereas oral cultures allowed the rich interplay of all the senses, print culture abstracted writing from speech and promoted the visual component of the human organism. The dominance of written forms of communication cultivated a rationalised culture that was linear, uniform and infinitely repeatable. Print culture replaces the sensuous play of oral cultures with a predictable and standardised mode of thought. Further, the hegemony of typography not only 'discourages minute verbal play' (McLuhan, 1962: 158) through the unification of grammar, spelling and meaning, but shapes modern forms of individualism. Book culture requires that reading practices are silent and attentive, that the text have an author, and that the translation of a shared collective culture is converted into one dependent upon individual forms of expression. As McLuhan comments, 'print is the technology of individualism' (1962:158). Print supplies the cultural resources for national forms of uniformity, while simultaneously giving birth to notions of individuality. In achieving this, the Gutenberg press converted space and time into the calculable, the rational and the predictable. The linear and logical emphasis of writing was mirrored in the uniform regimentation of clock time. The rationalising impact of the printing press paved the way for geographical maps, railway timetables, and notions of perspective in painting. According to McLuhan, the advent of print culture had both developed certain human senses (sight) rather than others, and shaped a particular form of human rationality. This, however, was all to change with the arrival of electric forms of communication.

The transition to electronic communication can be connected with a change in the experiential nature of modernity. This is best represented through the gradual displacement of hot media with cool media. What does McLuhan mean by this? A hot medium is one that disallows participation and is high in informational content. Conversely, cooler media leave more spaces for the audience to participate, and exhibit lower levels of information intensity. McLuhan explains:

speech is a cool medium of low definition, because so little is given and so much has to be filled in by the listener. On the other hand, hot media do not leave so much to be filled in or completed by the audience. Hot media are, therefore, low in participation, and cool media are high in participation or completion by the audience. (McLuhan, 1994: 23)

The most obvious example of a cool medium is the telephone. The telephone is a dialogic medium that normally requires at least two people to participate in communication. Conversely, print culture remains a hot medium in that the activity of reading makes fewer demands upon the subject in terms of shaping the flow of information. In McLuhan's terms the telephone 'demands complete participation, unlike the written and printed page' (McLuhan, 1994: 267). McLuhan is also aware that the telephone, by making its users constantly available, also has the effect of changing relations of power, and conceptions of the public and the private. Under the previous medium of communication, book culture was dependent upon reading practices that took place in private as opposed to public spaces, and knowledge production was undertaken by a small cast of authors. Cooler media, like the telephone, decentralise the production of knowledge in that they involve a wider range of participants and thereby democratise the formation of opinion. Interestingly, McLuhan argues that it is a characteristic of 'bookish' intellectuals to wish to extend so-called enlightened perspectives into societies in more backward regions. This, if the argument is followed, is the effect of an increasingly outmoded form of communication that depends upon centralised forms of knowledge production. The new media, such as the telephone, have ended relations of dominance in communicative relations and have in effect produced a system which no central authority can govern.

Similarly, McLuhan argues that television is cold whereas cinema is hot. The social practice of sitting in a cinema effectively isolated from other members of the audience disallows audience forms of participation. The activity of film viewing, as one might expect, for McLuhan bears a strong family resemblance to the passivity imposed upon the audience by book reading. The medium of film is centralised and authoritarian, requiring the film maker to transform the audience into another world (McLuhan, 1994: 285). Alternatively, where a hot medium like film spells out meanings, the cooler practice of watching television leaves more work for the audience to do. Television, as a more decentred medium than film, allows for the expression of regional dialect, and as the picture quality of most television sets was poor at the time McLuhan was writing, he argued that this converted spectators into more equal partners in the production of meaning. Television, in this respect, cultivated what McLuhan called 'depth participation' (1994: 321).

The reconstitution of media into electronic forms of communication also has implications for the reworking of space and time. Previously McLuhan had largely followed Innis by arguing that whereas oral societies were time biased, literate cultures were space biased. However, the displacement of print by electronic circuitry rendered Innnis's earlier reflections redundant. Space and time had been annihilated. To understand this we would have to reconsider McLuhan's view of the media. Print culture promoted individualism inasmuch as it implied a privatised mode of reception. If an individual wished to read a book she would actively have to seek it out. But under modern conditions, according to McLuhan, cultural forms 'pour upon us instantly and continuously' (McLuhan and Fiore, 1967:16). The interaction between modern subjects and communication networks is no longer confined to a few lonely hours before bedtime. Today the lives of the globe's citizens are wrapped around a seemingly endless encounter with material and symbolic modes of communication. Newspapers are read on buses and trains, car radios are tuned to the morning news, joggers listen to talking books while exercising and people make love in front of the television. The mediated experience of modernity is one of 'a whirling phantasmagoria' (McLuhan, 1951: v). For McLuhan, modernity is best characterised as the unceasing relocation of information in time and space. Here communication systems put us in constant and immediate touch with different perspectives. The co-ordinates of time and space have vanished, to herald a world where the sense of individualised detachment fostered by a book culture has given way to one where everyone is 'profoundly involved with everyone else' (McLuhan and Fiore, 1967: 61). The explosion of the new media has disrupted the visual bias of written forms of communication, returning the globe's citizens to a shared culture that has much in common with that of oral societies. The global village has swept aside the hierarchical, uniform and individualising culture of print production and replaced it with a more tactile culture of simultaneous happenings.

McLuhan, prefiguring much of the current talk on the death of the nation state, comments:

> Department sovereignties have melted away as rapidly as national sovereignties under conditions of electric speed. Obsession with the older patterns of mechanical, one-way expansion from centre to margins is no longer relevant to our electric world. Electricity does not centralise, but decentralises. (McLuhan, 1994: 35–6)

Just as Foucault (1980) and modern feminist movements have argued that power is everywhere, so, McLuhan suggests, are the tentacles of mass communication. A culture driven along by electricity does not flow from any one place or location, but is quite literally organised into networks that have no connecting centre. The technology of communication, therefore, extends our central nervous system into a sensuous global embrace with the rest of humanity. This renders redundant temporal (past and present) and spatial (near and far) distinctions. Those most in touch with the new electronic environment have relinquished the old means of perception delivered by an outmoded print culture. McLuhan represents the new media as in line with the most *spaced out* representatives of 1960s counter-cultural movements. The new mode of perception, for those tuned in enough not to have dropped out, eradicates social difference and involves human beings in a drug-like embrace of togetherness.

These are important points, to which I will return. For the moment, I want to indicate that for McLuhan the elimination of space and time is tied to technological advances in mass communications. If we take a look at our morning newspaper we can immediately see that it inhabits a radically different form to that of the traditional novel. In place of the linear progression of a narrative we are confronted by what McLuhan calls a 'communal mosaic' (McLuhan, 1994: 204). A newspaper has a multiplicity of authors and a variety of features and sections (sports page, fashion section, foreign news, editorial) that resist the single point of view evident in the book. The collage-like layout of the modern newspaper will also contain a number of items that have been transmitted from contexts far removed from those who either read or produce the newspaper. The speeding up and globalisation of news-gathering practices mean that temporality and distance will become progressively unimportant in governing newspaper content. Further, McLuhan explicitly argues that, as regards content, it is the consumers rather than those who own and control the means of production who are determinant (McLuhan, 1994: 216). As space and time, as well as patterns of ownership, become irrelevant to the content of the newspaper it is the audience's need for participation that shapes this process. This is nurtured by the fact that modern forms of communication enable audiences to travel through time and space. Before the mass production of photographs, travel was practised 'to encounter the strange and unfamiliar' (McLuhan, 1994: 198). Now, returning to our morning paper, we can familiarise ourselves with the Grand Canyon or the Eiffel Tower by glancing at the travel pages. But just as space has been abolished so have linear conceptions of time (McLuhan, 1969:122). Under electronic forms of communication the globe has become both historically and spatially visible. When we scan the newspaper we may be moving our eyes across stories from different parts of the world and events from human history. A single newspaper might contain articles regarding a new film on the Russian revolution, photographs of what our city looked like in the 1920s, or a feature on youth culture's attempt to revive the 1970s. This is why McLuhan suggests that the practice of reading a newspaper enables us to travel in time and space without leaving our own home.

These reflections lead on to McLuhan's concept of implosion. In preliterate cultures, he argues, 'there is no art in our sense, but the whole environment is experienced as unitary' (McLuhan, 1969: 31). The socially and sensorily integrated world of oral societies, as we have seen, was radically altered by the rationalising impulse of print. This led to the production of a minority, hierarchical and specialised expert culture. The emergence of the public sphere in the eighteenth century, as Habermas (1989) has shown, was intimately tied up with the production of a literate bourgeois society. But while Habermas ambivalently highlights the communicative potential of literate forms of production, McLuhan views this development as creating a centralised top-down culture, which encompasses rigid boundary distinctions. The specialisation of print separated the domains of aesthetics, politics, economics, and the public and the private. The vertical and horizontal relations of these spheres has, however, been radically redrawn through the impact of electronic communication. The new media technologies have restructured social life to the extent that you do not need to be an expert to take part. We now inhabit an overlapping world that has obliterated cultural hierarchies and the separation of spheres. The globe has imploded vertically, temporally and horizontally. Humanity, McLuhan goes on, has collapsed in on itself, returning to the village-like state characteristic of oral societies.

The domain of politics is no longer readily separable from the sphere of communication by which policy is made public. The point about the speeded-up culture of modernity is not that it expands the power of a political establishment that is able to colonise public discourse. Instead the implosion of the media of mass communication into the political domain brings about a society where the media is politics and politics is the media. When the French President flew out to the former Yugoslavia he did so not to attend the signing of a politically important treaty or to engage in discussion with the leaders of the civil war. Mitterand's visit was intended to focus world public opinion on the suffering of those caught up in the conflict; notably he achieved this by being driven through the war-torn streets while being shadowed by the global media. McLuhan and Fiore (1968) make the point that our political representatives can literally make or invent the news. Further, the corresponding implosion of the public into the private has brought an end to the public sphere. The private realm of critical reflection is continually breached by new media that demand attention, hereby hooking the human organism into the global tides of opinion formation. Cultural implosion has converted a rational public into an interactive mass or, as McLuhan occasionally puts it, an electronic circuit of energy.

Not only has the media imploded into politics, but showbusiness has imploded into education. We could argue that young people's current obsession with video games makes the book work associated with traditional forms of education seem unexciting and dull. Educational institutions are now utilising film, television and video as part of the instructive process. According to McLuhan, this will eventually produce hybridised cultural forms that are both entertaining and educational. The notion of the hybrid is an important one for McLuhan. This is because it encourages us to abandon linear patterns of development for the consideration of spatial constellations. Magazine production, has, according to McLuhan and Powers

(1989), been transformed by colour television. The emergence of glossy covers, colour pictures and more user-friendly layouts has come about as the medium of magazine production has responded to technological developments in television. This point would have been missed had our analysis been content to trace through the linear emergence of magazine production. McLuhan fruitfully suggests that the historical development of a particular field of media should be related to other fields of cultural production. The technical hybridisation of media forms has produced radical effects, restructuring related fields of production. To enforce this idea, I would draw attention to the hybridisation of music cassettes and the novel into talking books, the merger of television and computers in the development of Me TV, the integration of television and video found on MTV, and McLuhan's (1994: 231) own example: that the high production values of the cinema have, changed the nature of advertising. These comments build into McLuhan's overall view of the media as being like a hurricane that has torn apart stable relations of time and space, while the hybridised and imploded culture of post-literate societies are continually shifting the contours of modern experience.

> As soon as information is required, it is very rapidly replaced by still newer information. Our electrically configured world has forced us to move from the habit of data classification to the mode of pattern recognition. We can no longer build serially, block-by-block, step-by-step, because instant communication ensures that all factors of the environment and of experience co-exist in a state of active interplay. (McLuhan and Fiore, 1967: 63)

Space and Time:
Technology and Cultural Studies

The views of Marshall McLuhan were originally applauded by some and criticised by others. I do not intend to uncritically defend his perspectives here, although they remain germane in mass communication theory because of their concern with issues related to space and time. These themes remain important, given the current lack of attention to them within much media and sociological theory. Along with Adam (1990), I think that concerns around social or media time should avoid positing theoretical dualisms. By this she means that constructed social time should not be pitted against so-called real or natural time. Adam argues provocatively that time is best seen as a multifaceted concept where no absolute distinctions can be made between symbolic and natural time. Adam summarises: 'It is not either winter or December, or hibernation time for the tortoise, or one o'clock, or time for Christmas dinner. It is planetary time, biological time, clock and calendar time, natural and social time all at once' (Adam, 1990: 16).

A hermeneutic concern for the way media inform the experience of temporality, that also avoided subject-object dualism, should be concerned to investigate the means by which time structurates social action. However, while it as at least arguable that social theory has a reasonable pedigree with respect to questions of time, the same cannot be said of spatial relations. Edward Soja (1989) has shown that social theory has consistently privileged the investigation of social being and time over that of space. In a theoretical vein similar to that of Adam, Soja suggests – that space, when it is considered at all, is often conceptualised as a reified and objective product. Just as time is interwoven with human actions and meanings, so space does not merely act as the undifferentiated background of human interaction but is socially created and transformed by such activity. Space and time are not the *empty containers* of social activity, but both enable and constrain human action. Further, spatial and temporal relations, as McLuhan well understood, do not stand apart from social practices, but are both produced and reproduced by them. This of course does not commit me to defending the specific way in which McLuhan represented the transformation of space and time in his theory of media. But given McLuhan's concern to discuss notions of space and time in connection with the media, and accepting these themes are currently under-represented in the literature, the question now needs to be asked: how do we account for the resistance to his writing within cultural and media studies?

There are two related reasons that are usually offered in opposition to McLuhan's perspectives. The first, which has been most consistently outlined by Raymond Williams (1974, 1985), is the objection that McLuhan's technological determinism acts as an ideological justification of dominant social relations. McLuhan's analysis of the medium of communication, Williams claims, is isolated from broader sociological and cultural contexts. This in effect *desocialises* media analysis in that McLuhan renders invisible the ways in which dominant authority relations structure cultural production, content and reception. In effect, McLuhan renders such questions irrelevant, as the social impact of cultural technology is abstracted from the analysis of specific social relations. The charge that McLuhanism leaves unquestioned global capitalist relations has been a consistent theme of some of McLuhan's sternest critics (Finkelstein, 1968; Nairn, 1969). This strain of analysis can be related to Stuart Hall's (1986) argument that McLuhan's cultural disposition towards the media of mass communication has much in common with uncritical forms of postmodernism.[2] McLuhan's writing turns from the critical-literary perspective evident in his early writing towards a more euphoric position. This stance parallels some of the developments evident within French postmodernism, which has similarly advocated the-abandonment of cultural critique. Here the critic is accused of lacking an adequately serious disposition, and of advocating a form of consumerist lying back and enjoying the proliferation of discourses within the global village. There is much in these charges.

McLuhan, for instance, has very little to say about the globalisation of capitalist relations that make the global village imaginable. Further, the extent to which the transnational development of communications technology can be tied into the fostering of capitalist patterns of organisation, control and lifestyle is also neglected. The progressive commercialisation of public space, as the Mattelarts (1992) have argued, has meant that hegemonic modes of dominance can be tied into the shift from public to private operators, and from national to transnational ones. These issues can also be connected to the realisation of the cultural rather than technical forms of hybridity that are currently being promoted by globalisation processes. If on one level we are witnessing the international spread of an homogeneous capitalistic culture, at another there has occurred the eruption of different identities. This is a product of capitalism, in that post-Fordist forms of production need to produce different lifestyle orientations on the part of consumers, as well as being evidence of the symbolic capacity of complex, unstable identities to remake themselves through a global bricolage (Robertson, 1992). The political emergence of hybrid ethnic identities has occurred underneath the disciplinary discourses of the nation state, while articulating connections with a more globally oriented commercial culture. At the local level, therefore, one can detect a turning away from the uncertain flux of modernity into more definite social identities, and a more emancipatory, less reactive, recognition of difference (Hall, 1991).

Both Williams's and Hall's criticisms draw our attention to the fact that McLuhan's attempt to understand the networks of communication is of an overly *technical* nature. His concern to address the technical media of communication means that the meanings that are generated by the intersection of global, national and local relationships are, to take Williams's phrase, 'distinguishable only by their variable sense-ratios' (Williams, 1974: 127). This is a similar point to the one made by Miller (1971) in his classic study of McLuhan. Meanings, Miller contends, are not governed by the technical outgrowth of the senses but by linguistic practices. Following Saussure, I would argue that linguistic meaning is not determined by technical conditions (the relationship between signifier and signified is arbitrary) but by the intersubjective nature of language. The interactive nature of, say, a television programme has more to do with whether it is an open or closed text, or whether the programme is invested with *relevance* by the audience. The communicative nature of television is not, therefore, determined by the technical medium. Also like many of the postmodernists who follow him, McLuhan displaces attention from the impact that relations of power and force have within the social-historical world. His theoretical neglect of mass communication's role in the production of symbolic meanings and the maintenance of dominant social relations unnecessarily brackets off critical questions related to the organisation of institutions, culture and ideology.

And yet, while all this is true up to a point, I am left with the impression that the baby is being thrown out with the bathwater. While the cultural critics are correct to point to the limitations of McLuhan's analysis, their own concerns also contain certain allusions. Critical analysis within mass communication – since McLuhan – has paid very little attention to those questions which could be deemed central to his engagement. This might, for the sake of convenience, be compressed into a single question. How has the development of media of communication reshaped the perceptions of time and space within contemporary society? This issue, under charges of technological determinism, has been dismissed from mainstream cultural theory. The way McLuhan addresses these issues is certainly open to question, and in this respect the charges of technological determinism carry a good deal of critical force. Yet I would argue, along with Carey (1989), Meyrowitz (1985) and J.B. Thompson (1990), that cultural media, regardless of their actual content, have had a radical impact on the nature of social life. The above authors, like McLuhan, argue that media of communication restructure time and space and thereby help shape inter-subjective social relations. In this way, viewed less deterministically than McLuhan often presented himself, his writing remains full of insight.

McLuhan offers an interesting analysis of the way in which the introduction of the telegraph transformed human intersubjective relations. He reminds us that, like the telephone, the telegraph makes us continually present and accessible to other persons for communicative relations. The technical medium of the telegraph, for instance, allows us to maintain intimate social relations across time and space, while also structurating those relations. In short, the telegraph does not govern the cultural content of our personal messages, but it does play some part in helping to form them. McLuhan (1994: 256) offers the example of a number of Oxford undergraduates who, on reading that Rudyard Kipling was paid ten shillings for each word he published, telegraphed him. Their telegraph message contained 10 shillings and asked for one of his best words. Kipling promptly replied, 'Thanks'. We can judiciously argue that while technical media do not determine cultural meanings, as McLuhan implies, they do play some role in helping to form the lifeworld relations characteristic of modernity. J.B. Thompson (1990) notes that the transmission of culture in a society dominated by mass means of communication largely takes place without the constant forms of feedback that are distinctive of everyday talk. However, the one-way interactive flow of the television allows new forms of resistance on the part of the audience, in that they are distanciated from the producers of the message. Whereas television makes present the back regions of those who appear on television, my own reactions are absent. When George Bush collapsed into his soup his actions immediately became available to all those watching television, but what is absent is the apparent mirth and enjoyment of the television audience. The cultural technologies and media of everyday life have served to restructure much of modern experience. This discussion should warn against certain trends within poststructuralism that view social and technical relations as radically separable from the production of meaning. Again, while the meaning of last night's six o'clock news is not determined by certain technical apparatuses, it might make a difference to producers and consumers alike whether the information was heard second hand down the telephone, on television while trying to keep up with *Star Trek* on a different channel, or listening to the radio while putting the children to bed. To illustrate these arguments further I will briefly outline the contributions of two other thinkers similar to McLuhan. Both Jack Goody and Anthony Giddens place at the centre of their analyses of historical change a concern for the media of communication. Arguably, they do this in a way that avoids some of the problems that we encountered with McLuhan.

Oral, Print and Modern Cultures:
Jack Goody and Anthony Giddens

The aspects of Goody's (1977; Goody and Watt, 1968) writing I shall view refer to the distinctions he expertly draws between literate and oral societies. The novelty of Goody's approach lies in his insistence that the main differences between the two cultures are to be located within the specific media of communication. Similarly to McLuhan, Goody argues that the significance of these technological factors can be judged independently from ideological considerations. The differences in the communicative acts representative of oral and literate societies have far-reaching consequences for the sociological nature of the respective cultures. Generally speaking, oral societies have a much more pragmatic disposition towards language than is usually evident within literate societies. The social transmission of culture, as one would expect, predominately takes place in face-to-face interaction, where knowledge is primarily geared towards maintaining the existing set of social relations. Such is the need to maintain tradition across time rather than space that knowledge that does not perform this function tends to be quickly discarded. The transition from a predominantly oral to a literate/oral culture involves the storage of knowledge in written forms. This process allows the emergence of a more critical disposition in that subjects are freed from an overarching concern with the oral transmission of knowledge. The objectification of culture in writing also creates the conditions for critique as it becomes easier for readers to perceive logical inconsistencies and contradictions. If I decided to read this book out to an assembled audience over a number of days it would undoubtedly be difficult for those listening to become aware of some of the problems that remain under-theorised. Conversely, as reviewers and current readers are no doubt aware, the formulation of critical forms of understanding is enhanced, especially given the complex nature of many of the arguments, by the discussion's availability in writing. Further, as most of the people who sit down and read this book will be unknown to the author, this too enhances the possibility of critical forms of reception. Goody remarks that the advent of writing allowed for the more impersonal means of assessment that are characteristic of modern bureaucracies. Writing will permit those who are distant in time and space from the author to discuss a set of arguments without the results being automatically fed back to the producer of the text. This may produce a certain anxiety within the author, but it also involves a definite break with the more personal forms of interaction evident in oral cultures. Hence Goody deconstructs the oppositions between the civilised and the non-civilised that are traditionally associated with the contrasting forms of life in literate and oral societies, without advocating a form of cultural relativism. It is, according to him, the distinctions apparent within the means of communication, rather than radically different mind sets, that account for the relatively closed nature of oral societies.

These somewhat compressed reflections throw an interesting critical light on McLuhan's writings. Goody, along with other writers (Chartier, 1989; Thompson, 1990), argues that the transition from a predominantly oral to a print culture is more discontinuous than McLuhan allows. Goody agrees with McLuhan that print had an individualising and specialising effect upon culture, and that it also creates hierarchies of knowledge and social closure. These cultural changes, however, exist alongside the continued importance of an oral tradition. Writing did not so much replace an oral culture as both transform and modify it. Parents still pass on folk memories to their children, and other groups maintain a sense of the past through the performance of popular songs, ballads and stories, not all of which are written down. For all of McLuhan's claims to want to break with the linear grip that print has on the modern psyche, his discussion of the successive stages in the development of the mode of communication (oral, literate, electric) maintains a segmented shape. Print supplements oral culture rather than replacing it.

Goody emphasises the communicative possibilities that are opened up by print. McLuhan, as we saw, tended to view this development negatively as producing sensorily impoverished, uniform and homogeneous forms of life. This bleak reading of print culture unnecessarily discounts some of the more emancipatory opportunities that have flowered in the wake of written communication. As Goody amply demonstrates, the fixing of discourse into print has aided a form of rational, critical consciousness it would be difficult to imagine contemporary life without. Print culture, we may conclude, in opposition to McLuhan, is best represented dialectically. While it certainly had a rationalising impact on the production of knowledge, it also secured the reflexive grounds for counter-factual forms of engagement that have transformed the trajectory of modern cultures.

Anthony Giddens's (1990, 1991) theory of radicalised modernity represents one of the most original and far-reaching attempts to contemplate some of the transformations taking place in the modern world. In pursuing this theoretical project he represents modernity as a runaway juggernaut, where every attempt to order its path produces unintended consequences causing it to spin further out of control. For this reason, we can never gain total control over society. In light of these reflections, Giddens argues that modernity changes at a much faster pace than any prior society, that it has extended its global reach, and finally, that it has had a profoundly transformative effect on traditional social practices. I do not have the space to trace through the wider sets of issues ushered in by these remarks; here I want to concentrate on two areas that have been opened up by modern institutions which are central to Giddens's discussion.

First, contemporary societies have witnessed the development of a time-space distanciation that was not evident in pre-modern societies. By this Giddens means that within the pre-modern period time and space were always strongly located in terms of physical place. The turning of night into day or the passing of seasons served as localised markers of time and space. With the invention of clock time we could say that time has become separated from space, and that time and space have become empty phenomena. The pulling apart of time and space can be visualised in calendars, railway timetables and maps. These devices enable time and space to be co-ordinated without any reference to notions of place – they are abstract means of ordering social activity. The remembering of a birthday does not require the immediate presence of the person in question. The use of calendars helps us to keep track of important social occasions in ways that are not dependent upon concrete local factors.

This leads on to the second aspect of Giddens's contribution I wish to consider – the disembedding of social systems. Modernity, according to Giddens, is a post-traditional social order, where the 'emptying out' of time and space allows for the stretching of social relations. If we think for a moment about the globalisation of television networks this should become clear. While global does not yet mean universal, international media organisations are able to transport images and representations across time and space and on to the television sets of the globe's citizens. This memorably converted the Gulf War into a global conflict. In McLuhan's terms the globe has imploded in on itself, eradicating time and space. For Giddens, the relocation of information from localised contexts, evident within modern communication networks, is made possible via the uncoupling of time and space, and disembedding mechanisms such as technical media. These devices involve the separation of social relations 'from local contexts of interaction and their restructuring across indefinite spans of time-space' (Giddens, 1990: 21). For example, Giddens argues, expert systems exhibit many of these features, as the knowledge they deploy has a validity independent of the agents who make use of them. Expert systems are part of the fabric of everyday life and have the capacity of extending social relations in time and space. Every time I read a popular feature on health care, expert frames of reference are being recontextualised in terms of certain lifestyle decisions that I might make. The decision to stop eating meat might be informed by an article I read in a women's magazine, a leaflet attacking McDonald's, or my mistrust of the assurances offered by state-employed scientists – these are all examples of the way technical knowledge becomes routinely reconstituted in modernity.[3]

Giddens (1991: 24–7) explicitly recognises the role played by technical media in his short discussion of the cultural make-up of newspapers. It was the invention of the telegraph that allowed the early newspapers to separate space from notions of place. Up until this point, the content of the press had been determined by whether or not news items were close at hand. The telegraph's capacity to disembed information from social location meant that media content was less determined by proximity in space and time, while allowing newspapers to become much more event driven. The transformation brought about by the technical medium of the telegraph reshaped the nature of newspapers. Giddens markedly follows McLuhan by arguing that the restructing of time and space allows distant events to become part of everyday life, and reshapes modern media content into a collage effect.

The long-term impact of the changing contours of modernity has both unifying and fragmentary effects. The mosaic nature of the newspaper, for instance, both encourages the view that humanity shares a single world while making us aware of its diversity. Again, in a vein very similar to that of McLuhan, Giddens holds that the implosion of global forms of life enhances the notion that human beings currently share a number of opportunities and problems. I agree with Giddens, however, that social forces of unification are also accompanied by processes of fragmentation. As Giddens (1991: 188) argues, the act of reading a newspaper may on one level make us aware of issues related to globalisation, but on another it involves, given the amount of newsprint available, the conscious selection of certain information forms over others. The emphasis McLuhan places on the unificatory implications of communications technology and the relative unimportance of the meanings that these help generate leads him to bypass this point.

In other respects Giddens's remarks suggest similar criticisms of McLuhan to those offered by Goody. Goody and Giddens characterise oral cultures as being in the grip of traditional forms of life that integrate the time-space organisation of the village. The introduction of writing for Goody enables critical reflection – whereas for Giddens it has a similar effect in that it contributes towards time-space distanciation. This allows the production of knowledge to be bracketed off from the reinterpretation of traditional codes and practices. The decoupling of time/space from place and the critical appropriation of knowledge from tradition creates the conditions for the reflexive nature of modernity. We have already seen how the routine disembedding of expert forms of knowledge help sustain critical practices. Giddens writes: 'In all cultures, social practices are routinely altered in the light of ongoing discoveries which feed into them. But only in the era of modernity is the revision of convention radicalised to apply (in principle) to all aspects of human life' (1990: 38–9).

The reflexive arch of modernity heralds a world where ultimately nothing is certain or free from questioning, including reason. Reflexivity, or the altering of human action in the light of new knowledge, is deeply inscribed in modern institutions. Again McLuhan's reactive reading of the breakdown of tradition, and its quasi-return under electronic forms of communication, should be questioned. The new media of mass communication have not returned modern societies to a form of rationality evident in the pre-modern village. On this point, his writing is irredeemably flawed. McLuhan is right to argue that the media constitute new forms of involvement and spatial connection, but fundamentally mistaken in the extent to which he fails to make the connection between cultural media and reflexive questioning. To follow Giddens, then, we could argue that one of the primary mechanisms that has made new knowledge available has been the medium of mass communication. Various media of communication have flooded audiences' lives with perspectives that have been severed from previous locations within space and time. The critical examination of existing social practices is surely connected to the networks of communication that circulate revised forms of knowledge. Thus, for Goody and Giddens, notions of cultural critique have an intimate connection to technical media of communication. Cultural media act both as storage devices and as a means of relocating information through time and space.

These perspectives imply that technical media have played an important part in helping promote a more reflexive culture within modernity. To offer an example, American talk shows are often concerned with some of the most intimate aspects of modern life. Whether they are discussing child abuse, untidy partners or mixed race relationships they have a function in making public a range of social concerns that have until recently been shielded from the public gaze. While these issues are often dealt with in a sensational manner (in America intense network competition means that a variety of means of holding audiences is utilised) talk shows have recontextualised relations between the public and the private. The fact that these shows can be stored on videotape enables researchers to look at the ways sexuality and race are represented. This would of course be difficult if one could view the programme only once. The transportable nature of culture, in a global television market, means that such shows are potentially viewable by a vast audience. Talk shows, as Giddens indicates, offer a popular mix of expert opinion and audience participation. This enables viewers, in contexts radically different from the United States, to encounter discussions of issues that may be more repressively framed in their own national context. The recontextualisation of 'what constitutes a healthy relationship' partially takes such questions out of the hands of professional bodies and lays it open for public reflection. Yet the major problem with this analysis is that concerns with the way technical media serve to democratise reflexivity within modernity are overly separated from the quality of the conversations produced within talk show settings. As I indicated, the need to capture audience shares can lead to such discussions being colonised by glossy production values and elements of shock and surprise. This points beyond the concerns of this chapter but it should be evident that while technical media have had a certain democratising effect, in themselves they cannot guarantee informed levels of debate. This is not to deny the relevance of Goody's and Giddens's observations, although, it is crucial to the aims of this book to argue that the semiotic culture necessary for critically rethinking social life should be subject to certain normative considerations.

Goody and Giddens, as well as McLuhan and Innis, make the evolution of communicative systems central to an understanding of the development of modern societies. I would argue that the development of communication media is closely associated with the rise and fall of mass society. The decline of mass society has recently been associated with a number of cultural changes taking place in post-war society. These include changing work practices, the decline of traditional political parties, the waning of national traditions and the changing structure of the family. The change in the nature of technical media, as McLuhan was aware, also has implications for certain cultural relations. The degree of cultural integration experienced by early twentieth-century Western societies is often contrasted to a more fragmented present. The centralised and national nature of communication systems that accompanied the rise of the nation state is evident in the integration of citizens into vertical frameworks. The change in the centre of gravity of communication structures has correspondingly influenced the kinds of subjectivities that are evident today. The arrival of cable, satellite and more global broadcasting, the rapid emergence of a diverse magazine market, the commercialisation of the air waves, and the growth in the number of homes with video equipment have changed the axis of cultural production. Consumers now have a greater amount of choice and control over the cultural forms they may wish to purchase. This has enabled consumers to escape traditional forms of cultural production and bask in an unprecedented variety of semiotic material. The developments in media technologies have not only fragmented the audience, but have put limits on the extent to which communications media may be utilised for national manipulation and control. As networks of communication currently outstrip the capacity of nation states to regulate information flow, this poses restraints upon the imposition of ideology from above. However, media systems largely remain national in character, and such arguments falsely presuppose that commercial systems could not be equally utilised for purposes of indoctrination. What can be said with more confidence is that the proliferation of media outlets makes such strategies more complex than in previously existing modes of communication. That is, the breakdown of older social patterns of integration can be related to the technical systems currently available to a wide range of the population.

These concerns take us some way towards writing a history of modernity in terms of the development of media technologies. This project would seek to avoid the technological determinism evident in the writings of Innis and McLuhan, but would also critique functionalist or Marxist arguments that reduce communications structures to other formations. Equal care should be taken not to exaggerate the power of the media of communication. Indeed a more fully rounded appreciation of the role of the mass media in helping shape modern societies would include concerns around the media of communication, as Goody, Giddens and McLuhan demonstrate. However, where McLuhan, and Innis for that matter, goes astray is in his desire to replace a concern with the intersection of meaning and institutions with that of technology. The analysis that is being offered here would suggest that media theory should seek to maintain the tension between different but related levels of analysis.

More Critical Observations

The views of Marshall McLuhan have so far been met with relatively sympathetic forms of engagement. It is not, however, my intention to resurrect McLuhan's writing without offering a more forceful critical account. An adequate appreciation of McLuhan's work in relation to mass communication studies must recognise at least four other levels of criticism: (1) his misleading reflections on the nature of time and space; (2) the dialectic between unification and fragmentation evident in the media; and (3) the ways media technology can be utilised for strategies of surveillance. Finally, I will address, in preparation for a later discussion, (4) the implications McLuhan's theories have for the future of a specifically public space.

1. The implosion of the globe through the media of mass communication, in McLuhan's view, has destroyed time and space as meaningful constructs. The passage of information has resulted in the collapse of all meaningful spatial and temporal relations. Such comments are both essentialistic and highly exaggerated. If we take McLuhan's notion of space (although similar arguments could be made in respect of time) the writing of Henri Lefebvre (1991) offers some pertinent analysis.

According to Lefebvre, space is the product of both material and symbolic social practices.[4] We can talk about three different levels of spatial practice. First there are practices which directly involve the production and reproduction of specific spaces. The modern nation state can be conceptualised in this regard in that it usually attempts to regulate the passage of citizens across its borders by the enforcement of certain entry criteria. These practices help to reproduce certain notions of citizenship in a relatively durable way across time. Next, Lefebvre argues that there are certain representations of space that directly interlock with the production of space. The representational practices of contemporary architecture can be thought of in this way. While the joint agencies of money (capital) and power (state) are continually transforming the landscape of the city (spatial practice), they are in turn reliant upon the drawings and designs of architects to figure how this can be done. Indeed, in terms of the globalisation of specifically Western forms of technology and institutional practice, Lefebvre argues that capitalism has ushered in what he calls abstract space. Abstract space is governed by technological forms of reason and an imperialistic drive that flattens forms of difference and otherness. David Harvey (1989) has added that the spatial axis in relations between capital and labour remains crucial: whereas the liquidity of capital has come to dominate space, labour, at present, is better at organising resistance through local place. Finally there are what Lefebvre calls representational spaces: complex symbolic markings, such as art, that maintain a relative autonomy from the dominant relations of production.

In the first instance, Lefebvre's analysis at least makes us aware that there are different levels of spatial practice. McLuhan has imploded interrelated levels of spatial analysis to the transforming effects of electronic media. Lefebvre also makes us take note that spatial practices usually have a certain durability over time. This not only suggests that McLuhan's remarks concerning the end of space are essentialistic, but that they also act as a corrective to post-structuralist writers whose concern for hybrid identities – here I have in mind some of Hall's earlier remarks – has ignored the maintenance of more solid formations. The continued production of a specifically locatable national press is instructive. The social practice of buying a national newspaper arguably articulates a relatively stable identity that binds time and space. Further, in Lefebvre's terms, we are able to reconnect some of the spatial transformations brought about by the mass media with institutional processes. This returns to an earlier point: that the technologically simulated global village cannot be conceptualised outside a concern for those dialectical social relationships that have simultaneously commercialised and privatised public space. The more material concerns of Lefebvre remind us that the transformation of space is reliant upon institutional rather than merely technological frames of reference. On the other hand, it is difficult to visualise how Lefebvre's theory makes room for some of the capacities of technical media that McLuhan notably highlights. Lefebvre's materialist frame of reference would have to crudely tie in television's ability to recontextualise information across time and space with the interests of capital. We are perhaps on more secure theoretical ground if we argue that while the electronic media's global spread can be tied into the development of capitalism, some of the cultural implications enhanced by these processes are best conceptualised as properties of certain technical media.

But what of the way McLuhan represents time and space as instantaneous forms of communication? Marjorie Ferguson (1990, 1991) has pointed out that the *appearance* of immediate communication can act as a form of ideological manipulation obscuring the relations of selection that are involved in securing certain representations over others. Again it is McLuhan's exclusively technological paradigm that prevents him from producing more socialised reflections upon the mass media. In this vein, Ferguson suggests that certain social relations of image production can be tied into the selection of images and representations of others. The modern state, for example, is continually involved in the monitoring of the information that the mass media transmits to its citizens. This, especially during times of intense social conflict, can lead to measures of censorship, effective repression or active discouragement of the transmission of sensitive information. These are all cases in point. It is perhaps better to argue that the media has not abolished time and space, but radically compressed it. David Harvey (1989) argues that the global spread of capitalism has speeded up the processes of daily life through what he calls **time-space compression**. Such an argument should, as does Harvey's, stress the part played by institutions in disembedding certain images and impressions, and the role they play in relaying them across the globe, nation or locality without falling prey to the limitations inherent in a technological paradigm. As I have indicated, one could only argue that space had been abolished once media were no longer locatable within relatively stable spatial networks. Whereas the main news story on this evening's six o'clock news could be from any part of the world, it is still most likely to be concerned with the Western world or, for that matter, the nation. Further, despite the decline in the culturally cohesive power of the nation, within a European context news programmes are mostly broadcast within the borders of nation states, and more often than not they reflect its particular concerns. In terms of time-space relations, instantaneous communication is not so much our concern as the way institutional and technological matrixes intersect with the maintenance or disruption of local, national or global identities (Schlesinger, 1991).

2. One line of McLuhan's reasoning that is worth following is that the media of mass communication produce a world without strangers. By this he means that the new media, unlike a predominant print culture, have a democratising effect in that there is a less hierarchical entrance level. This serves to foster a sense of the imploded globe being the site of intimate connection. These ideas have been interestingly developed by Joshua Meyrowitz (1985). For Meyrowitz watching television is a private act that does not involve the level of public commitment that might be associated with purchasing a book, record or magazine. He argues, for instance, that although people might be reluctant to buy a magazine on

transvestism, they would have few qualms about watching a television programme on the topic. Television may not deepen our understanding of a variety of forms of life, but it at least offers a surface familiarity with others who do not share our immediate social locations. Meyrowitz views television as a form of public communication that cuts across a variety of social spheres, redefining boundaries of social interaction. Television, in effect, blurs relations of co-presence and distance, and what Goffman (1971) calls onstage and backstage regions. For a government minister stumbling over his words when confronted with questions concerning an alleged affair with his secretary there are consequences of this kind. Television makes visible the minister's embarrassment in ways he would rather have reserved for more private settings. The fact that we can view his discomfort has a demystifying effect on otherwise powerful people, reminding us that they are ordinary people like ourselves. The perceived ordinariness of politicians could also be linked to the much commented upon decline of deference amongst the citizens of Western democracies. Politicians will of course devise new strategies for coping with their more 'visible' relations with the voting public; concerted attempts will be made to hide back regions while seeking the means of reforming relations of distance.

Television, according to Meyrowitz, not only reformulates social relations between the people and politicians, but also between men and women and parents and children. Consistent with the discussion offered above, he argues that the medium of television has unified the distinct social worlds that previously existed between the sexes and across generations. Television has effectively demystified the public sphere of work and politics from which women have traditionally been excluded. Historically, a male-defined print culture has been used to ideologically mask these areas of social experience, effectively silencing and isolating women in the home. Similarly, television has given children access to a previously socially distant adult world. Children regularly watch soap operas that reflect upon many of the public and private problems adults routinely encounter as part of everyday life. These reflections are similar to those of Postman (1982), who argues that the invention of the printing press stratified adults and children into the literate and the non-literate. Part of children's rights of passage into an adult world was through a progressive familiarity with a grown-up book culture. In Postman's view, this situation has been transformed by the technical medium of television, which tends to eliminate the idea of a specific adult world. We now inhabit a publicly visible world with few topics that are not openly talked about.

The arguments of Meyrowitz and Postman share similar problems of technological determinism to those of McLuhan. They both, as does McLuhan, overstate the capacity of technology to promote social forms of unification. This is not to argue that television might not have had some of the effects that Meyrowitz outlines – but it is to suggest that television is best represented through a dialectic of unification and fragmentation. Since the late 1950s, argues Stephen Kline (1993), children have been explicitly targeted through television advertising by toy manufacturers. The commercialisation of children's culture was intensified throughout the 1980s, with television programmes themselves acting increasingly as advertisements for commercial products. Extensive psychological research, promotional campaigns and mass marketing have been employed by capitalist concerns in order to create easily identifiable characters. The colonisation of children's play, imagination and fiction by commercial agencies has been brought about through the integration of aesthetic and commodity production. Of course intensive marketing strategies often fail, or are resisted by children and parents alike. Yet the explicit targeting of segmented audiences should lead one to conclude that a more dialectical frame of analysis, one that conceptualises processes of unification and fragmentation, is necessary if one is to develop some of the more fruitful insights of Marshall McLuhan. Kline's argument is not only that television is used by children as a means of familiarising themselves with the adult world, but that they themselves have become an important market segment, utilised by capitalist strategies to expand an intensively competitive toy market.

3. Recently a number of mass communication theorists have suggested that communications networks make the social increasingly visible. J.B. Thompson and Meyrowitz, following McLuhan believe that these developments have opened up the possibility of more democratic social relations. However such reflections, in my view, contain a substantial blind spot in that they fail to address issues related to surveillance. Thompson's (1994) and Meyrowitz's (1985) considerations of the risks and opportunities accorded politicians through their public visibility interestingly develop McLuhan's arguments on implosion. But while McLuhan, Meyrowitz and Thompson pay attention to the means by which the actions of dominant groups are made visible, they neglect the way communication technologies can be used to scrutinise the actions of the less powerful. The writing of Michel Foucault could prove important here, although admittedly he had little to say on the historical development of communications systems.

Foucault (1977) calls disciplinary power the particular form of power and knowledge that characterises modern institutions. In pre-modern societies, like the *ancien regime*, it was the sovereign who made himself visible, while the subject population, those upon whom power operated, remained unseen. There occurs a distinctive reversal of this situation in what Foucault described as the modern carceral society. Here it is those subjects who are to be disciplined, observed and judged, whom the operation of power makes the most visible. Now it is power itself that seeks invisibility, while those who become its objects of control reappear through the reorganisation of institutional space. The state, in contemporary settings, relies upon a sophisticated dispersal of surveillance technology in order to watch over the individualised bodies of the public. The public makes itself present by allowing a sophisticated array of surveillance technology to record its actions, while those who monitor their bodies remain hidden from view. Activities as diverse as queuing in a bank, shopping in a mall or visiting certain sporting events routinely involve the monitoring of the crowd. These considerations should persuade us that communications technologies, in general, not only implode diverse spheres of social life, but also enable the scrutiny of the least powerful.

How do such considerations impinge on a social theory of mass communications? It could be objected that as most media products are consumed in relatively closed private spaces the activity of the audience is not usually subject to the mechanisms that Foucault describes. The point could also be made – one that Foucault does not address – that along with the widening of the normative gaze of the state came certain rights of privacy. These perspectives curtail some of the more exaggerated claims made by Foucault and his followers on the all pervasiveness of the carceral society. To this can be added the reflections of Thompson, Meyrowitz and McLuhan on the more democratic forms of life that are heralded by mass forms of communication. Norberto Bobbio (1987) has argued, in accordance with Foucault, that modern power aims to make itself invisible. The concealed nature of power violates democratic notions of representation and decentralisation. The idea of democracy, according to Bobbio, is to make more areas of social life visible and present rather than invisible and absent. Returning to Foucault, while the exercise of power may have been visible in pre-modern societies, what was invisible were the reasons as to why certain decisions were taken rather than others. The Enlightenment tradition, of which Foucault is so mistrustful, in Bobbio's analysis seeks justification and the open public operation of power that had previously remained secret. Foucault, in modern contexts, tends mistakenly to equate visibility with subjection, rather than with democratic forms of accountability. Foucault is not so much wrong concerning the utilisation of disciplinary power as misleading concerning the democratic possibilities opened up by what Thompson (1994: 41) calls *global scrutiny*. By this he means that the exercise of political power increasingly takes place upon a visible world stage. The media of mass communication make the actions of despotic states, such as the suppression of the Chinese pro-democracy movement, ever visible to the globe's citizens.

Yet, I would maintain that Foucault's account remains of great interest to students of the media. For instance, the popular press often utilises similar techniques to the disciplinary forms of power Foucault describes. Much of the content of the tabloid press has as much to do with normalising surveillance of the *private* lives of ordinary people as it has with the democratic mechanisms of publicity. Here, despite the arguments that are often made in its defence, the publicising of the identity of rape victims and the relatives of criminals, and the often racist reporting of riots has more to do with normalising forms of power than with the democratic flow of opinion. The edition of *The Sun* newspaper published on 20 October 1993 supplies two such examples. The first involves an undercover team of reporters who had *discovered* so-called wild sex parties held by university students. This report was meant to provide the backcloth to a discussion concerning date rape on university campuses. The newspaper not only misrepresents the issues of sexuality and power any complex discussion of the subject would have to encounter, but offers a lurid account of sexually deviant students. The same issue reports how a postman who had been caught by a photographer throwing a brick on an anti-racist march had been suspended by his employers. This, claims the report, had been a direct result of the newspaper publishing the photograph and inviting readers to identify the person in question. Both articles offer instances of the way that information technology can be used to create individualised cases of moral transgression for wider public disapproval. These reports, in Foucault's terms, attempt to impose regularised norms of behaviour on the populace by providing clear cases of deviant activity. Such examples, chosen at random, surely demonstrate that despite Foucault's limitations, an analysis of normalising practices should not be subsumed within an account that only admits of the mass media's role in serving to democratise public life. A more substantive theory of public media would seek to articulate communications technologies' potential to engender public, critical reflection as well as the dangers evident in disciplinary mechanisms.

4. McLuhan's account draws our attention to the relationship between information technology and the public sphere. The version of the public sphere outlined by Habermas (1989) is the product of a society dominated by print technology. Print, argues McLuhan, fosters the private space necessary for individualised reflection and opinion formation. By the same token, electronic forms of communication abolish a critical reflective realm by the implosion of social spheres and the fostering of a more interactive space. Here McLuhan's arguments have been interpreted in a somewhat conservative fashion by Postman (1985). Postman agrees with McLuhan that electronic media of communication have undermined a rational public space. The logical world of print has been displaced by a medium – television – that is ill equipped to enhance the values of a rational democracy. Television, as a visual medium, requires the use of few skills to watch it and promotes concerns with style rather than substance. Again, as Jenson (1990) points out, the technological paradigm Postman has inherited from McLuhan assumes that the meaning of television is determined by media of communication. Yet this does not mean that there is not a relationship to be established between technologies of communication and the public sphere.

Largely, I think McLuhan's arguments in respect of the public sphere are misguided. His analysis explicitly discounts the importance I assume in making a link between media of communication and a culture that promotes critical forms of discussion and debate. As McLuhan is well aware, electronic forms of communication have radically reformulated the public sphere. The increase in information provision and the general speeding up of our culture have made critical reflection more problematic. The increasing turn to what McLuhan describes as cool media can be perceived in the development of video, computer games and, ultimately, more interactive forms of television. This not only changes the balance between the providers of information and the audience, but has far-reaching individualising effects that erode notions of the public. These processes have consequences for democratic forms of public culture. It is not enough to argue, as does McLuhan, that media like television are democratic because they are relatively decentralised and allow participation. The concept of democracy is a shared contextual norm that covers a wide range of concerns. For instance, any culture that considers itself democratic would be required to provide the institutional basis for a plurality of perspectives and challenging forms of drama and debate. It is at least questionable whether these are the primary concerns of those currently marketing the new interactive future.

Zygmunt Bauman (1993) has recently offered the notion of *telecity* to explain some of these changes. Telecity, Bauman argues, is where objects and subjects appear only as forms of pleasure and amusement:

> Strangers may now be gazed at openly, without fear – much as lions in the zoo; all the chills and creeps of the roaring beast without the fangs ever coming anywhere near the skin. Strangers may be watched robbing, maiming, shooting and garrotting each other (something one would expect strangers being strangers, to do) in the endless replay of TV crime and police dramas. Or they can be gleefully gazed at in the full flight of their animal passions. Or, better still, they can be moved around, play the scenario, or be put out of action by the slightest move of the joystick. They are infinitely close as objects; but doomed to remain, happily, infinitely remote as subjects of action. In telecity, strangers are sanitised and safe. (Bauman, 1993: 178)

The television screen may allow us to go travelling without leaving home – but its integration into privatised leisure patterns means that otherness will be encountered by modern subjects only if it poses no serious sense of obligation. Although exaggerated, as it is hard to imagine a future where human beings no longer have any feelings of obligation and solidarity towards one another, the concept of telecity highlights certain cultural dynamics in the future technological developments of **virtual reality** and MeTV. In both cases, images and representations are selected that will fit into the subject's own lifestyle tastes and preferences. The space opened up by telecity is one based upon individual pleasure – one that allows the subject to wander through a variety of media texts without any strings attached. It is a disposition towards others. For instance, the idea of MeTV, currently being developed in the United States, would technologically empower the receiver to select films, documentaries and comedy shows on behalf of the viewer. On the one hand, this is a useful device for the viewer who, given the expected explosion of television networks and channels on the information highway, would find it difficult to make informed choices as regards programming preferences. But the more negative consequences might be that preselected programmes will do little to actively challenge the preconceptions of the audience: television watchers may become less tolerant of programmes they would not normally view, taking the elements of surprise and confrontation out of television culture.

Such negative projections would witness the end of public space and the enhancement of an atomised pleasure culture. However, such reflections remain futuristic, and the proliferation of television channels has potentially positive benefits. Instead of promoting telecity, we could argue, new technology will make available different kinds of programming for neglected sections of the audience. Just as newspaper and magazine production has been revolutionised by cheaper forms of technology (allowing the publication of feminist magazines, a black press and other radical publications) so the opening up of television will provide the same. While such projections are probably over-optimistic, especially given the limited circulation of alternative forms of print culture, as ever, it is difficult to predict future developments with any certainty. But unless public and communicative concerns are more forcibly underwritten my optimistic readings become difficult to maintain.

While I do not seek to defend McLuhan's remarks on the collapsing of public space, it seems plausible to suggest that the globalisation of information networks provides new possibilities and dangers for democratic cultures. Hence any attempt to rethink public space would have to retain a spatial emphasis (local, national, global). If these spheres are to be reformulated, the domains of the media of communication, content, and institutional organisation of culture would all have a part to play. Although these remarks are incomplete it should be clear that McLuhan's writing continues to offer challenging perspectives to those who are concerned to map out the contours of our culture.

Summary

McLuhan's analysis retains a contemporary relevance by introducing issues of space and time, implosion, and hybridity into media studies. His writing, emerging out of the context of Canadian social theory, has often been dismissed under charges of technological determinism and political conservatism. These arguments carry a good deal of analytic bite, but have been overstated by the supporting literature. McLuhan's contribution, along with those of Goody and Giddens, remains suggestive as to how media of communication have played a central part in the development of modernity. Both Goody and Giddens, as opposed to McLuhan, demonstrate the connection between certain technical capacities of cultural media and the reflexive forms of engagement characteristic of modernity. McLuhan's insistence that we have returned to a condition characteristic of oral societies was considered too partial and misleading. In the final section we saw that McLuhan's writing contained more substantial flaws than had appeared in the previous discussions. While his consideration of notions of space and time remains valuable it needs to be supplemented by a less essentialistic and more institutionally grounded approach. In addition, McLuhan's writing on the unificatory and democratising impact of electronic forms of communication needs to take account of corresponding cultural fragmentation and surveillance. Despite the limitations of McLuhan's approach, supporters of future more democratic cultures will need to reconsider the implications of the changing technological landscape for the future of the public sphere. We now need to look more closely at whether such notions have become extinct through the development of postmodernity.

Baudrillard's Blizzards

Postmodernity, Mass Communications and Symbolic Exchange

Postmodernism as a Heterogeneous Field

The concerns that are usually addressed under the banner of postmodernism are plural and can not be conceptualised in a unified discourse. Indeed, one would expect a philosophical creed that warned against the authoritarian impulse that lies behind the desire to unify and classify to be suspicious of attempts to name the intellectual field. And yet, although internally varied, postmodernism has achieved a certain cohesiveness in relation to a number of critical questions. A terrain of struggle has been mapped out over a number of crucial subjects. These include (1) the contestation of philosophical concerns such as objectivity and the referential function of language; (2) the fragmentation of modern subjectivity; (3) the preservation of difference against homogenising impulses; (4) the rejection of totalising perspectives (evident within much classical social theory such as Marxism) that seek to prescribe a universal human nature, or a means of grasping the social through one theoretical model; (5) the denial of teleological notions of social change; and (6) the scepticism of all utopian political stances that promise an end to social forms of antagonism. All of these themes will be touched upon here. Not surprisingly however, given the broad range of engagement, this ideal type is only inexactly realised by the theorists discussed. This warns against intellectually lazy attempts – of which there is much evidence – that either reject postmodern questions outright or fail to engage with the specific positions that are occupied by the main antagonists.

Jean Baudrillard has provided the most sophisticated postmodern critique of mass communication currently available. He has addressed the ways in which the experience of modernity has been radically altered by the growth of communications technologies, transitory fashions, theme parks, graffiti, and post-industrial lifestyles. For Baudrillard, the arrival of consumer cultures radically questions the distinctions usually drawn between high and low art, the profound and the superficial, culture and commodity, the signifier and the signified and – a point that will be of much concern in the later discussion – the idea of human needs and the current offerings of late capitalism. Related to these themes, Baudrillard's contribution in the context of theoretical perspectives in mass communication research has sought to develop the writing of Marshall McLuhan. Despite evident differences, Baudrillard radicalises concepts of implosion and instantaneous communication while squarely focusing his attention on the medium of communication. Baudrillard stresses the importance of the medium rather than the message. He and McLuhan part company over the latter's optimistic reading of the new global forms of interconnection that electronic communication makes possible. Baudrillard's much more pessimistic reading of the situation credits the postmodern rush of information with eliminating the subject and thereby creating indifference rather than participation. The dominant culture of postmodernity, within Baudrillard's analysis, has no critical immanence and requires only the most cynical forms of engagement.

The following account will respectfully restore Baudrillard to his intellectual context, and then, moving on, I will reverse many of his key assumptions. But, first, a word or two about some of the stylistic difficulties Baudrillard's writing poses the critic is worthy of mention. Baudrillard's often ironic and playful disposition, especially evident in his later writing, makes his work difficult to summarise. This, coupled with an avant-gardist politics means that Baudrillard's discourse seeks to evade incorporation in texts such as the present one. But however little sympathy I might feel for Baudrillard's politics, my argumentative strategy suggests that for the critic to respond to his theoretical assaults the discursive contexts of Baudrillard's own medium have to be hermeneutically uncovered. It remains to be seen that my own method of interpretation is for Baudrillard part of the problem, not the solution.

Baudrillard, Althusser and Debord

Three major works that have appeared on Baudrillard have stressed his affinity with a range of writers including Bataille, Marx, Mauss and Nietzsche (Gane, 1991a, 1991b; Kellner, 1989). These authors will inform the backdrop of my own discussion, but I want to place the initial emphasis elsewhere. While teaching in Nanterre in France during the late 1960s, Baudrillard contributed to a journal called *Utopie* which offered a mixture of situationism and post-structuralist Marxism. The two most important figures in these areas of theoretical practice remain Debord and Althusser. An understanding of both these authors is necessary to an appreciation of the early and late Baudrillard.

Baudrillard's initial formulations can be read as a debate with humanist and structural Marxism. In the French intellectual scene during the late 1960s the efforts of Althusser dominated these debates. The characteristic features of Althusser's Marxism are his rejection of socialist humanism and his pathbreaking writing on the concept of ideology. For Althusser, socialist humanism, which stemmed from the writing of the early Marx, was both essentialist and teleological. This philosophical creed represented the working class as the privileged subject of history. It was the historically given task of this subject, through revolutionary action, to realise the essential nature of human kind. Socialist humanism was essentialist to the extent that it held a fixed definition of human nature and epistemologically privileged the working class. The historicist twist in this Hegelian schema gave history an end point in the overcoming of alienation and the self-realisation of the working class. In contrast, Althusser argues, human beings are not constitutive agents who preside over an ultimately manipulable reality. They are in fact socially constituted subjects who are allotted places in the already existing social structure. Humanism's fundamental theoretical error lay in the belief that human beings have a nature that is not determined by existing social practices (Althusser, 1977).

Althusser's reflections on ideology sought to explain how Western capitalist societies reproduce dominant institutional relationships. The requirements of the economic system for labour power are satisfied outside the dominant mode of production, mainly in ideological state apparatuses such as the education system, family and the media. Labour power is reproduced under conditions of ideological subjugation. Ideology, if Althusser's propositions are followed, converts human beings into subjects. Ideology lets us mistakenly recognise ourselves as autonomous self-determining agents, whereas in fact we are subjects formed through social and psychic processes. Ideology, therefore, is not the mirrored inversion of the real, but our imaginary or symbolic relationship to our shared conditions of existence. Althusser's strength lies in his insistence that ideology is prereflexively bound up with the functioning of the dominant social order. Watching the latest Levi jeans advertisement I am addressed as an individual consumer with my own *unique* passions and desires. The ideological effect of the ad lies less in its specific cultural content and more in its ability to interpellate me in this way. Ideology is not so much bound up with misrepresenting the real as it is in the processes of mis-recognition encountered by the subject. It is not false consciousness. Rather it is a material practice produced by ideological state apparatuses. Thus the Levi ad hails me as a hedonistic consumer rather than a collective member of an exploited social class. It lets me think I am a sovereign consumer rather than the effect of ideological processes (Althusser, 1984).

Notoriously, despite his comments on false consciousness, Althusser develops this thesis by making a rigorous distinction between science and ideology. He dissects society into four main practices: economic, political, ideological and theoretical. Theoretical practice, as a scientific practice, has three distinguishable levels – raw material, means of production and the end product. Just as the worker uses her labour power to transform nature into a commodity, so the theoretician applies Marxist science to a mixture of concepts and facts to produce knowledge. Marxism's scientific status is dependent upon the writing of the mature Marx, who reputedly rid his work of humanist categories such as need, alienation and species-being. These claims are currently very unpopular, even amongst sympathetic critics. For example, Perry Anderson (1980) has argued that Althusser's structural functionalism means that he is unable to account for notions of class struggle. As E.P. Thompson (1978) pointed out at the time, Althusser's formulations reduce human agency to the level of pre-programmed social structures. Agents may not act in conditions they fully understand or, following Marx, in conditions of their choosing, but one must accept, particularly from a Marxist perspective, that human beings are capable of acting reflexively and creatively in order to alter their social conditions. Other commentators, such as Benton (1984) and Elliott (1987), have pointed out that Althusser's notion of theoretical practice is both authoritarian and circular. We only know Marxism is a science because Althusser tells us so, and the working class are effectively reduced to cultural dupes of the system. These problems aside, Althusser's critique of humanism and ideology helped shape the intellectual climate of Baudrillard's engagement with Marxism and cultural theory. Baudrillard's emphasis upon the decentred subject, ideology and the ideological bankruptcy of humanism all seem to have their roots here.

Debord's (1987) analysis of capitalist society differs markedly from the professional theoretical production of Althusser. Debord was a member of the Situationist International (founded in 1957) that sought to merge avant-gardist artistic agitation with Marxism. Here the concern was not to produce scientific theoretical practice, but to extend Marx's analysis of economic production to encompass cultural and media production. The emphasis is placed upon the writing of the early humanist Marx. The private ownership of the means of production was the root cause of the worker's alienation from herself, from her fellow human beings and the product of her labour. As it became separated from labour, the commodity took on an objectified existence, thereby alienating the worker from her true self. Debord claims that the intensification of these processes has not only alienated the worker in the public but in the private as well. The commodification of media and culture produces images and representations that are similarly thing-like in appearance. The pictures that we watch on the television news each evening have taken on an autonomous appearance that seems to bear little connection to everyday living. This is how, Debord would argue, we are able to watch the forms of mass bombing exhibited during the Gulf War with seemingly so little political effect. The problem is that the spectacle gives human misery and suffering the appearance of unreality. The spectacle is ideological because the masses are separated from the means of image production and forced into a form of stupefied passivity. They live in enforced distraction, which conceals the power relations that determine existing social relations. Due to the pervasiveness of the spectacle, the situationists sought to develop artistic forms of rebellion that resisted incorporation into the dominant system of image production. This included a number of shock techniques that were intended to awaken the revolutionary spirit of the people. They demanded that art be taken out of the galleries and develop a more reciprocal relationship with everyday life through street art, poster campaigns, wall poetry and the imaginative use of graffiti (Plant, 1992).

Debord's (1990) later writing has usefully extended the analysis with respect to space and time. Debord writes:

> Spectacular domination's first priority was to eradicate historical knowledge in general; beginning with just about all rational information and commentary on the recent past. The evidence for this is so glaring it hardly needs further explanation. With consummate skill the spectacle organises ignorance of what is about to happen and, immediately afterwards the forgetting of whatever has nonetheless been understood. The more important something is, the more it is hidden. (Debord 1990:13–14)

The abolition of historical knowledge has been achieved by a global alliance between capital, nation states and media professionals. The world of sound bites, instantaneous news, fluctuating fashions and three-minute pop videos has eradicated our sense of history. The restless and shifting nature of media discourse can only occupy matters of serious importance for a couple of seconds at a time before moving on. The old bourgeois public sphere based upon print culture and face-to-face interaction has been replaced by an instantaneous one-way discourse that leaves no room for reply. Such is the relentless speed of modern communication systems that the subject is no longer capable of constructing a stable version of the past. History and social context has disappeared within the white noise of media babble. Debord forcefully argues that the reification and fragmentation of the social in addition to the disappearance of critical debate and historical knowledge serves the class interests of multinational capital.

Debord's polemical writing exhibits many of the features of Baudrillard. For the present, I want to draw attention to two similarities. The first is their mutual emphasis on the medium of communication. For Debord and Baudrillard the kaleidoscopic chaos evident within the myriad of media channels and discourses provides the landscape for media analysis. Baudrillard, however, dispenses with concepts such as alienation and reification, given their connection to more humanist forms of Marxism. Instead, what he takes from Debord is the recognition that the form rather than the substance of media messages is a central feature of modernity. Baudrillard and Debord are both taken with the explosion of voices that demand to be heard but that do not require a response. Secondly, Debord and Baudrillard mutually advocate an avant-gardist political strategy. This shuns orthodox political attempts at patient alliance building for more polemical and explosive strategies. Baudrillard's later writing does not so much communicatively engage with the reader as shock and deride what he sees as naively held humanist beliefs.

Postmodernism, Symbolic Exchange and Marxism

In this section I want to concentrate on what I take to be the main themes of Baudrillard's theoretical writing. Following Kellner (1989), I think it is useful to organise Baudrillard's writing into two distinct, but related, phases. The first involves Baudrillard's provocative critique of Marxism and his arguments concerning the development of consumer society. Here Althusser's influence is at its strongest, although Baudrillard interestingly reworks some of his central assumptions. After the production of *Symbolic Exchange and Death* (1993a; first published in 1976) Baudrillard progressively came to abandon critical Marxist analysis. It is from this point on that the themes of implosion, simulation, mass media, fatal strategies and symbolic exchange come to displace more conventional theoretical categories. Baudrillard, through a more explicitly post-industrial analysis, argues that real relations of production and consumption have been replaced by a sign system.

The roots of Baudrillard's turn towards the analysis of signs can be found in his first two publications, *The System of Objects* and *Consumer Society*.[1] According to Baudrillard, the arrival of consumer society requires a radical reconstruction of critical theory. Consumer society has effectively displaced moral categories such as those based upon deference and thrift and replaced them with the hedonistic search for satisfaction. But if the market has a certain democratising effect, it also serves to erect new barriers of social exclusion through what Baudrillard calls the 'object/sign system' (Baudrillard, 1988a: 23). Baudrillard argues that before goods (objects) can be consumed they must become signs. The meaning of objects is established through the organisation of signs into codes. It is only through these codes that human beings come to realise their sense of self and their needs. The codes themselves are hierarchically ordered, being used to signify distinctions of status and prestige. As Baudrillard argues: 'a need is not a need for a particular object as much as it is a "need" for difference (the desire for social meaning), only then will we understand that satisfaction can never be fulfilled, and consequently that there can never be a definition of needs' (Baudrillard 1988a: 45).

The object is not consumed by a subject whose needs are fixed by a universal human nature or biology. Consumption – if this argument is followed – is also not the result of the disembedded subject's pre-constituted desire for the object. Social goods are consumed not to satisfy pre-existing needs but to signify social distinctions. This argument by necessity renders obsolete critical formulations of real and false needs, and primary and secondary needs. Such binary categories, in Marxist theory, produce both a form of subject-object dualism and a notion of the subject who is cultural on one side and biological on the other (Baudrillard, 1981a: 68). These philosophical dualisms and discredited humanisms are replaced with an analysis that views human needs as the effect of the social system. Baudrillard, therefore, follows Althusser in arguing that the subject is constituted through social classifications and ideological processes. But, in distinction to Althusser, for Baudrillard the main ideological apparatus is consumer capitalism. This acts as a form of social control. First, classificatory distinctions that are associated with objects have an atomising impact on the consumer. Returning to our earlier example of the individual being converted into a subject by television advertising, Baudrillard would argue that the coded discourse that becomes attached to the product has no relation to reality. Mark Poster (1994:178) argues that, for Baudrillard, 'language became intelligible only from the standpoint of its structure; language then constituted the subject, not the reverse'. Elsewhere, Poster (1990) claims that in Baudrillard's terms television advertisements help to shape a new language and as a consequence new subject positions. If the advertisement were to portray a young man wearing a pair of Levi jeans the aim of the ad could be to associate the product with youth, sexiness, masculinity and fashion consciousness. For Baudrillard, there is little point in arguing that the symbolic associations of the jeans are an expression of inauthentic or false needs. Instead, critical analysis should investigate the cultural connotations that are drawn upon within the advertisement. The ideological effect of the advertisement lies in the way cultural distinctions are articulated and in the way consumers are addressed as autonomous subjects. The other way consumer society maintains relations of dominance is through the privatisation of the consuming public. Baudrillard argues that individualised consumers of commercial culture are separated from one another by privatised leisure practices. Baudrillard, on this point, muses that the isolated nature of television viewing makes it difficult to imagine collective forms of resistance against television advertising. The system is caught in a fundamental contradiction of having to produce individualised consuming subjects and yet fostering forms of bureaucratic control to ensure that citizens meet their fiscal obligations. Although Baudrillard does not develop this, his critique remains dialectical enough, at this point, to appreciate that consumer society is fraught with systemic contradiction and conflict.

Let us now turn to Baudrillard's most concerted attempt to formulate a critique of the historic legacy of Marxism. *The Mirror of Production* (1975) argues that Marxism reproduces a social imaginary which reflects that of capitalism. The emphasis that is placed upon political economy fails to theorise notions of signification, is ethnocentric in its understanding of other societies, and reduces social practices to productive practices. Baudrillard's starting point is that the linguistic turn of contemporary philosophy has abolished the distinction between signifier and signified, or the real and the symbolic. There is no longer an extra-discursive reality that we can assume that language concretely represents. Linguistic practices do not so much reflect the real as actively constitute it. So far, so good. The problem lies in Marxism's implicit assumption that it can adequately textualise the domain of political economy. This assumption is now questionable, given that language does not refer back to any objective reality. What Marxism actually produces is a version of human potential and historical society that is over-determined by the code of political economy. Baudrillard argues that the symbolic code offered by Marxism establishes men's and women's primary identity as that of producer. In this social construction people would only make love with the aim of producing children rather than giving one another pleasure or establishing intimacy. Thus, while Marx does offer a theory of economic production, he is unable to account for social practices that do not mirror the logic of production. Language itself is not produced by some and consumed by others, but is exchanged through reciprocal social practices. Marxism's totalising logic is particularly marked in its consideration of historical societies other than capitalism. The symbolic code generated by historical materialism presupposes that the semi-autonomous sphere of economic production has a similar degree of separation in other societies. The ethnocentric bias of so-called critical theory masks the ways in which the economy is often deeply embedded in the cultural life-world. This idea, popular on the French Left during the 1960s (Castoriadis, 1987), argues that Marxism's scientism blinds it to its own cultural prejudices, which it then reads back into other societies.

What Baudrillard calls the revolution of the sign is granted equal importance to the revolution of political economy. Both Marxism and defenders of capitalism tend to subordinate a range of activities to economic ones and produce normalising codes of appropriate activity. As a consequence, Marxism has been unable to connect with emergent social struggles that are primarily symbolic in character. The most pressing political issue of the late twentieth century is not the economic exploitation of the proletariat but the imposition of an exclusive dominant code. Feminism and black politics are less concerned with socialising the means of production than with disrupting the ideological dominance of white, heterosexual men. Marxism's tendency to reduce these issues to the operation of a material base symbolically reinforces an ethnocentric and masculinist code. Further, the cultural dominance of Marxism within workers' movements elevates to a position of value the very sign of their own slavery. That is, the capitalist equation of the worker as reducible to her labour power is reflected by the primacy given work by Marxism. Work, for the Marxists, is not simply the site of oppression but the essential activity that will come to define a more liberated human being in the future.

Baudrillard's critique of Marxist productivism has many parallels in the New Left. Writers as diverse as Williams, Gorz and Habermas have criticised certain versions of Marxist theory for reproducing the dominance of economic reason. These writers have argued for a revitalised critical theory that would seek to *socialise* some of the more destructive aspects of the colonising power of the economy. Marxism's stress upon economic productivity, they argue, institutes a particularly impoverished version of the plural capabilities of human beings and fails to specify the cultural limits of economic forms of reason. Conversely, what makes Baudrillard's contribution distinctive is not his critique of economic rationality, but his emphasis on the code. Baudrillard's argument is not so much an attempt to rethink the relations between economic, political and cultural practices – which is the case with the aforementioned – but an attempt to suggest that the analysis of cultural codes has become the central project for critical theory. This poses Baudrillard's critique of Marxism with a problem. In his argument that critical theory should abandon Marxism's tendency to reduce the social to the sign of political economy he is assuming what he claims to be denying. If Baudrillard could not make a theoretical separation between the domain of theory and that of practice, he would not be able to argue that Marxism inadequately represents certain social struggles, linguistic exchange or history. That is, Baudrillard is still assuming that language can map the real. Unfortunately he resolves this dilemma by strengthening his claim that the real and sign have now imploded into the symbolic. Just as the unconscious would not exist without Freudianism, so Marxism symbolically produces the proletariat. Language, Baudrillard confidently concludes, has no referent and produces the real.

These ideas are developed in *Symbolic Exchange and Death* (1993a). Whereas the mode of production had been a point of reference for critical thought, Baudrillard resolutely claims that this is a thing of the past. Previously his thought had hinted at the possibility of rethinking the connections between a political economy of culture and the structural relations of consumption. This mode of analysis has been foreclosed by Baudrillard's assertion that the sign has now become emancipated from any system of reference. Rather than examining the relations between production and consumption, the economic and the cultural, and the material and the symbolic, Baudrillard proposes we focus on the functioning of the code. In this respect, labour is no longer a form of power but a sign amongst other signs. As Baudrillard comments: 'labour power is initially a status, a structure of obedience to a code' (1993a: 12). Capitalism has passed from the phase where labour was exploited to one where it is designed, marketed and consumed. The era of production ended in 1929 with the Wall Street crash, and from this period on production and consumption became caught up in a fluid spiral that targets neither profits nor needs. Capitalism then is less about material social relations than about the imperatives of certain identity formations that are necessary for the functioning of the system. As the signifier and the signified have become detached so have commodity production and profit and wage levels. Money has become a speculative phenomenon that can be gambled on exchange markets or roulette tables without signifying anything outside itself.

Here Baudrillard is certainly articulating some of the features of contemporary capitalism. Money, through the internationalisation of money markets, is becoming a free-floating signifier. By this I mean that the deregulation of money markets has progressively weakened capital's commitment to a sense of place. The more money becomes detached from the real processes to which it used to refer, the more it becomes generated through options, swaps and futures (Lash and Urry, 1994: 292). For Baudrillard, the more money becomes detached from the principles of political economy the cooler a phenomenon it becomes. Money is no longer about the circulation of commodities but is essentially about itself. Further, within this process, consumers have become part of 'the automatic writing of the system' (Baudrillard, 1998: 58). The consumer is continually mobilised into the consumption of an increasing quantity of goods. Indeed without the symbolic stimulation of the appetites of the consumer the system would collapse. In this respect, consumption is less about choice and more about duty.

The problem with Baudrillard, however, is that he makes capitalism too symbolic and not material enough. Of course the production of commodities now involves significatory considerations that were absent from mass-produced and more streamlined forms of production. And yet Baudrillard pushes this insight too far. Post-industrial economies produce objects that are materially as well as symbolically consumed. The most important feature of my toaster is not its design but its ability to brown bread. While it is true that late capitalism has witnessed the explosion of a number of differently designed toasters, all with different target audiences, this factor does not override their functional use. Most consumers, I would have thought, would rather their toasters worked reliably. This argument can be traced back to Baudrillard's earlier remarks on human needs. If needs are interpolated by lifestyle distinctions, then Baudrillard is correct that the code is all-important. But, as we shall see later, human beings arguably have material and symbolic needs that are not wholly determined by the system of cultural distinctions under which they are living.

For Baudrillard, the issue confronting labour movements in post-industrial economies is not the replacement of capital, but its more efficient functioning. Workers struggled against capitalism in order to gain the status of 'normal' human beings, and once this was attained they sided with the bourgeoisie against deviants and outsiders. In Baudrillard's terms, the most important function of Marxism's and capitalism's concern with political economy is that it operates a symbolic dominance over life and death. What Baudrillard means by this is that the status of being a productive worker is significatory of citizenship in post-industrial society, the fundamental law of society being the code of normality that seeks to occupy 'all the interstices of life' (Baudrillard, 1993a: 34).

Domination, in such a system, comes from being excluded from the code and processes of gift exchange. The working class occupies an ambivalent position in Baudrillard's theory as it helps define normalising conceptions of citizenship while being dominated by the forms of symbolic exchange instituted by capitalism. Baudrillard follows Mauss (1990) in arguing that the gift is a form of reciprocity in which the honour of giver and recipient is involved. Mauss studies a number of archaic societies (Polynesia, Melanesia and the American North-west) where the exchange of social goods is bound by forms of collective obligation. While culturally diverse, all of these societies exhibited features of reciprocal exchange or potlatch. The notion of potlatch has three interconnected forms of social obligation: to give, to accept and to reciprocate. This chain of mutual recognition symbolically binds small-scale hierarchies by creating relations of obligation. Mauss points out that the head of the tribe reaffirms his position by the act of giving more than can be returned. Other members of the tribe have an obligation both to accept and to return the gift. If someone fails to do so this usually means that this particular member of the community loses status and his or her rank as a free person. Reciprocal gift exchange is the practice which maintains relations of social solidarity. Mauss argues that processes of symbolic exchange could provide modern capitalist societies with organic forms of solidarity that mediate the cold abstraction of commodity exchange.[2] Baudrillard is both pessimistic and nostalgic in building upon Mauss's anthropological insights. Capitalism maintains its dominance over the worker not by exploiting her but by offering the gift of work that cannot be returned. Baudrillard argues, in an important passage, that

> If domination comes from the system's retention of the exclusivity of the gift without counter-gift – the gift of work which can only be responded to by destruction or sacrifice, if not consumption, which is only a spiral of the system of surplus-gratification; a gift of media and messages to which, due to the monopoly of the code, nothing is allowed to retort; the gift, everywhere and at every instant, of the social, of the protection agency, security, gratification and the solicitation of the social form which nothing is any longer permitted to escape – then the only solution is to turn the principle of its power back against

the system itself: the impossibility of responding or retorting. *To deft the system with a gift to which it cannot respond save by its own collapse and death.* (Baudrillard, 1993a: 36–7, original emphasis)

I have quoted at length as this excerpt further demonstrates Baudrillard's estrangement from Marxism and highlights some of the future directions of his social theory. The relationship between worker and capitalist is no longer one of exploitation but of unequal gift exchange. The difficulty for Marxist theory is that wage levels no longer correspond to production processes, so labour is no longer the source of all value. That the worker, on the other hand, is unable to return the gift means she is placed in a subordinate position. We can see what Baudrillard and Mauss mean if we consider the example of charity. Charity is arguably a form of unilateral gift, on which the recipient has no claim and for which the donor had no obligation. In terms of the distribution of value, charity tends to stigmatise the receiver and elevate the giver. Thus the gift of work, television images, radio signals or loaves of bread is a one-way relation of power. Other than unequal gift exchange, the code of capital is dependent upon the deferral of the death of its workers. In this way, the dominance of the code compels citizens to both work and consume; this can only be short-circuited by premature death or violent suicide. That is the logic of the system cannot be undermined by different or alternative coded readings of consumption. In an overdeveloped society neo-liberalism is resisted simply by consuming less (Baudrillard, 1998). As capitalism cannot be materially overthrown, it is only through the symbolic denial of the performance principle that the dominant code can be disrupted (Baudrillard, 1993a: 123).[3]

Here, through his advocacy of ritual death or consuming less, Baudrillard proposes a strategy, like that of the situationists, that cannot be reincorporated back into the system.[4] We are now in a position to understand why Baudrillard suggested that the masses crowd into the Beaubourg centre in Paris until it collapses beneath their weight. Baudrillard asserts that genuine culture is 'secrecy, seduction, initiation and symbol exchange' (1982: 3–13). The official culture of the Beauborg disallows these. It represents the gift of official culture (which has always held ordinary people in contempt) to the masses. As the masses are not in a position to return this gift, the only revolutionary slogan appropriate is MAKE BEAUBOURG BUCKLE. Elsewhere, Baudrillard (1993a) celebrates forms of graffiti that appeared around New York that had no meaning. He seems to be attracted to this form of inscription as it allows a response that is outside officially sanctioned modes of expression. Figural signs on walls that defy meaning both resist the incorporation of the bourgeois art world and allow for symbolic exchange. Similarly, his own writing does not actually advocate that the masses take over Beaubourg. His aim is to suggest a more subtle cultural logic. For example, the principle of utility is also undermined by fashion whose short life cycle encourages an atmosphere of 'play and futility' (Baudrillard, 1993a: 95). The cycles of new commodities, like Baudrillard's own prose, remind one that nothing lasts, yet everything has a chance of being revived. The constant abolition of new forms of music, books, clothing, newspapers expresses a repressed desire for death. This desire, which Baudrillard attempts to rework, is neutralised in that it is continuously postponed through endless renewal that disallows exchange.

In addition to Mauss and Debord, Baudrillard's reception of Bataille informs his stance (Baudrillard, 1987a). What Baudrillard takes from Bataille is the need to resist the principle of utility that has been ushered in by the capitalist class. In opposition to this principle, which is shared by Marxism's concern to preserve use value, Bataille proposes an aristocratic critique in the form of the notion of sacrifice. Thus Bataille and Baudrillard argue for the subversion of capital through the anti-utilitarian logic of waste, sacrifice and destruction. All previous Marxist revolutions have simply contributed to the expansion of instrumental forms of reason. Baudrillard, by linking Bataille and Mauss, proposes a form of exchange that breaks with the dominance of the logic of capital and proposes an alternative moral economy. This is a predominantly nostalgic and avant-gardist strategy, and Baudrillard is not proposing that capitalism be reformulated in these terms. His is the politics of the permanent margin. In the admittedly unlikely event of his reflections being taken up by a social movement, thereby risking incorporation into the dominant code, he would most likely pack his theoretical bags and move on.

Such a strategy is partly necessitated by Baudrillard's view that the logic of political economy produces conformism at the level of everyday life. Again, this can be negatively contrasted with the contributions of say Habermas and Williams. While these writers were concerned with the forms of rationality evident within capitalism, they perceived that the social system contained a more emancipatory logic. Whether this was embodied in speech acts, the need for autonomy or collective social movements, the social system was represented dialectically. The prospect of immanent forms of critique are foreclosed by Baudrillard's exaggerated assertions with respect to the code. That contemporary societies remain riven with competing rationalities remains under-appreciated by Baudrillard. In this context, it is difficult to see how Baudrillard would account for socialist, anti-militarist, feminist or green movements that offer alternatives to reifying modes of thought. These concerns have traditionally sought to undermine purely calculative forms of reason by building communicative relations of solidarity with others. They have also addressed some of the key existential and social problems that currently face humanity. With this in mind, I shall later argue, that Baudrillard's discursive polemics have more in common with some aspects of the New Right than with attempts to build reciprocal relations against domination.

Baudrillard's more recent writing has developed a different symbolic strategy around what he calls fatal theory (Baudrillard, 1990a). There are, Baudrillard proclaims, two kinds of social theory. There is banal theory, where theorists claim to be able to master and give a stable representation of the social. The other form of theory available to practitioners, Baudrillard modestly argues, is his own particular brand of fatal theory. Fatal theory is not so much a method as a disposition. Baudrillard explains: 'the object is considered more cunning, cynical, talented than the subject, for which it lies in wait. The metamorphosis, the ruses, the strategies of the object surpass the subject's understanding' (Baudrillard, 1990a: 181). Going over to the side of the object and the disappearance of the reflective subject is apparent in his work on American culture (Baudrillard, 1988b). One of the reasons that Marxist critics like Kellner (1989) have reacted so violently against Baudrillard is that he seems to erase any trace of suffering, exploitation, racial segregation and sexism from an appreciation of the American scene. Gane (1991a), painting a more sympathetic portrait of Baudrillard, argues that this is not an exercise in depth hermeneutics but an attempt to say something about the culture he is writing about. Both Smart (1993) and Turner (1993a) agree with Gane, but point out that Baudrillard neglects the dark side of American culture and ignores its global dominance. Turner (1993a), pursuing Gane's earlier remarks, claims that the experience of the reader encountering Baudrillard's text is similar to that of the tourist. Instead of condemning Baudrillard for a lack of seriousness, Turner suggests that we read him as embodying a culture of cruising and channel hopping. The reader is able to glide through Baudrillard's text as a tourist would through a theme park or a shopping mall. That is, Baudrillard neglects the other side of America because he wants to shock the reader into appreciating that critical forms of distance have disappeared.

For Baudrillard (1983), subjects no longer project their desires on to objects; instead the distance that lies between the two has imploded. Ultimately subjects now occupy a world where the cultural flows of information have swallowed up private space. Our most intimate moments are ritually made public through media technologies. There are no longer any taboo subjects: everything is revealed and everything is discussed, no matter how trivial. The implosion of everyday life into the media is described by Baudrillard as a form of pornography. Modern culture can be accurately described as an *obscene* culture where the world has become immediate and transparent in that it is devoid of any secrets. The close up universe of the television screen has eliminated the prospect of critical reflection, as subjects become reduced to terminals of a bland, fast-moving culture. Cultural overproduction means that the amount of information produced exceeds the interpretative capacity of the subject. The object has made the subject extinct. If we imagine a man sitting in a bar surrounded by a bank of television sets, advertising posters, the global press and the constant chatter of the radio we can capture something of Baudrillard's remarks. The man sips his beer while taking note of the *permanent electrocution* of media technologies, without any one medium attracting his full attention. The cool cynicism of our beer drinker has seen it all before. Beneath the cacophony of global information flows he remains 'deep frozen' (Baudrillard, 1993b: 32).

Finally, Baudrillard's (1993b) most recent addition to his cultural theory has sought to develop a principle of evil. The code, as we have already seen, is bent upon eliminating notions of radical Otherness. Such Otherness can now only be expressed in communicative forms that refuse to be reasonable or to idealise the goodness of human beings and uphold values of rationality and democracy. The principle of evil is meant to articulate a form of symbolism that does not fall into the soft culture of permissive society. By way of an example, Baudrillard (1993b: 83) defends his right to call a cripple a cripple. Again this deliberately offensive strategy becomes caught in Baudrillard's own contradictions. Such a formulation is premised on the notion that critique is possible after all for the super-theorists amongst us. His own writing, like much of modern advertising, is geared to attract an audience by distinguishing itself from the serious tones of most cultural output. Like the latest beer commercials, the more outrageous they are, the more attention they attract in a field of overproduction.

The French McLuhan:
Simulations, Hyperreality and the Masses

Baudrillard's most important contributions that specifically address the media are easier to summarise. While a concern for media and communications permeates his writing, he rarely focuses his attention exclusively on the operation of different media. The earliest translated essay I have been able to trace is a product of his concern with the explosion of signs within consumer society (Baudrillard, 1990b).[5] Baudrillard mainly concentrates his analysis on television, which is important in two senses. First, as a product of consumer society, television as an object is a 'codified element of social status' (Baudrillard, 1990b: 73). The cultural content of television was of secondary importance to the object's function of establishing cultural differences between different class fractions. Elsewhere, Gane (1991a) reports that Baudrillard argues that television's physical location in domestic settings articulates certain status differences. In lower-class houses, the sitting room or living room is organised around the television set, which is usually made a central feature. By contrast, the bourgeoisie have a tendency to hide or disguise their television sets; this is probably due to it being taken as a sign of vulgarity and mass culture. Secondly, taking his lead from McLuhan, Baudrillard considers the medium of communication a central feature of media culture. Given television's location within the domestic sphere, a form of superficial play arises that Baudrillard calls 'ludic curiosity' (1990b: 79). Television offers a form of depthless involvement that translates the world into easily consumable chunks of social 'reality'. The medium's primary ideological effect, as we saw in my discussion of advertising, is that it offers the illusion of an unmediated appropriation of the social world. The medium's capacity to disconnect signs from social contexts gives the viewer the impression that she is able to view the world from her sitting room. Thus the viewer, remembering Baudrillard's Althusserian heritage, misrecognises the social world as a transparent phenomenon. Television is not about the subject's communication with a real world of objects, but concerns the articulation of subjects and objects through chains of signification.

As Baudrillard's writing on the media develops, he becomes increasingly less concerned with their symbolic function and more with the technical media themselves. This is because access to the mass media is no longer a positional good, but has imploded into a mass culture. Baudrillard (1981b), at this stage, seeks to develop a theory of the media through a discussion of Enzensberger and McLuhan. He claims that Marxism, due to the dominance of the code of production, has never adequately accounted for the medium of communication. Enzensberger, while producing a more sophisticated theory than most, similarly fails to view the mass media as a deformed version of symbolic exchange. The central problem of the mass media does not lie within the power relations that govern the production of messages, but with the medium's 'unilateral nature' (Baudrillard, 1981b: 170). Baudrillard's emphasis upon symbolic exchange means that Enzensberger's democratic impulse to place the technical means of production in the hands of ordinary people ends up being a form of totalitarianism. Like the official culture of the Beaubourg, modern media technologies require no reply on the part of the audience. To those who would insist that audiences often participate in the production (radio phone-ins or studio debates) and in the consumption (interpretative responses to television discourse) of media, Baudrillard argues these are marginal phenomena. The media cannot be democratised because the technical capacity of the system of communication remains univocal. Baudrillard negatively contrasts print and electric forms of communication with more reciprocal forms of exchange such as graffiti. As a cultural form graffiti is transgressive in that it breaks the fundamental rule of the media by allowing for social response on the part of the public.

The foregoing discussion implies that Baudrillard's fatal theory is constantly undergoing revision and reformation. Fatal theory, Baudrillard (1993c) says, does not have any doctrines to defend, only strategies. One such strategy with regard to Baudrillard's offerings on technical media has been to push an argument to the extreme. Given these considerations, Baudrillard wants to further reverse some of the more optimistic pronouncements of McLuhan and Enzensberger on the media. The argument that the media actually forbids response implies an anti-media struggle on his part (Baudrillard, 1985). In keeping with his previous pronouncements, he argues that media theorists can no longer proceed with the assumption that certain aspects of human nature are denied expression through the media. Indeed, McLuhan's own claim that new media technologies allow for greater forms of participation and unification is dismissed. The proliferation of information and the silencing of the masses has lead to the disappearance of meaning altogether. Cultural forms, in Baudrillard's provocative analysis, that used to signify social distinctions, have evaporated amongst the scrambling of communication. The science of semiology has been replaced by that of the 'liquefaction' of the social (Baudrillard, 1993c: 84).

If we take the example of opinion polls, they actually produce opinion in an era when the public has disappeared. This is not a form of manipulation, but characteristic of the implosion of public polls and private opinion. The private space of opinion formation since the decline of print culture has become engulfed by mass-mediated processes. This formulation, originally McLuhan's, means that we are no longer able to tell whether voting patterns influence polls or whether polls influence voting. The opinion poll only requires a pre-programmed response in terms of a certain binary logic. Thus the dominant code of mass communication, like that of opinion polls, is one of yes or no, and for or against. We are asked to buy a copy of the latest bestseller, endorse the Conservative party manifesto, vote for our favourite film or remain silent. Baudrillard, completely reversing his Marxist leanings, argues that the power of the masses lies in their refusal of meaning and participation:

> this silence was a power, that it was a reply, that the silence was a massive reply through withdrawal, that silence was a strategy. It was not just a passivity. It is precisely a means of putting an end to meaning, of putting an end to grand systems of manipulation, political and informational. (Baudrillard, 1993c: 87)

This power, is not hot, like political forms of struggle, but cool. This melancholic form of cultural disdain seems to mirror Baudrillard's own conceptions of popular culture. In place of those cultural theorists who wish to view ordinary people as forming complex readings and understandings of popular culture, Baudrillard offers the couch potato. The speeding up of media messages, as we have seen, has carved up our experience of space and time. Understood pessimistically these processes have led to an increasing sense of the depthless and disposable nature of modern culture. If nothing lasts forever, then nothing is worth believing in. These information spirals have left black holes in their wake which are occupied by the masses. That is, in response to the hysteria of information the silent masses have produced their own anti-media strategy. Seemingly the only way to resist the over-proliferation of information involved in radio talk shows, advertising imperatives and interactive television is to refuse to get involved. This in itself produces a media spiral in that the more inactive the masses become the more the media seek to persuade them to join in, spend money, and ultimately submit to the dominant code. For Baudrillard the silence of the masses is not passivity but an active withdrawal.

The other main strand of Baudrillard's (1988a) media theory is his concern with simulations and the hyperreal. The progression towards the modern age of simulations has moved through three historical stages. According to Baudrillard (1993a), the period between the Renaissance and the industrial revolution can be described as the age of counterfeit. Signs, in this epoch, signified order, rank and prestige. This, notably in Shakespeare plays, opens up questions of the true nature of the person that lies behind the mask. The next stage, the order of production, which accompanies capitalism, makes possible the infinite *doubling* of objects. Walter Benjamin (1973) famously argued that capitalist production had destroyed the aura of the work of art. In the age of film and photography, Benjamin suggested, it made little sense to talk of an original print as this could be endlessly reproduced. Baudrillard presses these insights further in the final stage: the current age of simulation. The possibilities opened up by the new media technologies hold that culture no longer copies the real but produces it. The real is an effect of television, computer screens, virtual reality and stereo head-sets. The movies we watch on television are now part of an intertextual culture drawing inspiration from other genres of popular music, pulp fiction, classic tele-serials and other film features. These forms obviously do not reflect an already constituted real, but help constitute the shape of much of postmodern culture.

For example, lets take Princess Diana's infamous confessional address in an hour-long television interview to demonstrate many of these features. The interview touched upon Diana's relationship with her husband Charles, bulimia, self-mutilation, extra-marital affairs and her relationship with the media. The audience's impression of the Princess is likely to be formed through a variety of newspaper and magazine articles, gossip columns and radio talk shows that have discussed the subject. Diana in this regard only becomes known to the audience through a mediated culture. Even if Diana were to meet members of the public face-to-face it is likely that they would relate to her through the way the media have simulated and constructed her image. The audience, Baudrillard would remind us, have no authoritative account of the Princess to rely upon in making their judgements. The Princess therefore exists as a simulated media personality where truth and fiction can no longer be teased apart. Hence the point is not whether Charles or Diana were at fault in their separation, but that such discussions have destroyed their aura and mystic. It is the medium rather than the message that has had most impact. In such a climate, Baudrillard might well argue, what would be the point in writing another story about the 'truth' of the Royal Family? Diana's confessions into the camera merely offer the simulated 'presence' of the real long after it has disappeared. Again, the point is not what Charles and Diana are 'really like' but how they are symbolically coded in postmodern popular culture. The global obsession with the private lives of the Royals is then merely a cynical form of entertainment that has erased the distinction between myth and reality.

The over-inflation of media discourse that surrounded the Royal marriage can only be read cynically in that the audience is denied the possibility of re-ordering truth and fiction. Yet they are placed in a position whereby, according to Baudrillard (1983), the public are 'obliged' to make up their minds by the dominant binary code. The media achieve this effect in a number of ways. As we have seen, the system of mass communication has instituted a one-way flow of information from sender to receiver. For Baudrillard this non-dialogic relation effectively forces the audience to have an opinion about the Royal family. The media also use other means to simulate public debate through a variety of opinion and telephone polls. Instant polls and other devices are used to construct instantaneous opinion. Baudrillard writes:

> They have broken down reality into simple elements that they have reassembled into scenarios of regulated oppositions, exactly in the same way that the photographer imposes his contrasts, lights, angles on his subject (any photographer will tell you: you can do anything, all you have to do is approach the original from the right angle, at the right moment or mood that will render it the *correct answer* to the instantaneous test of the instrument and its code). It is exactly like the test or the referendum when they translate a conflict or a problem into a game of question/answer and reality thus tested, tests you according to the same code, inscribed within each message and object like a miniaturised code. (Baudrillard, 1983: 120–1)

We can no longer negotiate a path between truth and fiction, the real and the simulated, and surface and depth. In a world which cancels critical self-constitution, we have little choice other than to play with fragments of postmodern culture. The postmodern, therefore, is the abandonment of the modernist goal to find the inner truth behind appearances. The paradox here is that just at the point when the world becomes overrun with information, it becomes empty and devoid of meaning. Modernity, the era when different interpretative criteria could be employed to demystify meaning, is finished.

Simulation leads to a certain nostalgia for the real. This emerges in the popularity of true life stories, autobiography and so-called infotainment. The simulation of the real produces the hyperreal. Baudrillard offers the examples of fans of soap opera who take the performers to be the embodiment of their characters or crime stories that frighten the audience into staying home at night. We might add that the 1993 film, *In the Name of the Father*, offers a further example. The film tells the story of two members of the Birmingham Six who were wrongly accused of committing an act of terrorism. The narrative is based upon the autobiography of Gerry Conlon, one of the defendants. Accompanying the film's release there was much controversy in the press concerning the truth value of the film. Some claimed that so-called real events had been misrepresented, thereby detracting from the main purpose of the film in exposing the corruption and racism evident within the British establishment. Baudrillard's contribution to this debate would have been to point out that we can make no such distinction between the real events the film was commenting on and the film itself. He would argue that there is no dialectic between image and reality, there are only signifying practices (Baudrillard, 1987b). What would be the point in making another film closer to the so-called truth? This would only enhance the reality effect of the film and heighten processes of misrecognition. Instead it is better to attend to particular genres that claim to enunciate the real, thereby moving the analysis beyond truth and falsity. Yet what is important for Baudrillard is not so much the content of media messages (questions of simulation and the **hyperreal**) but what he calls the 'imperialism of communication' (Baudrillard, 1998: 146). By this, as we shall see, Baudrillard intends to draw attention to the media imperative to increase the amount of channels, opinions, voices and information irrespective of the number of people who are actually listening or engaging. Increasingly within these new information circuits the media seemingly engages with itself rather than the population. This upholds a principle of mediation rather than communication.

Baudrillard and Jameson

It is currently becoming fashionable to proclaim that Baudrillard is not a post-modernist after all (Gane, 1991a, 1991b). Such claims are at best displacements. It is true that his writing has been impacted upon by a diverse range of theorists, many of whom I would be reluctant to label postmodernists. But Baudrillard has something to contribute on most of the themes that map out the field of post-modernism. Baudrillard's rejection of ideology, truth, representation, seriousness, and the emancipation of the subject has a strong family resemblance to the concerns of postmodernism. To develop these themes, I will offer a dialogue between Baudrillard and the writer I take to be the most sophisticated postmodern theorist today, Fredric Jameson. The critical comparison will seek to highlight shared themes and confusions, and the reasons why I consider Jameson's writings superior. As a backdrop to these reflections, I will highlight Jameson's most recent con-tributions to theories of culture and media. I shall concentrate on one of Jameson's major works to date: *Postmodernism or, The Cultural Logic of Late Capitalism* (1991).

Postmodernism, as the title of Jameson's book indicates, is the cultural expression, or what he calls logic, of a particular phase of capitalism. Jameson notably prefers the term 'late capitalism' to Baudrillard's term, 'post-industrialism'.

This is because Jameson takes the global collapse of culture into economic forms of production as the starting point for his analysis. The effacing of high modernism and mass commercial culture has been achieved by the colonisation of the cultural sphere by the operation of the market. The integration of aesthetic production into commodity production has delivered the new cultural dominant, postmodernism. The aim of classical modernism was to shock and deride the bourgeoisie through cultural production. In the postmodern era, modernist formations have become canonised in university departments and have lost their subversive temper. Meanwhile, contemporary art forms, like punk rock, that seek to subvert the system are quickly made safe through their commodification. Most artistic production has now become tied to the marketplace and takes achievement to equal commercial success. For Jameson, the depthless fluidity of much of modern culture is the consequence of multinational capitalism.

What then are the distinctive features of postmodernism? One way of illustrating this is to compare it with other modes of artistic production. Jameson offers a comparison between Van Gogh's well-known painting titled *A Pair of Boots* and Andy Warhol's print, *Diamond Dust Shoes*. Van Gogh's work invites a traditional interpretative approach that refers to its context of production and possible moment of transcendence. The vivid colours of the painting offer a utopian gesture, while the content speaks of material deprivation. Such an interpretation could not be made of Warhol's effort. For one, the shoes in the print are a random collection of objects that float free of any larger context. Jameson muses that the shoes could have been left behind after a dance hall fire or be the ghostly remains of a concentration camp. The fact that we have no way of knowing, Jameson argues, is also embodied by Warhol's artistic disposition, which he describes as 'gratuitous frivolity' (Jameson, 1991: 10). These concerns mirror those of contemporary theory that have become suspicious of depth models of interpretation. The notions of signifier and signified, and sign and referent, have been replaced by concerns with discourses and codes. Warhol's shoes, in distinction to Van Gogh's, have no stable or obvious relation to the domain of the real. An interpretative approach could return the peasant's boots to a notion of totality that is absent from Warhol's project. The freeing of regimes of signification from their original material contexts is a crucial part of the global postmodern culture.

The superficial culture of the market has also erased the notion of individual style. Again, developments in modern theory around the death of the subject have run parallel to the disappearance of the 'inimitable' styles of modernism. The commodification of the social world has led to the proliferation and fragmentation of social codes. Since discursive heterogeneity has become the norm, modern culture is best represented as 'blank parody' or pastiche. By pastiche, Jameson means that social codes can no longer be the subject of parody in the traditional sense. Parody implies, by definition, a critical reception of the social codes and norms being utilised by the cultural producer. This is no longer possible, as the fragmentation of cultural styles has not only dispensed with the idea of individual creative genius, but with the notion of linguistic normality. Pastiche is 'without the satirical impulse, without laughter, without that still latent feeling that there exists something normal compared to which what is being imitated is rather comic' (Jameson, 1988a: 16).

If we return to the film *In the Name of the Father*, Jameson would probably point to the variety of linguistic, stylistic and musical codes that are used to signify the 1970s within the text. These codes are currently being utilised by a number of popular cultural forms through a nostalgic rerun of the 1970s period. The cultural artefacts that are generated by the means of representation becoming detached from their original social location (the splitting of signifier and signified) herald a breakdown in temporality. The film, under Jameson's reading, is less about British injustice, and more concerned with the schizophrenic array of codes that are no longer able to represent a past as the other of the present. The 1970s become a form of pastness that is conveyed through certain 'imaginary and stereotypical idealities' (Jameson, 1991:19). In a move reminiscent of Baudrillard, the real 1970s have been symbolically erased through the intertextual play of codes that seek to semiotically simulate the decade. Historicity is erased, as part of the pleasure of watching the film is the decoding of the music, long hair and flared trousers. Given the current revival of these fashions, it is difficult to map past and present. The pastness of the film is contradicted by the nowness of the cultural codes. The 1970s revival currently sweeping global culture has collapsed definite stylistic distinctions that could be made on the basis of period. For instance, musically we are currently experiencing the rebirth of 1970s soul, punk and Abba (including bands that imitate them) all at the same time. The endless recycling and mimicking of old styles has become a central feature of corporate music culture. According to Jameson, the fracturing of signifiers and signifieds evident within this process means we are now living in a perpetual present.

Elsewhere, Jameson (1988a) argues that the electronic media generally, through its rapid turnover of news and event, quickly relegates recent experiences to a distant past. In a manner similar to Debord, Jameson suggests that the ideological effect of the media comes through its form rather than its content. The conversion of reality into autonomous regimes of signification and the electronic speed of information circulation deprive the subject of a sense of historical process. However, as a dialectician, Jameson argues that the media and modern culture also contain a more critical potential. He readily accepts that the new forms of public visibility heralded by communication technologies have restrained certain repressive regimes, while media events, like President Kennedy's murder, retain a utopian impulse. The new communication technologies contribute both to a pervasive historical amnesia and occasionally to more collective forms of communion. Unlike Habermas, Jameson does not prefigure utopia through the structure of language, but through the symbolic representation of collectivity. The film *In the Name of the Father* contains collective expressions of solidarity through the resistance of the Irish Catholic working class, and in a closing scene, where the prisoners are finally released from prison, moments of euphoric optimism. Such representations hold out the utopian possibility of a more collective sensibility that is denied expression within the reifying culture of commodity capitalism.

The sliding fragmented culture of film production, while articulating moments of transcendence, is unable to represent the global mode of production. Such is the dominance of the complex fragments of the object that subjects cannot adequately locate themselves in an external world. Just as the work of art is no longer able to conceptualise the whole, so the phenomenological experience of the subject is unable to position itself within the global co-ordinates of capitalism. The relation between the social structures of late capitalism and our social experiences has become more polarised. The growing complexity of systemic levels of analysis has meant that the subject becomes 'limited to a tiny corner of the social world' (Jameson, 1991: 411). In this vein, Jameson describes postmodernist architecture, represented by the Bonaventure hotel in Los Angeles, 'as a total space that repels the city that surrounds it'. What Jameson calls his principal point is that the hotel is both populist, in that it denies the elevated language of modernism and, even more crucially, that its spatial arrangements disorientate the subject. Such is the fragmented design of the hotel that it even gives customers problems locating the shops. This local example proposes that capitalism's cultural features have begun to trespass upon the more instrumental focus of accumulation. Spatially disorganised capitalism demands a new radical form of politics Jameson calls cognitive mapping. Such a venture would realise that while the real cannot be directly represented it could be mapped. New cultural forms are required that are able to represent the spatial dimensions of multinational capitalism and that can help to build a new class consciousness. This is especially necessary in a spatially confused culture that has witnessed the suppression of critical distance. Like McLuhan, Debord, and now Baudrillard, Jameson accepts that the information barrage of modern communications has collapsed private spaces of critical reflection. However, what makes Jameson's account distinctive – particularly in this company – is his insistence that this is the result of the pulverisation of the cultural by the economic. Given the pervasiveness of global capital, cultural autonomy and aesthetic mediations have finally collapsed. It is only through Marxist science, and potentially radical art, that this situation can be grasped. The interrelations of locality, the nation and the globe can only be thought at this level, while the subject remains fractured and isolated.

There seem to be many common points of reference for Baudrillard and Jameson, such as the disappearance of the real, the linguistic formation of the subject, the importance of consumer culture and the erosion of depth. They also offer similar arguments concerning the historic periodisation of culture and distinctive forms of space.[6] The main difference between Baudrillard's and Jameson's accounts lies in the notion of political economy. While Jameson persists in the idea that economic relations have become increasingly important in the organisation and control of cultural production, Baudrillard takes this as a sign of the dominant code. Seemingly, Baudrillard's need to distinguish the logic of production from that of symbolic exchange, coupled with his desire to replace the real and the symbolic with the code, blinds him to the extent to which the former has reordered the latter. The coupling of so-called economic relations and symbolic representations means that Jameson is able to explore the increasingly complex forms of their interrelationship. The globalisation of consumer capital, Jameson rightly comments, has fostered new relations of social control and internationalised class domination.

Yet, like Baudrillard, he also argues that the new mode of production and the development of hyperreal space has outstripped the capacity of social subjects and classical social theory's ability to represent it adequately. In Jameson's terms, this necessitates a redrawing of the relations between theory and practice, while Baudrillard erroneously runs these two levels together. In fact, despite the sophistication of Jameson's cultural theory, he remains a traditional Marxist in certain respects. His argument that the dominance of the capitalist system depends upon the psychic fragmentation of the proletariat can be traced back to the early Lukacs. This dimension is stressed against those critical theorists, taking their inspiration from Gramsci, who argue that the actual meanings generated by capitalism ensure its dominance. Jameson, on the other hand, insists that it is both cultural and material forms of separation that ensure the dominance of multinational capital. Just as important as cultural fragmentation, in this frame of reference, is the radical separateness of the practices of consumption and production (Jameson, 1991: 315). The reification of these social domains ideologically erases the less fortunate from the imaginary of dominant social groups. This, particularly in a culture that has lost its ability to express historicity and totality, materially prevents the development of geographic relations of solidarity.

Jameson's ability to stress the interrelations of material and symbolic and theory and practice is an advance on Baudrillard's concern for implosion. Baudrillard sees no danger in throwing out all such distinctions. From his perspective, Jameson's critique of the colonisation of culture is simply another addition to the gallery of those who are caught up within the mirror of production. In contrast to Baudrillard's reductions, Jameson's more spatially oriented theory retains the ambition to articulate the continued importance of capitalism to the production of culture. The difference between Jameson and Baudrillard in this regard is that Baudrillard refuses the distinction between the level of theories about the world and actual social practices that take place within it.

Of course Jameson's formulations encounter their own difficulties. Here I will mention only a few. Reading Jameson's prose I am nearly always struck by its American origins. His emphasis upon the economic dominance of the cultural sphere seems to make less sense in other social contexts. At one point, Jameson (1991) claims that Habermas's theory of communicative action has no more than a local significance within a certain national context. This is because within German society the principles of liberal democracy have only a weak institutional footing. My claim here is that Jameson's own theory says more about American culture than it does about the global culture. Said (1993) has argued that it is a characteristic illusion of the pretensions of American intellectuals to assume their own nation to be the centre of the globe. Jameson, despite being a Marxist, offers much of the confidence that is usually associated with an imperial vision. While he partially protects himself from this objection by arguing that postmodernism has not yet fully arrived, his theory lacks an appreciation of certain cultural and institutional mediations that restrain the economic. Such a concern, in a European context, would want to address the state funding of traditional artistic practices, the development of public cultural policy and the shared tradition of public service broadcasting. These institutional formations operate within a relatively decommodified zone. That Jameson ignores these institutional levels says as much about the culture he is working within, as he does about Habermas. Indeed, Said (1993) has forcibly argued that it was the very lack of a democratic public sphere that proved so crucial during the Gulf War. The tight control over instituted public dialogue, in the American context, was instrumental in securing public support for the war. By ignoring these levels Jameson arguably makes a fetish of reification. The extent to which other determinants and hegemonic features of late capitalism impact upon the production of public cultures never fully occupies Jameson's analysis. Further, the image of a largely passive world being overrun by a commodified postmodern culture has little to contribute on the cultural relations between different world regions. As we shall see, in the following chapter, many post-colonial thinkers have criticised similar ideas of media imperialism. For example, many critics have pointed to the fact that time/space compression has lead to an increasingly hybridised global culture. Rather than simply introducing an increasingly commodified culture such concerns have also introduced critical political agendas such as cosmopolitanism, multi-culturalism and associated struggles for cultural recognition (Gilroy, 2000). Such political concerns are arguably poorly appreciated by blanket concerns with global commodification.

The other feature I want to point to is Jameson's seemingly unreconstructed Althusserianism. It has never been clear how Marxism has been able to justify its status as a science as opposed to an ideology. This concern is particularly marked in Jameson's writing, in that he wishes to preserve a notion of ideology critique. If we take Jameson's writing on utopia it seems that any image of the collective has a positive significance. Terry Eagleton (1990: 404) argues that such is Jameson's attachment to the transcendent qualities of images of human solidarity that we could be forced to attend to the utopian potential of a racist rally. In addition, given the importance Jameson places upon the fragmentation of the self, it is not clear what the sources of utopian impulses are, or even how Marxism can claim to provide a *stable* analysis of historical developments in consumer capital. That Jameson makes such comments and refuses to adequately consider the grounds of his critique flies in the face of much critical theory. Williams and Habermas have signalled a retreat from theories which claim a scientific superiority to other reflections. It is Williams's and Habermas's project to make commonly available more democratic forms of communication. This would make ideology critique a practice of everyday life. A democratic revival of public institutions would seemingly allow Baudrillard's masses to communicatively rethink their interests in the light of other considerations. Here interests are not immediately self-present to agents, or the privileged property of American professors, but can begin to emerge only after full consideration in a variety of democratic settings. Jameson's theory remains, therefore, overly constructed around the reificatory aspects of consumerism without seeing the pressing need to develop a more normative democratic theory of media production and reception.[7]

Baudrillard's Irrationalism

Since Nietzsche's time, attacks on Enlightenment concepts of reason have become common. In more recent decades they have become familiar through French social theory. Here I have in mind Foucault, Derrida, Lyotard, and of course Baudrillard. Such intellectual strands have pointed to the connections between power and knowledge, underlined the myth of the disembedded subject and emphasised the limitations of instrumentalist reason. Baudrillard seems to have pushed these currents much further than his rivals. He not only emphasises the situatedness of the subject but its complete disappearance into the object. In criticising the epistemological focus of modern philosophy, he disregards conceptions of truth and claims to rightness altogether. Baudrillard's avant-gardist fatal strategies not only reduce the operation of media to their technical functions, but also apparently deny the possibility of reflexivity on the part of the audience. Here I will forcibly reverse Baudrillard's sustained attack on critical and radical perspectives such as the one defended in this volume. Crucial are four analyses that I have already mentioned: (1) the necessity of truth claims for a critical theory of ideology; (2) the importance of a culturally materialist approach to language; (3) the theoretical limitations of what I shall call Baudrillard's avant-gardist and technological approach to the media; and (4) the continued relevance of conceptions of human need to cultural analysis. Despite these limitations I will, where appropriate, credit Baudrillard for at least asking important questions that have previously been eluded within media sociology. Here I have in mind some of Baudrillard's more insightful comments on the forms of subjectivity that are likely to be developed by interactive media technologies and the overstated interpretative activity of the audience. Baudrillard's concentration upon the mediums of communication also has a certain validity, although my overall sense is that he takes and adds little to McLuhan's more innovative contributions.

1. Baudrillard's attack on reason, as I have indicated, has its roots in Nietzsche's anti-humanism. The replacement of Marx by Nietzsche in contemporary French social theory has undoubtedly opened up some interesting perspectives – this seems particularly true of Foucault – but in hands such as Baudrillard's this is used to legitimise a more reactionary project. Baudrillard's (1993c: 209) most provocative remarks concerning his anti-humanism and anti-feminism have their roots in this philosophical resource. In an important essay, Sabina Lovibond (1990) argues that much postmodernist theory, taking its lead from Nietzsche, and here I would include Baudrillard, opposes rationalism on the grounds of an unrepentant masculinity. Nietzsche characterises rationalism as a form of slave morality that was the cultural expression of the resentment of the masses. Running against the grain of Nietzsche's more enthusiastic supporters, Lovibond affirms that Nietzsche's aristocratic social theory dispels democratic movements because of their questioning of so-called natural orders of rank. The aim of feminist and socialist movements has traditionally been to open up rational critiques of domination. Critical theory, Lovibond wisely reasons, has interests in replacing relations of force with those of communicative understanding and truthfulness. For Nietzsche, and we might also say for Baudrillard, in a world that had abolished distinctions between appearance and reality and removed the grounding of morality, this left the social open to virile intervention. The social is for Baudrillard and Nietzsche a meaningless chaos, which leaves the critic free to create *his* own values. In the face of an empty universe, Nietzsche advocates a form of masculine agency through the will to power. Similarly, Baudrillard argues that the simulation of the social through new media technologies has imploded questions of truth. What use is truth, Baudrillard asks, in a world where Mickey Mouse has become as real as George Bush? His discursive strategy in conveying these ideas similarly depends upon the kind of robust agency that his own version of the subject explicitly denies. Baudrillard has apparently inherited, from Nietzsche and some of his followers, a version of the subject that is subsumed by the object and yet sufficiently centred to advocate *harder*, less feminine forms of theorising.

These confusions aside, I want to address Baudrillard's remarks on the idea of truth. On Baudrillard's view, notions of truth can be dispensed with since the signifier and the signified have been riven apart. This means that there can be no relationship between concrete events and regimes of interpretation. Baudrillard it seems can't quite make up his mind whether the real world is becoming like the movies, or whether the movies are becoming more like the real world. In discussing films about the Vietnam War, therefore, Baudrillard (1987b) is able to claim that the war never actually happened. This is distinct from Jameson's writing on postmodernism, where the more plausible claim is made that we only have access to the real event through certain regimes of signification. In my understanding, this does not seek to deny that the series of actions that we might call the Vietnam War have a similar ontological status to a film about the war. Whereas Baudrillard's point is that a film about the war is just as much a simulation as the war itself, Jameson's view is that the historicity of the real is made schizophrenic by floating signifiers.

Baudrillard, it must be said, certainly has a point, in that pop videos, Hollywood cinema and crime detective stories do not reflect the real. Hence they should be regarded as forms of significatory production in their own right. His arguments seem less plausible – dare we say absurd – if one is considering a documentary film about single parent families. If such a film claimed that all single parent families produced delinquent children we would quite rightly feel justified in our indignation that such a view is false. This is not to argue that documentaries, like other forms of film production, do not work within certain codes, but they are capable of making truth claims. Further, films about Vietnam are also capable of articulating truths. Oliver Stone's trilogy of films on Vietnam is concerned with the universal theme of the needless human suffering that modern technological war generates. The films are arguably more truthful representations of the conflict than, say, official American propaganda released during the war. To make this case, argues Christopher Norris (1990), inevitably involves us in a form of ideology critique where certain representations are deemed to misrepresent reality. In Baudrillard's reading, the only difference between the films of Oliver Stone and various forms of propaganda is that the propaganda claims to be more real. For Baudrillard such notions are always misunderstandings of the nature of symbolic production. This evades the problem that all films and documentaries are apparently social constructions, and yet some are more truthful than others. To always reduce such formulations to the level of misrecognition, as does Baudrillard, is to deny the subversive power of popular film, documentary and commentary.

2. The idea of simulations and the hyperreal raises the question as to whether Baudrillard can adequately account for the role of culture in social life. If texts only have reality effects how are we to assess the truth of Baudrillard's own pronouncements? It may be, as Baudrillard argues, that language does not reflect the real but actively constitutes it. Still, does this fact mean that cultural forms are unable to open up interpretations of the social world? It is noticeable that the further Baudrillard moves away from reference to a material world the further these

questions are repressed within his writing. Here I disagree with Baudrillard's thesis that the real has disappeared only to be replaced by its symbolic mourning. Returning to the work of Volosinov (1986) and Raymond Williams (1979b, 1980, 1982) I will argue that language and cultural forms are both material and symbolic in character. This may seem a marginal point to make, yet a cultural materialist perspective can offer a different view of the subject to that which is maintained by Baudrillard. The application of cultural materialism also has implications for the way we interpret culture and for reworking conceptions of human need. The discussion will then flow into some of Gadamer's (1975) and Ricoeur's (1981) remarks on the referential moment of text, which Baudrillard's and Jameson's writing obscures.

Volosinov and Williams argue that language is a material and symbolic social practice. The reproduction of the sign is the product of the interface between human action and social structures. Both writers criticise Saussure's *arbitrary* separation of the structure of language from the way it is reproduced in social settings. Saussure gives language a fixed objective character that is abstracted from the living speech of human beings. The dialectical emphasis of cultural materialism argues that linguistic production cannot be reduced to the subjectivity of an isolated agent or the predetermined structures of language. Language is the collective product of intersubjective social relations. Volosinov (1986: 26) famously argues that the psyche is formed through language that lies at the *borderline* between biology and the external world. These linguistic processes are reducible neither to human biology nor to the structural imprinting of human society. In other words, the dynamic structuration of language cannot be resolved by pointing to the biological foundation of human beings or a closed objective system of language. The emphasis is placed upon the creative capacity of human subjects to collectively modify language through the reworking of previously existing structures. In this way, human action is not opposed to an *external* constraining linguistic structure since the rules of language are the precondition of such activity. These practices, as I have indicated, are at once material and symbolic. The sign has to be materially produced by making sounds in the air, impressing marks on paper, or by making certain bodily movements. Its symbolic quality or the meanings that are generated through an ensemble of signs are multi-accentual. The sign is the subject of semiotic warfare, with different social groups attributing different meanings to a variety of social accents. Williams (1979b) and Volosinov (1986) both argue that dominant groups will tend to insist that the sign is uni-accentual. Hegemonic formations will represent the sign as having a reified and fixed quality that is not the result of historical processes. The capacity of human beings to interject new meanings through certain material forms is a source of optimism for both these writers.

This account differs from Baudrillard's in that language is seen as the site of struggle for extra-linguistic social forces. Baudrillard's insistence that the sign has no referent means that the production of material forms such as films, newspapers, television programmes and magazines is not properly understood as a field of hegemonic struggle. Yet neither Williams nor Volosinov automatically assumes that the social relations of production have a pre-determined or a negligible impact upon linguistic production and reproduction. In this, Williams tends to emphasise the role of public institutions, whereas Volosinov, rather like Bourdieu, ties symbolic articulation into class backgrounds. While these themes need further elaboration, what is clear from such formulations is that the production of the sign, considered as a social practice, has to be related to external social relations. To place, as does Baudrillard, such extreme stress on the disjuncture between the symbolic and the real fails to account for these relations. Language and culture are always already the result of certain social relationships of realisation and consumption. One of the many frustrating aspects of Baudrillard's writing is his turn away from a recognition of these features. That is, the symbolic may not be determined by the real but it certainly impinges upon its production and reception.

Much of modern media culture continues to have a referential nature yet Jameson and Baudrillard offer an analysis of media culture by stressing the production of intertextual codes and media of communication. *In the Name of the Father*, however, is not just an example of intertextuality, as Jameson and Baudrillard might suggest. While these perspectives remain important they appear to ignore more traditional hermeneutic concerns with the world view that is discursively opened up by a text. Put another way, the film in question could be considered a comment upon the forms of injustice that have historically been granted Irish suspects under English law. The dimensions opened up by the text are potentially a critique of real social relations. In opposition to those who wish to deconstruct the text, or those, like Baudrillard and Jameson, who mainly attend to its features as a cultural form, a more hermeneutical appreciation would seek to look at the critical horizons that are raised by attending to *what the text is trying to say*. Baudrillard is unable to respond to this critical feature of textual production because he implodes poetic commentary on the world into actual social actions and relations. What Gadamer (1975) and Ricoeur (1981) call the referential moment of the text is both essential to an appreciation of the audience's relation to a variety of texts and again adds a subversive dimension to cultural politics. Of course semiotic plurality is now variously encouraged and incorporated by the structures of consumer society. But if we consider the partial entry into mainstream culture of feminist perspectives our conclusions need not be so pessimistic. The rise of feminist publishing houses and the feminist movement generally has transformed a variety of popular texts aimed at women (Ballaster *et al.*, 1991; McRobbie, 1994). The ideology of femininity incorporated by women's magazines has been challenged by the impact of feminism. It certainly remains the case that the broad range of magazines aimed at women mostly address their target group in their role as consumers and primary carers. Yet there are visible shifts in that some magazines at least pay lip service to a number of feminist concerns, ranging from more emancipated definitions of sexuality to health and women in employment. These material cultures offer the possibility of new identities and subjectivities that cannot be understood without attending to the relation between textual content and extra-textual movements and relations. While such texts barely seek to politicise relations of sexual dominance, the feminine subject has become a more unstable construction and spaces for more autonomous forms of development have thereby been opened up. Again I would want to stress that such developments should not be overstated – although what is important in this context is that Baudrillard's and Jameson's concerns leave these issues unwrapped.

3. If the analysis developed thus far is correct, Baudrillard's view of media culture overstates some aspects to the detriment of others. Additionally, it seems to me, underlying his concept of fatal strategies lies a masculinist avant-gardism that holds in contempt any fellow feeling amongst human beings that might generate relations of reciprocity within the life-world. Raymond Williams (1989c) has traced a similar structure of feeling through the early modernist movement to the New Right. His analysis of Strindberg and Nietzsche argues that the culture of the modernist avant-garde emphasises an individualistic revolt against the bourgeoisie. The modernist concern with feelings of alienation, fragmentation and exile have now become intertwined with a rightist discourse of the atomised individual that seeks to deny more empathetic and solidaristic connections. The stance taken by Baudrillard's writing advocates a form of individualism on the part of the writer that is not available to the modern herd. This seemingly colludes with some of the more elitist aspects of the modernist avant-garde outlined by Williams.

Similar assumptions can be seen underlying Baudrillard's concern that the technical apparatus of mass communication converts the people into an irresponsible mass. Bauman (1992a), Hall (1986) and Kellner (1989) all argue that Baudrillard's writing contains an anti-hermeneutical bias. Baudrillard arguably represents the masses as an apathetic homogeneous body that refuses media strategies to elicit participation and identification. According to these perspectives, he lacks an appreciation of the semiotic plurality of popular texts that are ambiguously read from a variety of subject positions. Here I am reminded of Williams's (1965) related remarks concerning those who seek to reduce the culturally diverse body of the people to a unified category like the masses. For Williams the *masses* have no referent outside of the symbolic productions of certain intellectual traditions and artistic formations. Such representations, along with those of the reified individual existing independently of human connections, offer a reductive analysis of the actual lived complexity of modern life. In Williams's terms, Baudrillard's argumentative strategy on the level of theory and practice isolates lay actors from their intersubjective contexts and constitutes nothing less than a form of technological determinism. These objections carry a definite relevance. Yet Smart (1992), in Baudrillard's defence, has argued that his point is that the masses are rendered silent by the one-way nature of the technology. The masses, Smart would agree with Williams, are in any case a simulation of Baudrillard's own writing. What is missing from those who characterise Baudrillard as an elitist is an appreciation of his discursive strategy. In this sense Baudrillard has produced an alternative to the hegemony of the dominant code that encourages audience activity and participation. Hence Baudrillard locates a form of refusal in the reluctance to consume or participate more generally. The problem again arises from the way Baudrillard formulates the issue. If the masses themselves are purely a simulation, I am entitled to ask why I should accept Baudrillard's pronouncements. In relation to media sociology, Baudrillard's deep pessimism acts as an antidote to some of the semiotic dizziness of the audience theorists. In this sense, his writing does retain a certain descriptive relevance in its version of consumers of popular culture growing ever more distracted and cynical, and yet aware of the intertextual references evident in popular fiction, television series and films. But his reflections remain impressionistic and, taken on their own terms, would have to resist the empirical referent I am suggesting here.

Baudrillard's other strength, like McLuhan's, is his stress on the role of technology in the formation of intersubjective relations. Again like McLuhan, he makes a fetish out of the technological aspects of media communication. That modern communications systems have instituted a specifically one-way version of communication remains an important insight. Concerns around democracy and ideology within media studies have all been built upon this assumption, although for the most part it has not been explicitly recognised. The institution of so-called mass societies was based upon certain national forms of cultural homogeneity that were in turn enabled by centralised communications technologies. Today, with the advent of personal stereos, satellite stations and video recorders, technologies have individualising effects. The new forms of social control suggested by such developments are less the integration into a mass society and more cultural fragmentation. The Gramscian paradigm that privileges notions of ideological incorporation is of course still relevant, but any concern with hegemonic effects of popular culture will have to be mediated with a concern for the crumbling social space of late capitalism. Of course, Baudrillard does not make the connections that are being suggested here; he is perhaps more important for some of the questions that he raises.

For instance, McLuhan's and Baudrillard's insistence that instantaneous or obscene communication has rendered the public sphere obsolete retains an analytic purchase. Any attempts to remake the public sphere, such as those of Williams and Habermas, would have to accept that certain limitations are imposed by modern information flows and the silencing of the vast majority of the population. Baudrillard and McLuhan legitimately point to the move from print to electronic culture as having certain implications in this respect. The simulated information blizzards characteristic of modernity mean that reflexive responses on the part of the audience are caught up into an increasingly individualised speed culture. But this does not necessarily eliminate the subject's capacity for critical reflection in terms of the good and the just, as both McLuhan and Baudrillard imply. More plausible, it seems, are Debord's and Jameson's claims concerning the decline of historical narratives – although such concerns would have to explain the resilience of nationalism in the modern age. Such an appreciation, however, does place limitations on the attempt to form communities of exchange solely, through the media. Defenders of the public sphere could point to the fact that Baudrillard's obsession with technology conservatively brackets off issues concerning its democratic institution. How, we might ask, could we ensure that issues of public relevance are widely discussed from a plural number of viewpoints? Further, given the fragmentation of the public, how do we make sure the most important questions of our time reach into spaces where people work, look after children, relax and form their opinions? Such questions both presuppose a democratic reformulation of our culture and lead to less media-centric views of the social than those offered by McLuhan and Baudrillard.

From a different angle, the fast-flowing world of media images has been interpreted both too optimistically (McLuhan) and too pessimistically (Baudrillard). My own disposition resembles that of Jameson, though I argued that his account remains constructed too closely around the problem of commodity reification. Such a dialectical view would accept with Baudrillard that the daily turnover of *unique* events in the media fosters a sense of impermanence and depthlessness. In this modernity helps foster a thin culture where nothing seems to have enduring value. Yet the explosion of semiotic culture has correspondingly witnessed a new search for depth and meaning within and outside of the dominant commercial culture. The development of global communications offers the possibility of new relations of solidarity with those who are distant in time and space. Such a dialectic – and this leads me back to my preoccupation with the public sphere – makes the case for free systems of communication more urgent than ever before. The opportunities and dangers that face the globe's citizens presuppose the necessity of having access to high-quality information, drama that promotes critical reflection and filmic reports that elicit a response on the part of citizens. Citizens have a definite need to have a critical awareness of the increasingly complex social conditions within which they live and die. This necessitates both a radical democracy and an open communicative system of exchange as free as possible from the dominance of money and power. Unfortunately Baudrillard's nihilistic social theory renders such issues irrelevant.

4. I began this chapter tracing through the roots of Baudrillard's anti-humanism. We have seen that this was informed by Althusser's critique of the early Marx and, much later, by his interest in Nietzsche and Bataille. A connecting thread through Baudrillard's social theory has been his insistence that the subject has disappeared into the object. Moreover, Baudrillard argues that a concern with human needs is both philosophically bankrupt and anachronistic in the age of cool electronic cultures. Nonetheless, I would insist, the idea of human beings having needs that are socially and historically mediated remains an important concern. Otherwise, if Baudrillard's pronouncements are followed, one could never argue that social systems fail to satisfy the needs of their citizens. To be sure, unless some version of human need is defended, it is difficult to see why I should want to criticise the structures of late capitalism at all. The supermarkets may be full of consumer goods, but this does not mean that their food is not poisonous or that it is within everyone's reach. More to the point, our radio stations may be full of celebrities expressing themselves, but this does not mean they are skilled at challenging our perceptions of AIDS or poverty. Here I shall maintain, somewhat unfashionably, that human beings in the late twentieth century have both material and symbolic needs.

The idea of human needs is rejected by Baudrillard for two main reasons. First the notion, Baudrillard correctly summarises, has a close relationship with theories of human nature. For Baudrillard ideas of human nature are caught up with the *normalising* operation of the dominant code. Marxism and capitalism share a similar view of humans as being essentially productive workers, which reinforces a form of species racism against those who fail to attain this status. Baudrillard's other criticism was that notions of need depend on a version of the human subject that is not properly social. Baudrillard argues that needs are dependent upon the subjects' distinctions from other consumer groups and are an effect of the social system within which they live. Thus needs discourses are ideological – not a term Baudrillard is very fond of – in that they reproduce the exclusivity of the code and split the subject into natural and social needs. I consider both of these assumptions misguided.

The first argument that conceptions of human need and nature are necessarily exclusive is surely false. We could perhaps agree that certain formulations operate in this way, but this is not necessarily the case. For instance, Norman Geras (1983) has argued that Marx, contrary to Althusser's pronouncements, never rejected a view of human nature and that he was right not to do so. Marx defends a universalistic conception of human beings through a theory of material and social needs. Unless needs for food, shelter and health are met, human beings are unlikely to survive for very long. They also, according to Marx, have social needs for human association, creative labour and diverse social pursuits. These needs may be differently expressed within different cultures, but they are in essence universal.

While I am not necessarily interested in defending Marx's theories on human need and nature – it is difficult to see what is inherently racist about his views. Baudrillard himself presumably needs food to survive and thinks that a writing career gives him a greater capacity for creativity than monotonous manual labour. In terms of communication theory, as I have indicated, if an idea of human beings as having needs for community, knowledge and creative expression can be defended, as I believe it can, this will have implications for the organisation of the dominant means of communication.

Baudrillard's other objection is similarly flawed. This said, the idea that theories of human need are prone to philosophical dualisms certainly has some resonance. Such a view was certainly true of Marx, since one of the problems with capitalism was that it reduced factory workers to the degraded status of animals. It was the barbarism of nineteenth-century capitalism that prevented workers from fully realising their intrinsically *human* nature. Such a view comes close to a form of specism that codes animal needs as base and human needs as lofty and noble. However, to say that there are problems with the way Marx formulates human needs does not, in my view, call for the outright dismissal of the concept. The notion of universal material needs that human beings share as a species is self-evident and points to a deep prejudice against ontology in Baudrillard's thought (Bhaskar, 1991). If such needs were governed by the system we could not claim that a society that was starving its citizens was failing to meet their needs. On the point of philosophical dualisms, Ted Benton (1993) claims that these can be avoided if we consider each species to have a certain historically given potential. Humans and cats share certain biological conditions (limited life-spans, bonds with other animals, sexual activity, etc.) yet have different species potentials. For example, only human beings are capable of linguistically sharing their need interpretations through the instituted mechanisms of the mass media. This species potential is obviously dependent upon certain levels of historical development and cannot be adequately conceptualised as an expression of their biology (Doyal and Gough, 1991). Yet the difficult question remains how we democratically decide in a mediated age what constitutes human needs. For Baudrillard such universal constructs are likely to cancel the space for radical Otherness. My argument, on the other hand, is that a radical politics in respect of the human needs for community and dialogue continue to have important consequences for the ways in which we choose to organise the dominant systems of mass communication.

Summary

Baudrillard is mainly concerned with the technical features of mass communication. Along with the pervasion of simulated culture, and his own anti-humanism and uncompromising polemics, this was the main concern of the chapter. But, like McLuhan, Baudrillard initially offers the prospect of an attentive concern to specific technological media before crushing them together under more abstract forms of analysis. Baudrillard seems to have much to offer on the impact of new forms of communication. Yet given his derision of notions of the public, political economy, and his impressionistic analysis of media cultures, his contributions require more substantial support. The problem here is that Baudrillard's extreme anti-empiricism undercuts such a possibility. However, Baudrillard's social theory continues to have a radical purchase given his emphasis upon questions of simulation, hyperreality and the imperatives of the dominant code within modern consumer society.

New Media and the Information Society

Schiller, Castells, Virilio and Cyberfeminism

The development of new mediums of communication are inevitably accompanied by fresh modes of theorising. While this gives rise to new and original waves of thinking it can also provide space for more predictable narratives. The development of **Internet** technology, digital television and cyberspace are no different in this respect. The camps of thinking that have accompanied these new technological developments have either been welcoming, in terms of the social and technical opportunities that seem to be offered, or cynically suggested such narratives offer nothing new. For example, most of the writing on the Internet has either pointed to the ways new technological forms are linked into the accumulation of capital, commodification and the disappearance of public space, or has optimistically pointed to the communicative possibilities that are suggested by horizontally rather than vertically organised information structures. Within these arguments lies a deeper debate as to whether we are witnessing a transformation away from an industrial society to an information or network society. This argument, first proposed by the sociologist Daniel Bell (1973), argues that knowledge and information are becoming the key factors in economic and social development. The central argument here is that productive and distributive processes within the economy are increasingly driven by knowledge-based inputs. In this way, the development of new media technology needs to be linked into the transformation of the economy, and related changes within politics and culture. Many writers, as we shall see, prefer the term network society to information society. Van Dijk (1999) has argued that the most important structural change impacting upon new media is the convergence of telecommunications, data communications and new and old media. Within these circuits of information we are witnessing the digitalisation of communications accompanied by the convergence of television, telephone systems and the Internet. The second related change has been the shift towards interactive forms of media that allow two-way forms of communication. These twin changes move contemporary society from the age of industrialism and mass culture into an era governed by networks and interactivity. Their co-ordinates point in a different direction to the debates as to whether or not we should become technological optimists or pessimists. The idea of a network society offers a different model of the capitalist economy, a rethinking of the link between communications and politics, and consideration of the changes taking place within our cultural life. The network society then is the attempt to provide a social theory of mass communication that takes both the rise of the new media and the shift to knowledge-based societies seriously. New information and communication technologies do not bring about a new society, but they provide the means that make it possible.

Here, mainly through an investigation of the work of Manuel Castells, I will seek to investigate these and other claims. The idea of a network society is a significant attempt to connect the study of the media of mass communication to the changing nature of society. The age of new communication technologies and information offers the possibility at least of a theory that dispenses with some of the limitations of Marxism and postmodernism. However it is true to argue that arguments in respect of either a network or information society have their challengers. As I indicated in Chapter 1, many Marxist writers are resistant to the idea that the capitalist economy (the main driving force behind the provision of communications) has changed that much. In this respect, we shall look at the arguments of Herbert Schiller in terms of the capitalisation of communication systems. Further, the writing of Paul Virilio argues that the projection of a culture of interactivity is largely a myth that is leading to the disappearance and annihilation of the phenomenological capacities of the human subject. That is the information society is a speed culture that is gradually leading to increased levels of cultural impoverishment as society becomes overrun by euphoric technological determinism. Finally, I look at one of the most significant academic and political movements of the information age, cyberfeminism. Here the concern is with large structural transformations, which are linked into a concern with gender divisions and masculinist ways of thinking. Cyberfeminism has developed substantial ethical and political concerns in respect of who benefits from technological change, and how our culture decides to represent and encode technology more generally.

Herb Schiller and Media Imperialism

For the American theorist of the information society, Herb Schiller, it is the West's dominance of economic relations that leads inexorably to cultural forms of dominance. However it is arguable that the character of global capitalism and culture has changed considerably since the 1960s and 1970s. Schiller (1991, 1996) argues, in the latest restatement of his media imperialism thesis, that the 1960s represented the apex of American economic and cultural power. Since this period, the globe has become increasingly complex with competing centres of economic power and activity. The American response to these challenges has been to move its efforts more forcefully into the cultural industries through the development of new communication technologies. These developments have aided the increasingly global spread of American multinationals, the deregulation of public networks and the spreading commercialisation of the mass media.

In Schiller's (1996) most recent defence of this argument he focuses upon the capitalist driven nature and commodification of American popular culture before transferring this model to the rest of the world. The globe it seems is being remade in America's own image. American capitalist culture, according to Schiller, is one of the purest currently in existence; its internal development in post-war society is being fostered by the expansion of credit, rampant consumerism, advertising and the systematic displacement of traditional forms of constraint. Capitalism American style has largely arisen in a national context that lacks any recognisable tradition of social democracy and where working-class labour organisations have only the weakest public presence. Such an environment has fostered the integration of information and culture into the dominant structures of the finance economy. Popular culture in America is driven by capitalist accumulation strategies. Economic forces are the main structures behind technological developments such as the super information highway and the Internet, and they also help determine the super-ficiality of much of mainstream mass culture. The dominance of the economic system over other social spheres helps foster a culture of conformity rather than critique, of sensation rather than substance and technique rather than reflection. Cultural concerns, other than for a small intellectual elite, are run, managed and determined by the parameters of economics. For this reason, American culture carries ideological messages of consumerism and promotes acquisitive behaviour in the host and the world population in general. Mass forms of entertainment, therefore, act as a form of compensation for a disintegrating communal life while encouraging the displacement of critical questions connected to a divided society. Schiller argues that the expansion in entertainment services not only provides new markets for advertisers, but masks important social issues such as the growing underclass, widening social divisions and a spiraling prison population. In prime-time television the economic losers are rendered invisible. Mass culture thereby insulates the well off from the poor, and is utilised increasingly by private as opposed to public interests.

Schiller maintains that while America has declined in terms of its overall position within the world economy, it has maintained its hegemony over the globe's culture. Since the 1980s, culture everywhere has become increasingly Americanised and penetrated by economic reason. The increasing integration of media products into the global market, and the rapid deregulation of public cultures have promoted worldwide processes of Americanisation. This has been achieved thorough the direct promotion of American products, and the local copying of American television styles and formats. Just as American capitalism was able to marginalise oppositional structures at home, so with the running down of public cultures abroad it has been able to penetrate into new markets. Commercially driven media, which are the main carriers of American products, are currently overrunning a passive world. Significantly it is the global economy rather than the nation-state which is the new mechanism of governance. In the face of networks of global capital the nation is struggling to maintain its cultural autonomy and preserve the distinctiveness of internally constructed social identities. Indeed the development of global communications has been driven less by individual states than by the world's rich and powerful seeking to cordon themselves off from the poor. In this reading, again mirroring developments within American society, the globe's wealthy consumers will become the targets of accumulation strategies, thereby repressing questions concerning deepening global inequalities that will inevitably be avoided by overtly capitalist controlled media structures. A world dominated less by the governance of the nation, and more by the commercial imperatives of global capitalism will foster a social environment where a few prosper and many are marginalised.

Schiller then would need to argue that many of the Internet's most radical enthusiasts neglect the way that the new media is integrated into a global capitalist economy. For instance, Julian Stallabrass (1996) argues that the super information highway and cyberspace will not offer a utopian domain of free communication, but the perfect market place, able to operate through space and time at the flick of a switch. Those who are currently excited about the future possibilities of the Net are failing to ask who will control the information, to whom it will be made available and in whose interests it is likely to be run. The answers to these questions can be traced back to the needs of global capital. For instance, so-called virtual communities are places built upon irony and play, unlike real communities which are places of obligation and responsibility. If within cyberspace we are able to disguise our identities this effectively denies the possibility of a genuinely democratic communicative exchange, where the particularity of the 'Other' has to be engaged. Instead it creates a 'kingdom of information, whose palatial halls we may wander without fear, free from chaos, dirt and obscurity' (Stallabras, 1996: 67). Cyberspace becomes a zone of irresponsible consumption where the poor will never appear as subjects in their own right and only very occasionally as 'objects' for discussion. Indeed the desire to create 'virtual' communities over the web both points to the disappearance of 'real' communal relations, trampled under the atomising effect of commodity capital, and to the fact that humans desperately need a sense of belonging and will create it with whatever tools they currently have to hand. The human need and desire for community is what the advocates of cyber solutions are currently manipulating. The democratic and communal potential of much of the new media turns out to be an old con trick performed by capital's need for new markets and enthusiastic consumers. Notably Schiller's views take these arguments a step further by linking new media developments to American capital. Key corporate interests such as Time Warner, America Online and Microsoft have indeed been the driving force behind the development of the superhighway (Street, 2001).

Mattelart and Mattelart (1992), on the other hand, have broken more decisively with the argument that the main role of media cultures is the legitimation of a declining American empire. This however is not to doubt the universal and global presence of American media products. They report that between 1970 and 1981 only France and Japan succeeded in securing a majority share of their domestic market in film (Mattelart, 1984: 20). Further, in 1982 American advertising firms held the top 30 of the 50 places in the global market. Yet the most marked change since America's overwhelming cultural dominance of the 1960s has been the arrival of a multi-polar world. In particular the 1980s have witnessed the development of new cultural exporters in both the 'Third World' and the so-called developed world which has changed the shape of international image markets. For instance, in Brazil the formation of the audio-visual conglomerate TV Globo was set up through a series of local initiatives and without the involvement of substantial amounts of foreign capital (Mader, 1993). While it depends upon revenue from transnational advertisers, the company grew in the 1980s, experiencing financial turnovers equivalent to those of the combined efforts of French television channels. Other more detailed analyses of global media flow have revealed a more complex picture than the one offered by advocates of American media imperialism. For instance, just as economic analysis has questioned the supposed unity behind concepts like the 'Third World', media analysis has also become more attuned to its complexity. According to Reeves (1993) it makes little analytic sense to put Brazil and India into the same categories as some of the poorer African nations. In 1985 India produced 912 feature length films and Brazil 86; this not only overwhelms Africa (where the numbers are so low they are often not recorded) but also European nations like France (151) and Italy (73) with strong traditions of independent cinema. These figures disrupt simple assumptions that economic development has any direct and unmediated impact upon the production of cultural goods. Hence the argument that cultural development can be assumed to 'mirror' economic development can no longer be seen to apply. The shift in perspectives hinted at by these structural changes has lead Mattelart and Mattelart (1992) to argue for the abandonment of the media imperialism thesis. They argue that while the dimensions of political economy remain important in the production of culture it should be tied to a more specific appreciation of the intersection between different global regions and local conditions. They now argue that while the media imperialism thesis has been historically important in raising the consciousness of those nations outside the rich capitalist club, the theory no longer adequately maps (if indeed it ever did) global communicative relations. Further, the Mattelarts hold that media imperialism always had its weaknesses, in that it consistently failed to account for the cultural relations within 'Third World' states and the uneven distribution of capitalist technology. In order to account for global relations the 'media imperialist' thesis needs to be replaced by a different theoretical paradigm.

More recently Mattelart and Mattelart (1992) point towards the increasing commercialisation and economic penetration of shared public spaces as the most promising contender for the new paradigm. Such arguments have the added advantage of ditching ethnocentric notions of Westernisation and talk instead of a multi-polar commercial culture. The problem for those interested in global political economy is no longer primarily the imposition of cultural homogeneity through Americanisation, but concerns the transformation and privatisation of public spaces in a world economy. These transformations, especially within Europe, have undermined national public service models of media production through processes of deregulation and the need to compete within international markets. From a political economy perspective, globalisation concerns processes of liberalisation, commercialisation, privatisation and internationalisation. The coming together of large media conglomerates and new information technology defines a communication field marked by commercial rather than state regulation (Mosco, 1996).

Whatever the adequacy of these reflections I think the main stumbling block for the media imperialist thesis lies in its economic essentialism. Those who advocate forms of media imperialism like Schiller largely derive their studies from economic dependency theory. The flaw in this argument is that cultural identities and processes are thought to reflect material social structures. For Schiller, if America were the dominant cultural power in the 1960s, this is a direct reflection of its economic standing. Further, if we can demonstrate the global nature of American culture then it is quite proper to assume that the world's peoples are being ideologically indoctrinated by its influence. Hence, Schiller's hermeneutic both misrepresents global economic trends and marginalises other more 'cultural' patterns. For example, Robertson (1992) has pointed towards a growing political and cultural realisation that critical questions related to AIDS, nuclear disasters, and ecological degradation are truly global questions. The rich and powerful are, of course, in a much better position to be able to shield themselves from the negative impacts of such developments, but there remains a sense in which they are *everyone's responsibility*. These dimensions arguably offer a different understanding of the new identities being fostered by processes such as the technological development of the media that cannot be captured by patterns of consumerism alone. Indeed, we might go further, and suggest that the intensification of the capitalist economy has produced both cultural homogeneity as well as cultural difference. For example, in terms of the media of mass communication we can point to the development of niche marketing where consumers are explicitly targeted depending upon lifestyle criteria, income bracket and other information. Yet we can also read this argument in reverse and suggest that the expansion of commodity capitalism into the cultural arena has developed globally recognised products from Coca-Cola to Disneyworld. The point here is that we need not make a choice between homogeneity and difference but learn to understand how they inform one another. Further, we might even point that the image of a single (in this case American) culture over-running the cultures of the globe is fostered by an imagination shaped by colonialism. This is a Eurocentric analysis. Post-colonial theorists question such images in the name of hybridity, multiple identity and diaspora. Popular culture considered along these lines cannot be contained within the frameworks of Americanisation or nationalism. With these features in mind Pieterse and Parekh (1995) have called for the 'decolonisation of the Western imagination'. Often the West is represented in one-dimensional terms such as Americanisation or McDonaldisation. This fails to appreciate both the internal complexity of 'Western' cultures and their relations with other parts of the world. Further, as my own research on the televising of the Rwandan genocide revealed, much popular culture reinforces discursive binary distinctions between the 'civilized' West and the barbarism of the 'Other' (Stevenson, 1999). Like assumptions of blanket media imperialism or Americanisation these discursive constructions serve to mask more complex narratives of exile, cultural entanglement and migration. Media studies has yet to take onboard Edward Said's (1993: 401) comment:

> The fact is, we are mixed in with one another in ways that most national systems of education have not dreamed of. To match knowledge in the arts and sciences with these integrative realities is, I believe, the intellectual and cultural challenge of the moment.

The impact of audience studies and more ethnographic approaches to cultural studies have added new levels of complexity. These studies have discredited simplistic assumptions that the meanings of popular culture can be understood independently of the audience that makes sense of them. In global contexts this argument speaks less of cultural imperialism and more of difference, polysemic meanings and diverse patterns of identification. Yet it would seem that if these reflections are carried to their logical conclusion they would cancel any concern with structural and institutional levels of power and authority. In short, while many of these studies focus attention upon the fluid practices of the audience, they tend to displace a concern with the 'effects' the media might have on the sustenance of collective identity and the impact that a political economy of culture might also have on these levels. If our level of attention is focused upon the different inter-pretations offered of popular programmes our analysis is likely to reveal how different ethnicities, nationalities, genders, age groups and social classes interpret a diversity of media products. Absent is the way that wider structural and institutional changes continue to inform the 'life-world' contexts of the users of mass communication. This points to an understanding of media that rethinks the predominant arguments of neo-Marxists that the economy has causal effects on the levels of cultural identity, and the so-called 'new revisionists' who assume a more radical disjunctive between these different levels. Instead what is being insisted upon here is that the media should be seen in terms of a wider cultural political economy connected to levels of structure, power and identity. That is, despite the emergence of various specialists within media theory and analysis, we need to be open to the possibility of theoretical developments that seek to connect questions of political economy, the semiotic complexity of the audience and new patterns of political engagement. Here we need to look beyond arguments that oppose the cultural meanings generated by ordinary practice of interpretation and the so-called 'harder' features of political economy. Again media theory has much to learn from the post-colonial levels of analysis in this respect. That is we need to find alternative ways of representing the past and present, which are free from monopolizing attitudes and which recognise the diversity of ways in which different cultures and world regions are positioned within a continual intercultural dialogue. The problem with Schiller's defense of media imperialism is that it neither captures the recent developments within the capitalist economy nor the negotiated horizons of political actors. However, as we shall see below, this is precisely the terrain that the recent theoretical innovations of Manuel Castells have sought to capture. Whereas Schiller is content to describe the progressive commodification of media cultures, Castells more specifically focuses upon the interconnections between economy, politics and culture within the information age.

Informationalism, Networks and Social Movements:
Manuel Castells

Manuel Castells (1996, 1997, 1998a) has come the closest of recent writers in opening some of the important political features of contemporary media cultures. Arguably, unlike the perspectives presented this far, Castells outlines a view of contemporary media cultures that both deconstructs the polarities of the earlier discussion while connecting them to processes of substantial social transformation. Castells argues that the emergent 'information society' is primarily born out of the changing relationship between global capitalism, the state and new social movements. However he is equally clear that the development of new media, the diversification of media messages, the implosion of politics and the media, and the development of the politics of 'scandal' have all had far reaching effects upon the public sphere.

Castells argues it is the development of the 'informational economy' that is central to his attempt to rethink the dynamics of post-industrial society. In this new economy it is the application of knowledge and technology in customised production that best ensures economic success. The technological level of the enterprise is a much better guide to its competitiveness than older indices like labour costs (Castells, 1989). The rapid development of informational technology in the 1970s in Silicon Valley, USA enabled capital to restructure itself after the impacts of a worldwide recession. 'Informationalism' has allowed organisations to achieve increased flexibility through more knowledge-dependent and less hierarchical structures. New technology has enabled large structures to co-ordinate their activities world wide, while building in reflexive inputs to both quickly respond to the current state of the market and benefit from economies of scale (Castells and Hall, 1994). Hence whereas industrialism was oriented towards economic growth, informationalism is more concerned with the development of knowledge and the creation of networks. The digitalisation of knowledge bases allows information to be processed and stored across huge distances. Thus capitalism is becoming less dependent upon the state and more upon the ability of a common informational system to transmit knowledge across distanciated networks (Castells, 1996). Within these processes old capitalism (the pursuit of profit) and new capitalism (new information technology and new organizational forms) converge.

The dominance of the flows of capital as opposed to the locality of labour has heightened processes of social exclusion. The new informational economy is characterised through simultaneous processes of economic development and under-development. The 'black holes' of the informational economy include people who are socially and culturally out of communication with mainstream society. While informationalism has lead to the growth of employment within the higher tiers of management there has also been a substantial reduction in low skilled employment and heightened exclusion of the earth's poorer regions from the flows of global capital. These excluded zones (that cannot be mapped onto any simple North/South divide) have responded to such processes by operating 'perverse' forms of inclusion. This has fostered the expansion of illegal and criminal economies within inner city ghettos and the planet's most marginalised economies. This means that capital becomes ever mobile, tourists find different places to visit and the global media move our attention elsewhere. Networks are structured through the dynamic effects of interconnection and disconnection, delivering a global economy that is enhancing processes of economic polarisation both between and within nation-states. At the global level then the network society has produced a world where income differentials between the top 20 per cent and the bottom 20 per cent have leapt from 30 to 1 in 1960 to 78 to 1 in 1994 (Castells, 1998b).

The dominance of the informational economy has many definite cultural effects which are multifarious. Television in particular and the media in general have become central and defining institutions in modern society. Castells illustrates this by pointing to the fact that television currently frames the language and types of symbolic exchange that help define society. Unless a social movement, set of ideas, or commercial product appears on television it may as well not exist. From the advertising jingles we hum on the way to work to our opinions on the government's latest set of social policies, the media frames our sets of common understandings, knowledges and languages. The media then do not so much determine political agendas, but provide the background and context to political and social struggles. The centrality of modern communications in contemporary culture does not deliver a mass culture, but what Castells calls a culture of 'real virtuality'. The idea of a mass culture has now been surpassed by a media environment where messages are explicitly customised to the symbolic languages of the intended audience. The future will not so much be governed by a homogenous mass-produced culture repressing human diversity, but by a diversified popular culture where competitive advantage comes through product differentiation and audience segmentation. For Castells (1996): 'we are not living in a global village, but in customised cottages globally produced and locally distributed'.

The newly emergent information society is characterised by a media culture that is more individuated and less homogenous than before. The culture of 'real virtuality' opens out a world where popular moralities and perceptions opened by soap operas can have as much if not greater impact on modern sensibilities as the moral strictures of politicians. Indeed we can probably think of numerous examples where the 'popular' and the 'political' have become irreversibly intertwined. This might invoke soap opera's raising political questions, the development of so-called infotainment, politicians receiving media training, protests deliberately designed to attract maximum media exposure and the development of the art of media spin doctoring. Taken together these aspects and others speak of a new media and cultural environment that presses the case that unless you are on television then you are not in politics. Here I shall open out two such examples from the many that appear in Castells's three-volume study; they are the politics of scandal and some of the avenues social movements have explored by utilising new media technologies.

Scandal politics develops within the general context of an increasingly televisual society. This has come to the fore against a backdrop where political concerns are frequently played out and reported by the media as a cynical and strategic game. This privileges the presentation of political issues in a fast paced and punchy style, which in turn prioritises the culture of the sound bite. Further, the visualisation and corresponding trivialization of political issues through television gives an added emphasis to the 'personalities' rather than the substantive issues at stake in political debate. Television produces a kind of binary politics where complex positions are boiled down into digestible categories. The personalisation of politics and the decline of ideological contrasts between the major political parties, produces the grounds for the central forms of struggle in the age of 'informational politics'. In an era where distinctions between political parties are increasingly being replaced by more instrumental forms of manoeuvering that seek to interrupt themes and positions previously occupied by opposing political parties, the whiff of scandal can create a sense of political division and untrustworthiness. The fact that major political parties are both involved in expensive forms of image making while being simultaneously chronically under-funded makes them increasingly likely to accept money under the table. Once this form of corruption becomes central to the organisation of mainstream politics then this provides ammunition for journalists and opposing political forces to expose corruption at the highest level. Scandal politics, therefore, becomes a daily threat, if not occurrence.

Although Castells brackets off the analysis here it is not hard to imagine a social movement that seeks to attract support by constructing agendas and political teams that are 'above' scandal. Yet, if Castells is correct, such attempts are likely to prove fruitless. We might even further extend this argument by pointing to the future possible development of a kind of 'scandal fatigue' amongst the electorate. Just as the reporting of distant wars, famines and human rights abuses has arguably fostered compassion fatigue, so scandal fatigue could equally lead to an unshockable form of cynical indifference amongst the vast majority of the population. Scandal fatigue then would open out a situation whereby the public sphere became drained of meaning and politics detached from wider questions of value. At this point Castells's concerns come close to those of Williams and Habermas in respect of the closing down of public space and discourse. These are all evident dangers in contemporary media-saturated societies.

However if Castells retreads familiar themes within critical theory demonstrating how media politics has become detached from ideological positions, these agendas are in turn seemingly interrupted by a variety of social movements from below. Castells (1997) characterises a variety of social movements as developing highly skilful media techniques in fostering largely reactive and defensive responses to economic globalisation. By this he means that the movements under review do not so much articulate a vision of a future emancipated society, but a more conservative attempt to preserve current social identities. For Castells (1997: 69), 'people all over the world resent loss of control over their lives, over their environment, over their jobs, over their economies, over their governments, over their countries, and, ultimately, over the fate of the Earth'. The task then of any oppositional movement must be to connect local experiences to a more global agenda. Defensive reactions to globalisation can be seen in a range of fundamentalist and communalist political movements and cultural struggles the world over. As the democratic state becomes increasingly reduced to an empty shell the new sites of power lie in images and information codes. As Castells (1997: 359) puts it, the 'sites of this power are people's minds'. However given the new vitality given to information and culture in the network society, the mobilisation of peoples through information flows and networks are likely to be short lived. In terms of media politics, today's firmly held principles and beliefs soon become 'tomorrow's fish and chip paper'. This is not so much a question of 'dumbing down', more the informational logic of a new society.

For example, the Zapatistas in Mexico (who Castells describes as the first informational guerrilla movement) made skilful use of image manipulation (video, Internet, etc.) to convert a small local struggle for dignity, democracy and land into a movement that has caught the attention of international public opinion. Indeed the Zapatistas' media connections made it impossible for the Mexican government to use the state apparatus to forcibly repress their movement. This brings out one of the distinctive features of the network society; while the concentration of power and wealth is increasingly distinct from local contexts our collective forms of meaning are more readily to hand. The task of any oppositional movement must be to connect local experiences to a more global agenda, and absolutely crucial in this process is the media of mass communication, given its capacity to shift information through time and space.

Castells argues that new media technology can contribute to the building of networks amongst new social movements. This picture is further complicated elsewhere in discussing who actually uses the Net. Here Castells asserts that new media technologies reinforce existing social structures rather than transforming them. For instance, because access to the Net is dependent upon economic and educational factors it is likely to reinforce the cosmopolitan orientation of social elites, rather than destroying social hierarchies in the way that some commentators had been expecting. New media technologies therefore simultaneously reinforce relations of cultural capital, hierarchy and distinction while enabling social movements to publicise campaigns and connect with distant publics. This creates a fundamental division between social elites, who inhabit the culture of hyper-modernity, and a neo-Luddite tendency amongst the dispossessed where globalisation means job insecurity, crime and poverty. For Castells neither technological enthusiasm nor its opposite is likely to lead to new waves of social and economic development which reverse processes of exclusion.

Castells's concern for the cultural conditions of the public sphere in the informational age offers a more substantive agenda than questions simply linked to the granting of additional rights, describing the dominatory effects of capital upon culture and the tracing through of the 'effects' of technological change. Castells breaks with the view that we can coherently view the development of new media cultures in any straightforward way through the axis of domination or emancipation. Instead Castells's complex reading of modern informational cultures points towards a more nuanced position that views the evolution of media cultures and technologies in a structured field, capable of being transformed by political agency.

The Limitations of Informational Politics

At the time of writing Castells's work on the informational society is one of the most exciting agendas available within media theory. Castells's achievement is in linking together a wide range of evidence and insight that takes contemporary debates in media and communications beyond many of the limitations that have become associated with the existing paradigms in media studies. Whereas post-modern responses are inadequately concerned with the role of powerful media institutions and social questions, Marxist arguments overstate the determining power of the economy, and audience studies often fail to take account of wider social relations. Castells has been able to make a contribution to all of these areas of inquiry. In addition, his theory of informational politics is able to take account of the changing capitalist economy, technological innovation and social movements while bringing the study of media and communication to the centre of his analysis. This is a considerable achievement. However, despite my enthusiasm for Castells's venture, I want to make a number of critical points: (1) the concern that Castells's analysis suffers from a form of technological determinism; (2) the lack of an explicitly normative dimension in this thinking; (3) his analysis of the politics of scandal; and (4) his neglect of more cosmopolitan responses to globalisation.

1. Castells has attracted the attention of numerous critics who argue that the evidence for the economic impacts of new technology is not as pronounced as he

argues, and that his theory of informationalism is overly determined by technology. Both Webster (1995) and Garnham (2000) have criticised Castells in these terms. Their argument seems to be that Castells's analysis is overly concentrated upon changes in information technology , which then causes changes within the economy, politics and culture. Yet as Downey (2000) argues, Castells would probably respond that while he spends much of his time tracing through the implications of technological factors, his three-volume study actually points to the interconnections between the development of information technology, the diminishing power (if not influence) of the state, and the role of social movements. Indeed, while there is evidence of the shaping power of technology within Castells's writing, his emphasis upon the agency of social movements means that these criticisms are currently somewhat wide of the mark. Indeed perhaps Castells's key insight is not the impact of technology upon society, but the way that information technology has helped foster certain economic and social networks that have radically reconstructed the dominant features of economics, politics and culture. For example, viewed in terms of theories of cultural imperialism like those advanced by Schiller, Castells is arguing that globalisation is not Americanisation or straightforward commodification, but the development of interconnected networks. As John Urry (2000) argues ideas of cultural imperialism suppose that one larger world region is coming to replace less powerful places, whereas networks tend to emphasise interconnections and disconnections from a circuit. These features actually change the nature of social and cultural power within society where cultural features, symbols and images lose their connection to specific spaces and places. More important than the 'origin' of cultural icons and symbols is the way they are used to sustain, disrupt or call into question networks of social power. The point about the Internet in Castells's analysis is that it is mutually constituted through the power of global media conglomerates, its technological capacities, the flow of information and symbols that are largely beyond the capacity of states to regulate, and that it has become the organising centre for those who seek to resist global capitalism. As Castells points out, such an analysis takes us beyond the certitudes of either cultural or technological imperialism. The metaphor of the network helps us understand processes of cultural exclusion and disconnection in ways that are not available through ideas of media imperialism. Rather than a politics which protests against the homogenising effects of American culture, informational politics is attuned to a multi-polar world where the cultures of capital, the political establishment and social movements all compete for attention in a variety of popular and informational frameworks.

2. By viewing Castells in terms of the tradition of critical theory we might argue that he takes a less 'pessimistic turn' than is evident in Habermas and the early Frankfurt school.[1] What Castells most clearly provides is a social and historical understanding of the emergence of the 'information society'. Like Adorno

and Horkheimer's account of the culture industry and Habermas's notion of the public sphere, the 'informational society' opens out a new critical paradigm. Yet if one of the main agendas of critical theory is present another is absent. Missing from Castells's account is a more overtly normative analysis that would provide us with a critical standpoint from which to evaluate social change. In answer to this charge I think Castells would make two responses. The first is that implicit in much of what he says, there is an agenda that seeks to map out the possibilities for democracy and social justice. Secondly, that it is not for 'experts' like him to hand down blueprints for social change; the history of actually existed socialism has surely put paid to the desirability (or even feasibility) of getting social reality to conform to the wishes of the intellectual vanguard. Such reasons arguably cut critical theory off from the connections between media and democracy my book has at its core. To put the point bluntly: if it is worth arguing that the public sphere is becoming increasingly infected by a form of cynical reason and 'show' politics it is also worth making some broad suggestions on how we might begin to construct an alternative. Further, if the media is becoming increasingly central to the self-definition of democratic societies then radical change will only come through citizens increasing their involvement and participation within wider media cultures. The question as to how democratic societies help foster public involvement as opposed to private withdrawal, communicative concerns as opposed to instrumental strategies and publicly engaged pluralistic identities as opposed to passively construed cultures is central to the concerns of critical theory. In doing this we should indeed avoid adopting the legislative ambitions of the expert, while also side stepping thinking that fails to open new critical possibilities. It is not that Castells believes that the world could not be otherwise, but that he misses the implications a moral and ethical agenda could have for media and culture. If Castells opens out a more complex view of the media's position in modern society than was evident in the other perspectives under review, he also fails to develop a more normative response to the need to democratise media cultures

3. One of the many distinctive features of Castells's argument is his concentration upon questions of scandal in the context of the personalisation of media politics. Despite the strong features of his analysis, I think his account can be seen as misleading in a number of respects. That is despite the emphasis Castells places upon the politics of scandal, I think his reading is overwhelmingly one-sided in the context of a sociological understanding of contemporary media. Firstly, as is commonly understood, scandal involves the transgression of common norms and values. In Castells's terms there is a structural tendency towards a politics of scandal due to the common mediation of politics and the funding crisis of post-ideological political parties. Hence the politics of scandal becomes a central feature of the information age. Yet if we think for a moment, Castells's viewpoint poorly accounts for the sheer diversity of scandals (particularly those which involve sex)

that have come to dominate our media cultures. In this respect, J.B.Thompson (1997) argues that the social production of scandal has a deep connection with new forms of visibility that have accompanied the development of media cultures since the late nineteenth century. Before the arrival of the media an event was only public if it was staged before a number of individuals who were physically present. Increasingly with the development of eletronic media the publicness of actions is no longer tied to particular locations but depend upon their visibility within the media. This presents politicians and other public figures with new opportunities to communicate with distant others, but also with a number of risks. In a television age, politicians are obliged to concern themselves with the attempts to manage their self-presentation. In short, public figures are constantly open to the threat of scandal through the media as it is impossible to completely control their visibility in modern media cultures. Mediated scandals, which have gripped public figures from Richard Nixon to Prince Charles, and from Michael Jackson to George Michael, are all connected to the transgression of moral vocabularies and the new forms of visibility imposed upon public figures. These processes, we might add, gain new forms of intensification in a television culture that can replay incriminating material and contradictory evidence over and over again, fixing certain impressions in the minds of the public. This analysis then argues that scandal is more the product of televisual visibility than the underfunding of political parties or the simplification of political debate.

We might also add that we can read the processes of scandal in a more ambivalent way than is evident within Castells. For example, the media's ability to make private life public opens a number of complex ethical and political questions. From soap operas to talk shows the media have become increasingly caught up within complex cycles of mediation that bring the 'private' into the 'public' (van Zonnen, 1998). The lives of celebrities and politicians have to operate in public cultures whereby their private lives are increasingly scrutinised by the public media. It is however far too sweeping simply to link these features, in the way that Castells does, to the trivialisation of politics. Within his argument the more the media becomes concerned with the 'private lives' of media celebrities and politicians the more market driven and superficial our common cultures become. Such a view ignores evidence that stories of scandal can often lead to the dramatization of public morals (Bird, 1997). Stories related to sexual scandal can also be connected to gendered dimensions, discussions of masculinity and sexuality, and debates about personal ethics more generally. The rise of scandal politics, rather than being dismissed as progressively undermining a substantial public sphere, needs to be linked into a consideration of new forms of public visibility and the politicisation and transformation of the private sphere within modernity.

4. Castells, as we have seen, poses some difficult questions for those seeking to promote a cosmopolitan agenda. How do we ensure that cosmopolitan

orientations are spread more widely within society? Is it the case that those of a cosmopolitan orientation are most likely to be found amongst elites, within global cities and in fields such as education? How might more cosmopolitan dispositions become an ordinary part of everyday life? These questions are particularly pressing given the emphasis Castells places upon social movements as 'reactions' to globalisation. Yet in connection to these agendas we might criticise Castells for not being concerned enough to connect global dimensions to a cosmopolitan defence of human rights and cultural difference (Beck, 1992, 1998). We could argue within this framework that there is evidence of globally interconnected social movements that are not merely reactions to globalisation. Within this argument new media are not used specifically to defend territory against threatening forces from above. In this respect, it could be argued that those who seek to defend human rights, ecological sustainability and the recently published struggles of workers within sweatshops making fashionable garments all point towards the possibility of an emergent cosmopolitan agenda. The development of what we might term 'responsible globalisation' seeks to ask how the interconnections of global society might promote the interests of sustainability, justice and democracy. We shall see later, in our discussion of cyberfeminism, the potential beginnings of such a social movement.

Virilio, Speed and Communication

Despite Castells's arguments on the possibilities and exclusions of the information age many have chosen to view the arrival of a technological society through a more negative optic. Here the development of the on-line economy, instantaneous public opinion and a culture of sensation has robbed human-beings of the capacity for critique. In this understanding, it is not so much commodification that is the danger, but the triumph of technological reason. These much more pessimistic reflections have recently been refined within the work of French theorist Paul Virilio. Yet rather than concentrating upon the disappearance of modernity, Virilio has argued that its hyper-development has delivered an inhuman culture which is pushing global society ever closer to catastrophe. Hence whereas Castells explores the ambivalent possibilities of the new age, Virilio's work is better read as a rejection of the positive spin many have sought to place upon the mutual development of globalisation and technological change.

As we saw in Chapter 4, the temporal dimensions of media cultures have strong connections to processes of globalisation. For instance, in the mid-eighteenth century it used to take letters approximately forty days to cross from Europe to the United States. Today through the intervention of telephones, worldwide web and live broadcasts we have entered the age of instantaneous and immediate communication. The experience of what Giddens (1990) has called 'time-space' compression has meant that the increasingly 'event' driven nature of media reporting has become exaggerated in correspondence with its global spread. In this respect, some critics of media cultures have sought to emphasise the cosmopolitan nature of new media cultures. With the arrival of the Internet, mobile phones and muti-channel television cultures, the shifting of images and perspectives have invited the prospect of a more genuinely global as well as local sets of concerns. The media's ability to move texts and images through time and space opens the possibility of what J.B.Thompson (1995) has described as 'intimacy at a distance'. The audience's relation to media personalities is different from those with persons who are co-present. A non-reciprocal relationship of intimacy depends upon the scrutiny of the celebrity or news event by the audience and not the other way round. For many the media's capacity to enhance *connexity* holds out the possibility of enhancing surface forms of cosmopolitanism. That is, the globalisation of the media means that we are likely to become more tolerant of the 'Other', or that our capacity for reflexivity will become enhanced, or even finally that such developments will help foster a society of 'clever' people who are no longer bound by local geographies (Mulgan, 1997; Giddens, 1994; Urry, 2000). The problem with such projections from the perspective of Paul Virilio is that they are overwhelmingly optimistic. For Virilio such projections, and others, are part of an overwhelming positive reaction that media, and especially new media technologies, have received within the academy more generally. Virilio (1999: 12) argues 'it is necessary to determine what is negative in what seems positive. We know that we can only advance in technology by recognising its specific accident, its specific negativity.'

For Virilio the problem with those who seek to emphasise the positive aspects of new media is that it tends to lead to a concern for others who are distant, over those who are our immediate neighbours. Indeed Virilio has argued over a number of publications that the impact of new technologies of communication on the human senses is overwhelmingly negative. The 'real time' of modern media communications has fundamentally altered and distorted our shared conception of reality. Here Virilio makes some important links between technology and communications, war and speed. Within these co-ordinates virtual reality and the Internet are not completely new forms of communication, but the exaggeration of key aspects of modernity and the dominance of a form of technological fundamentalism. In this respect, John Armitage's (2000a) recent description of Virilio as a hyper-modernist seems accurate. That is for Virilio the emergence of new media of communication have distorted our conceptions of the 'real' while building upon the destructive developmental logic of modernity. Critical of Marxism, postmodernism and other conceptual approaches that have made an impact in the study of media cultures, Virilio describes himself as an urbanist. By this he argues for a regenerated politics of the city that tries to reconnect people with their immediate neigbours, themselves and nature. Virilio (1999: 48) argues that 'the main question is to regain contact'. We do this by recovering the practice of social intercourse, the conditions for an inclusive communal life, and as we shall see, most crucially of all, a livable temporality. Virilio in common with the cosmopolitan theorists mentioned above also wants to create a space for the 'Other' in democratic deliberation. Yet we can only achieve this in relations of co-presence, not by following debates over the television or by mailing discussion groups on the Net. New and old media in this respect are actually bound up with a set of harmful fantasies that would argue that we can escape from the fragility of the human body, our dependence upon nature and the more immediate sets of social relations in the communities in which we live.

In this respect, Virilio's writing, despite his arguments to the contrary, displays a connection to much of the dystopian commentary that has become connected to the rise of the Internet. For example, some critics have pointed out that new technologies promise to deliver us from a world beyond the constraints and frustrations of the material world and physical body. That is, according to Robins (1997), new media technology is invested in omnipotent fantasies and feelings. In the promise of **cyborg** relations, which melt the distinctions between humans and technology, what is being offered is the 'thrill of escape'. In the new media universe we are invited to choose new disguises and assume new identities, thereby distancing ourselves from 'real' human relations. The capacity of technology to magically solve human predicaments potentially offers us a 'magical' solution to the problems of self and community. The Net can both promote the warm feelings of community while we are being atomized. In cyberspace we become blind to questions of difference as we only encounter the privileged, retreat from the brutal realities of late capitalism, and avoid the burden of geography. On-line there are few real surprises and little that is unfamiliar. Rather than dealing with the otherness of the Other, cyberspace is based on the governance of corporate capitalism (Robins and Webster, 1999).

For Virilio, politics has been taken away from the people and is increasingly determined by the military, the state and technology. This has lead to a decline in meaningful public forms of participation and the increasing power and scope of social elites. The increasing speed of the transport of people, images and perspectives within modernity has all been driven by the need to dominate and control a territory with as few obstacles as possible. The power of modern warfare is actually dependent upon the development of new forms of information technology. As Virilio (1998:24) writes 'to possess the earth, to hold terrain, is also to possess the best means to scan it in order to protect and defend it'.

The main driving force behind technological developments connecting the rise of photography, television and the Internet has been determined by the military's requirements for more extensive wars. This has involved a shift in political boundaries from the localised politics of the city to a global geo-politics of domination and conquest. It is then the requirements of war rather than democracy that is best served by the emphasis upon speed and efficiency. For example, in Virilio's (1989) *War and Cinema* he points to cultural connections between the development of cinematic techniques and warfare. In the 1914–18 war cameras were used to take motion and still pictures from airplanes to help decide military tactics. Later, after the Second World War, spy satellites and other technologies were used as a means of military intelligence with weapons systems being systematically trained upon visible targets. This connects the desire to make subjects and objects visible with the need to destroy them as the enemy. However if new technologies of communication actually make the enemy more visible they also reduce their physical presence. Cinema helped convert war into a visible spectacle, films were deliberately made as forms of war propaganda, while 'honey tongued' announcers managed to blur the destruction of the bombers by developing personal relations with members of the crew (Virilio, 1989: 24). There was then no bombing without photographs and no mass destruction without cameras. Within this configuration the human eye, the camera and the bomb all become weapons of war.

The invention of cameras and photographs actually entails a reduction in the field of vision. For example, at one point Virilio compares the art of the painter Rodin to the visual effects produced by photographic images. Whereas a photograph freezes the image in time the work of art could seek to capture the complex temporality of motion. Electronic images do not bring the subject any closer to the world, but obscure the phenomenology of a complex field of vision. For Virilio (1994:13) the fusion of the eye and the camera leads to the human gaze becoming more fixed and predictable. Within this Virilio (1994:13) detects a totalitarian ambition within visual technology that he calls 'omnivoyance'. This term is linked to the desire to repress the complex negotiations of the human subject and replace them with normalising vision machines. The vision machine's evolution begins with the camera and ends with video equipment that places the public under constant surveillance. The development of computerised vision machines have finally dispensed with the human senses given that they are fully operated by machines. Virilio (1994:14) further explores the reduction in the complexity of the visual field through what he describes as the 'phatic image'. The phatic image is a definite image that has the ability to hold the gaze of the viewer. This is produced through visual technologies' ability to be able to illuminate, intensify and single out specific features of an image. Virilio argues that we can see the phatic image in Chaplin's silhouette or in the red lips of Marilyn Monroe. Virilio's point here is not only the power of the image which can be seen in everything from advertising to contemporary cinema, but the emphasis which is placed on the specificity of the image to the detriment of the surrounding context. It is as if when one scrutinises the image that the 'context mostly disappears into a blur' (Virilio, 1994: 14).

Hence what Virilio (2000a: 57) calls the 'industrialisation of vision' has not so much added new realities, but has displaced our sensitivity towards different temporalities and visual ambivalences within modernity. This has produced a 'dyslexic version of reality' (Virilio, 1995: 72). The real-time of television has come to dominate our shared definitions of reality. The showing of events 'as they happen' has meant that a society of images and spectacles has come to replace public forms of dialogue. Whereas the press, in France, were originally both read and talked about in the 'galleries of the cloitre des Cordeliers' (Virilio, 1995: 37), as the media became constituted through speed and technology it became displaced. As we shall see, 'with real-time technologies, real presence bites the dust' (Virilio, 1995: 57).

The speed of modern communications in this regard has a number of consequences. Firstly, speed destroys thought and the possibility of democratic deliberation. Ideas concerning the possibility of using technology to enhance democracy are mistaken. Speed technology produces a culture where communications are used to condition the responses of the public (Virilio, 2000b: 109). Secondly, the global spread of information and computer technology introduces the possibility of the 'terminal citizen'. By destroying temporal relationships between near and far, human beings become more concerned with the reality of the screen than the actual physical proximity of their more immediate personal and communal relationships. In this society becomes divided between two distinct temporalities which Virilio (1997:71) describes as the absolute and the relative. The radical divide is between those who live in 'real time', whose economic, political and cultural activities are driven by speed, and those who become ever more destitute while living in 'real' spaces. For the 'terminal citizen' virtual reality, an event-driven media and the frantic mobility of information has not come to supplement 'reality' but to replace it. Thirdly, the paradox of the information society is that it is simultaneously leading to an increase in virtual mobility and physical inertia. That is the 'terminal citizen' does not have to actually move about as technology is increasingly modeled to fit the contours of the human body. The new interactive space that is facilitated by the Internet, television and virtual reality means that the home becomes a cockpit that receives the world without the occupant having to move. We are then not so much in the age of mobility as the age of paralysis. This induces the subject into a 'vegetative state' or culturally induced coma, where the search is not so much for the possibility of public action, but the 'intensiveness of sensations' (Virilio, 2000a: 69). Fourthly, the speeding up of 'reality' in real time has an individualizing effect whereby information becomes increasingly focused in on the self. This process, coupled with the replacement of reality, means that we actually pay less and less attention to our ecological landscapes that support all life forms. The collapse of space then turns us inwards away from the world and into the increasingly simulated world of new technology, fun and cyber-fantasies. The televisualisation of reality does not so much deliver a cosmopolis but an **ominopolis**. This enhances the possibility of a global accident that could destroy large sections of humanity. As we become distanced from our own natural-ness and vulnerability the possibility of global catastrophes through economic collapse, nuclear war or the spread of viruses come ever closer. Technological imperialism pushes us closer to disaster while robbing our common human senses of the ecological sensitivity necessary to resist such changes.

Fifthly, the global spread of 'real time' technologies increases the possibility of a new phase of totalitarianism by putting us under constant forms of surveillance. These new forms of danger and control can be detected in the seemingly innocent practice of setting up live Internet broadcasts from the home to the recent war in Kosovo. Live cams set up on the Internet from people's kitchens and bedrooms are not about information or entertainment, but the exposure and invasion of the individual. The constant monitoring of human activity now takes place on a global basis and makes us all constantly visible, imposing upon us a 'technological vigil' (Virilio, 2000b: 62). The spread of new technologies of surveillance, from mobile phones (which abolish the distinction between public and private for employees) to the orbital surveillance of enemy territories, subjects us all to global forms of control. Control, as demonstrated by the war in Kosovo, is now not so much a function of state sovereignty, but the capacity to determine who occupies air and space. This enhances the possibility of global powers (like the United States) launching an information war through the presence of satellites (monitoring population movements) and live broadcasts providing citizens with disinformation. This control is also linked to the ability to pollute information exchange through disinformation. By disinformation Virilio (2000c) does not mean the control of information through shortage and distortion. In the Kosovo war disinformation was more the product of over information. That is the constant 24-hour supply of television news does not so much divide opinion as confuse it with contradictory data. Finally, the modernity of technology, having colonised public space, has the ability to invade the intimate regions of the human body. The development of genetic engineering and technological transplants into the body increases the possibility of the human body and psyche being fashioned by the needs of technology. By this Virilio fears that the biorhythms of the human body will soon be speeded up to match the temporalities of a technologised everyday life. The postmodern subject's craving for 'surplus excitement' will end in the abolition of distinctions between the inside and the outside of the human body. Virilio's warning here seems to be that once technoscience has penetrated the human body, altering the senses and physical being of the subject, then this will also lead to the annihilation of the possibility of critique.

Virilio and the Media of Mass Communications

Virilio's main contribution to contemporary debates in respect of the media of mass communication has been to add a sceptical voice in respect of technological innovation, and to focus our attention on the temporal dimensions of communications systems. However, as we shall see, while a critical engagement with Virilio is undoubtedly worthwhile, his contributions have a number of limitations. Virilio's writing is perhaps best read as a warning as to where technological change might lead rather than as offering a balanced account of the effects of technological development. Here I want to concentrate upon the suggestive comments he makes linking technology, speed and cultural impoverishment. Finally, I will end the discussion of Virilio by making some further critical comments concerning what I take to be the main limitations of his analysis.

Technology, as Virilio points out, is intimately concerned with speed and efficiency. The quickening of the time allowed for opinion formation can often lead to the production of superficial perspectives in place of those which could have taken a deeper and more substantial view. We might then be in a position to receive more information more quickly than ever before, but denied the interpretative opportunities to make the world more meaningful. For example, the increased speeding up of events interferes with our capacity to feel empathy and disappointment. The media it seems are always moving on, restlessly searching for fresh news and different viewpoints. This makes the achievement of responsible and meaningful forms of reflection increasingly difficult in the modern age. Yet it is a mistake to proceed as if the media only colonise society's shared capacity to construct meaningful relations with others. For instance, the culture of immediacy and speed can also feed the idea that we the nation, or international alliance, in a time of crisis, ought to do something. This can be invaluable if we are considering offering immediate humanitarian aid to the victims of a disaster, but can also have other perhaps more negative consequences, given that speed can be used to displace the necessary labour of democratic deliberation. The rapidity with which these decisions are made might mean that a wide-ranging public discussion has not yet taken place and that not enough 'quality' information has been made available to make a judgement. I am struck by a basic ambivalence between the need to receive information quickly and the consequences this might have for human reasoning. The wider point is that the temporal bias introduced by media cultures disrupts our capacity for critical reflection as well as providing a necessary service and influence on contemporary political culture. The issue here is to hold an intellectual concern regarding the lack of slowness in our culture against an appreciation of the 'political' necessity of speeding up information exchange.

So far I have treated Virilio's writing to only the most sympathetic forms of engagement. I have sought to argue that Virilio's work does indeed offer the supportive critic with the possibility of raising some key questions in respect of the temporal dimensions of contemporary media cultures. However we also need to recognise that Virilio's current projections are severely limited. Here I will mention four reasons as to why Virilio's work is unlikely to develop a productive cannon of research in respect of the media of mass communication. Virilio's limitations are: (1) his technophobia; (2) his neglect of the political possibilities offered by media cultures new and old; (3) his lack of analysis of the inter-connections between new media and identity; and (4) his failure to appreciate the ways in which new media is structured in a contested cultural field. I shall however keep these arguments brief as they have been approached in more detail elsewhere in the volume.

1. The most obvious limitation of Virilio's approach is his pronounced techno-phobia. To give one example amongst the many available in his work. The development of what Virilio calls a political economy of speed is such that at times he sounds as though the only way of resisting the totalitarian ambitions of technology is through technological abstinence. The political trajectory of such a position is both conservative and reactionary. Unlike say Castells, Virilio's politics and social theory fail to appreciate the ways in which contemporary society and culture has been unalterably transformed by the impact of new technology. There is then a lingering sense within Virilio's writing of a possible return to a society with low levels of technological development. While such views may indeed form part of a resistance to certain features of contemporary media and social devel-opment, they can hardly be expected to generate a sustainable political perspective working within the contradictions and ambivalences of the present. Indeed Virilio's position on the information society often comes close to the neo-Luddism described by Castells (1998b). Within this Virilio misses the opportunity to think more constructively as to how new technologies might become utilised by inclusive forms of social development. That is, if a globally sustainable planetary economy is to become possible it will be built through the new information technologies, not their abolition. The main problem here being that Virilio offers an excessively one-sided view of technology which 'substitutes moralising critique for social analysis and political action' (Kellner, 2000).

2. The development of the media of mass communications has gradually seen the decline of print as the dominant form of communication and the rise of an audio-visual domain. Virilio links the visualisation of the media into narratives of decline where our perceptions of reality are progressively undermined by a speed culture. As I have indicated, Virilio tends to see progressive political possibilities in reversing this process, with human populations better able to make contact with others through face-to-face communication and print cultures. While there is much that could be said on the superficiality of much visual culture and its

progressive underming of literate cultures, such an analysis is too sweeping. The popularisation of the media, which has accompanied the rise of television and its increasingly visual nature of media cultures, has also made public cultures and associated debates open to a greater number of people. While the visualisation of media cultures can indeed be linked into narratives of control and surveillance in the way that Virilio suggests, it can equally be connected into a progressive democratisation of everyday life. The visual bias of much media and communication provides social movements with considerable opportunities to interrupt the flow of dominant media messages, by staging dramatic media events and engaging in image manipulation. We can make a similar argument in respect of the development of the Net. As Dahlgren (2001) has argued the partial displacement of hierarchical forms of information that the Net makes available confuses the boundaries between who is and who is not a journalist. While these arguments have been carried too far by some Net enthusiasts the possibilities that 'ordinary' people have for constructing their own sites of images, information and discourse is greatly enhanced by the arrival of new media. Seemingly these and other democratic possibilities are missed by a critique which offers an overly one-sided view of new media technologies.

3. Virilio, as I have indicated, seeks to make a positive virtue out of his pessimistic reflections on new media. His argument positions him firmly against those who would argue in favour of the potentially liberating promise of the web. However Mark Poster (1995, 1996, 1997) argues that such reflections actually spell the inability of critical theory to understand the significance of new media. That is, critical theory is overwhelmingly concerned with whether or not the media limit or foster autonomous social relations, rather than investigating the ways in which media might constitute new subject positions. For Poster (1995:24) what is at stake is not the way new media help foster domination or resistance, but 'a broad and extensive change in the culture, in the way identities are structured'. That is virtual reality helps evoke new possibilities for the imagination given its emphasis upon play, simulation and discovery. The enthusiasm for the Net, then, is not an escape from reality, but from the dominant codes of modernity which sought to articulate a view of the subject as autonomous and rational. Within virtual communities subjects are able to explore the boundaries of different identity formations while pleasurably entering into previously unexplored imaginary worlds. It is new media's relatively decentralised structure that potentially turns everyone into a producer and a consumer of information that constitutes subjects as multiple and unstable. These possibilities dispense with the opposition between a 'real' and 'fictitious' community and enable participants to express themselves without the usual visual clues and markers. Such a situation encourages the proliferation of local narratives, the experience of different realities and a diversity of knowledges. Again if it is the unfixing of subject positions that excites Poster it is the escape from reality that seems to bother Virilio. The problem being that such is the strength

of Virilio's repudiation of new media he leaves unexplored the positions of those who have become its most enthusiastic advocates. Notable here is Virilio's dismissal of cyberfeminism. The limitations of this particular mixture of theoretical and political concerns aside, Virilio argues that cyberfeminism is a dead-end, given that it seems to celebrate 'the replacement of emotions by electrical impulses' (Armitage, 2000b: 51). What is notable here is Virilio's resistance to the idea that cybercultures could impact upon modern identity formations in ways which are not always reducible to humans being invaded by the destructive logics of technology. Such a position, then, fails to engage with the more ambivalent and more culturally complex features of identity politics in respect of the Net.

4. Finally, missing from Virilio's argument is an account of the way in which new media may become linked into the contestation of cultural identity. Virilio's analysis offers a picture of human subjectivity increasingly limited and crippled by the impact of technology. Here there is a strong family resemblance between Virilio and a host of cultural critics who argue that humanistic sensibilities are currently under attack by a technologically determined present (Roszak, 1986). Such perspectives offer specific narratives of decline, where more 'authentic' cultures are gradually replaced by technologically induced sensibilities. The development of what Postman (1993) calls a technopoly is ushered into place when common cultures are progressively shaped by the requirements of technology. A technopoly displaces questions of cultural value and quality by championing efficiency, objective measurement and quantity. Virilio's radicalness comes in taking these arguments further by suggesting such is technology's dominance over culture that it is actually pushing global societies ever closer to their own destruction. Without wishing to dismiss these perspectives out of hand, such viewpoints have a conservative bent and often underestimate the extent to which popular cultures are capable of sustaining a diverse range of tastes and sensibilities. Indeed, if we follow these critical points we might ask what is the social basis for technophobia? Andrew Ross (1994) argues that technophobia amongst intellectuals and experts can be connected to a fear that the development of technology will erode their traditional status and store of cultural capital. This fear (which is not without basis) is that the knowledge economy requires the creation of an obedient, instrumental and efficient knowledge class. While these are important considerations, Virilio does not demonstrate sufficient reflexivity in attempting to position his analysis within a wider social field. Put differently, we might argue that because Virilio fails to consider how his concerns can be linked to a traditional knowledge class, he thereby neglects to analyse different identity formations to his own.

Here we might follow Stuart Hall (1996) in arguing that contemporary cultural identities are increasingly multiple and diverse. Identities are constituted by different discourses, languages and histories and are not the 'effect' of technologies. In other words, Virilio's 'reading' of the effect of the penetration of information technology cannot adequately take account of a diversity of contested cultures and subject positions. Within this we might emphasise, along with Castells (see above) and Melucci (1996), that power within modern society is exercised through the production and exchange of symbols and not the erosion of human reality by technology. The establishment of master codes and symbols within global flows of information are increasingly likely to be contested in a diversity of spaces and places. Inevitably this means that the introduction of information technology opens the possibility for new forms of information that challenge, reinforce and contest the organisation of our understanding of the main features of human life, from questions of sexuality to global poverty. These perspectives invariably introduce both an awareness that modernity remains constituted through powerful centres of information and symbolic provision, and that such codes are increasingly drawn upon in a diversity of social and cultural contexts. The problem here is that Virilio fails to investigate the contestation of identities and codes, preferring to emphasise the 'brute' effects of technology.

Critical Questions within Cyberfeminism

We have entered into an informational and technological society from which there is no exit. This is not to say that individuals and collectives continue to dream about less complex social relations, but that the impact of science and technology has irretrievably changed our common worlds. These new social relations cannot be dismissed as technological determinism as they have opened out dominant social imaginaries, fantasies and projections whereby science has helped blur the distinction between reality and fiction. What once seemed to be the common culture of science fiction magazines is fast becoming normality. The ability to genetically modify humans, animals and plants, the development of intelligent machines and robots and worldwide instantaneous communication are radically altering what we take to be the 'real world'. The radical agenda that has become associated with cyberfeminism has sought to both positively and critically respond to these changes. Cyberfeminism has sought to bring our attention to the ways in which cultural narratives about technology have limited the material practices and cultural imaginations of men and women. The transformation from a humanist to a post-humanist world involves the deconstruction of assumptions that wish to mourn the passing of a technologically underdeveloped literary culture. In this reading, the technological is not the opposite of human values, but rather should be viewed as intermingled and co-extensive with the human. With the development of new media, cyberfeminists have taken the opportunity to deconstruct cultural understandings which position masculinity with technology and feminity with nature. Cyberfeminism has sought to redefine new media by seeking opportunities to criticise the exclusion and oppression of women, while simultaneously exploring the fantasies and cultural frameworks within which we commonly make sense of technology. This has involved a dual strategy of seeking to promote the equal access of women while redefining notions of technology which gives space to play, imagination and the feminine.[2]

It is in this context that Donna Haraway (1991, 1997, 2000) created the myth of the cyborg. As Haraway (1991: 154) puts it 'a cyborg world is about lived social and bodily realities in which people are not afraid of their joint kinship with animals and machines, not afraid of permanently partial identities and contradictory standpoints'. The myth of the cyborg is created out of the fictions, imaginations and discursive realities that have helped construct a world of domination and transgression where science is simultaneously reaffirming relations of oppression and calling into question binaries between culture and nature. The cyborg as a matter of science fiction and lived experience takes 'pleasure in the confusion of boundaries and responsibility in their construction' (Haraway, 1991: 150). The story of modernity that promised increasing domination and control over nature has been breached by the mixing of humans and non-humans. In this the boundaries between humans, animals and technology have become increasingly blurred and discredited. We are no longer as certain as to what counts as machine, human or animal. This means that our identities are currently constructed out of a number of differences which defies essentialist attempts to reconstruct boundaries that have begun to implode. The idea of the cyborg is intended to engage in a form of politics that is both more appropriate to an information society, while providing a critical analysis of webs of power which simultaneously delights in the ironies and complexities of transgression. In this respect, our politics needs to form a complex understanding of a range of inter-related organisms which are biologically, technologically and culturally constituted. For Haraway the feminist imagination should seek an ethical response to the ways in which technoscience operates in terms of global forms of power and the emergence of ambivalent zones between culture and nature. This does not involve an uncritical celebration of all things cyber or an ideological rejection of the operation of science, but the critical exploration of ambivalent possibilities and transformations. The research stimulated by Haraway's projections seeks to uncover the ways in which science, nature and culture have become progressively intermeshed in ways that destabilise a number of previously assumed oppositions. However, rather than follow Virilio, and portray the ways in which the 'human' has been invaded by the technical, the myth of the cyborg seeks to map the enculturation of nature and technology. Cyborgs deconstruct the hierarchy of humanity, technology and nature, unravelling the ways in which we construct our relations with beings both technical and organic.

This research agenda has provided feminists with a number of opportunities when it comes to rethinking their relation to new media. The argument was that earlier versions of feminism tended to view technology as intrinsically linked to social relations of oppression. These waves of theorising are often viewed by more contemporary theorists as positing an essential feminine identity against the ways in which women were exploited and controlled by modern technology (Wilding, 2001). However the metaphor of the cyborg offered opportunities to deconstruct technology and rethink it in respect of relations of domination and the possibilities of transgression. The attempt was to reconstruct feminisms in order to capture the role that technology plays within the formation of identity, domination and, of course, empowerment (Albright, 2001). These observations have, as we have already seen, arrived in a society that is currently going through a number of social changes in respect of technological development and globalisation. To such transformations we also need to add the third major shift of our time, which is the decline of the role of tradition in the definition of gendered and sexual identities. The increasing visibility of a diverse range of sexualities, the break up of the nuclear family, the impact of feminism, the increasing numbers of women in the job market and other factors have all sought to transform the role of women within contemporary society. The crisis of modernity which is largely the outcome of technological change, globalisation and gender quake is for cyberfeminism more a matter of possibility than loss and decline (Braidotti, 2001). In terms of the politics of identity cyberfemism takes its lead from theoretical developments which have sought to develop a critical practice by interrupting the dominant ways in which technology and feminity have become encoded within modernity. Through the subversion of the dominant codes which have sought to construct women as 'essentially' caring, nurturing and submissive, and technology as hierarchical, controlling and exclusive, cyberfeminism has sought to explore other possibilities.

Sadie Plant (1996, 1997) argues that whereas the first computers were designed by the military their commodification has opened them to different uses. The emergence of web-like connections amongst the users of new communication technologies has paved the way for the Net 'as an anarchic, self-organising, system into which its users fuse' (Plant, 1996: 174). Computers then allow for the emergence of autonomous, interconnected communities without a governing core. In this version of the network society, the development of connectivist communities hold out the possibility of a less patriarcally determined culture. While most commercial and state organizations remain hierarchically structured the Net fosters a less masculinist culture. Here Plant points out that the practice and the metaphor of 'weaving' best captures the pioneering spirit of the web. The weaving of links between different communities and individuals introduces a network culture that is both hostile to traditional forms of masculinity, while allowing women the possibility of experimenting with their identity. It is not that the practice of weaving offers the possibility of an authentic feminity, but more that it builds upon traditional feminine practices while offering the possibility of rethinking shared identities. Plant (1996: 181–2) summarises that 'cyberspace is out of men's control: virtual reality destroys his identity, digitalization is mapping his soul and, at the peak of his triumph, the culmination of his machinic erections, man confronts the system he built for his own protection and finds it is female and dangerous'.

However, such statements have been the cause of a considerable amount of debate and discussion within cyberfeminism. Wakeford (2001) has argued that despite the arguments that the Internet is 'female friendly', women often experience cyberspace as a form of male territory. This is largely because women continue to be a minority of Internet users, and marginalised due to the cultural dominance of masculinity on line. She argues that while the metaphor of weaving is useful, it is best utilised as a discursive strategy which suggests new and different meanings that can be potentially generated out of Net culture, and not the expression of an 'essential' link between women and the web. Similarly, Squires (1996) argues that within Haraway's writing the idea of the cyborg undoubtedly offers new opportunities for feminists to explore the contradictory sets of social relations and cultural frameworks ushered in by the Internet. The image of the cyborg refuses to repudiate technology in the desire to return to a set of more innocent and 'natural' social relations. However, the way that Plant chooses to explore this research agenda is open to question. What seems to have been forgotten is the way that information technology is involved in the alienation and exploitation of women across the world. Whereas Haraway offered the possibility of a more ambivalent reading of the narratives and practices of new technology, Plant simply argues that technological change offers a better world for women. Hence, despite the utopian energy that lies behind much cyberfeminism, it is worth reminding ourselves that the Net continues to be a zone of exclusion for many women across the world. Here we might consider the very 'real' digital divides that constitute cyberspace. Internet users are overwhelmingly white, male, middle class and concentrated within Western Europe and Northern America. It has been estimated that the average user of the Internet in the US in 2000 is a 41-year-old male who earns $65,000 a year. Further, as Segal (1999) has argued, despite technological innovations many women are under increasing pressure through the extension of working hours, the reduction of leisure time and the persistence of conservative gender ideologies which permeate both popular and Net cultures.

While these are important correctives to some of the feminist inspired technological enthusiasm we need to be careful not to cancel the cyberfeminist project altogether. Wendy Harcourt (2000) has pointed out that the Internet has provided women the world over with new opportunities to fight for women's rights by entering into transnational dialogue with women from other nations and cultures. Despite the fact that the Net is linked into large corporations and financial institutions it has provided feminist social movements with opportunities to exchange and share information about different campaigns and strategies. Further, Braidotti (2001) has argued that the Net continues to offer women possibilities to experiment with visionary passions and humour in ways that are not so evident within mainstream popular culture. Whether these possibilities are built upon to open up new and imaginative social spaces where a multiplicity of women and identities can become engaged it is perhaps too soon to tell. Yet viewed from the position of a social theory of media and mass communication, cyberfeminism's main weakness is its inability to consider the more instrumental features of Net cultures. As we have seen, cyberfeminism's main concern is to explore the ways technology becomes culturally encoded and to uncover its ambivalent opportunities. However, as Virilio in particular demonstrates, the Net remains part of a culture which emphasises profit, speed and effiency over other more cultural concerns. Here we might both welcome cyberfeminism's ability to investigate the ways in which the Net is scripted within a variety of gendered frameworks, while cautioning that it needs to continue to investigate some of the more 'restrictive' features of what earlier generations of critical theory called technical reason.

Summary

The arrival of new technologies of communication has offered new possibilities for the social theory of mass communication. We have witnessed the development of a number of provocative perspectives in this regard seeking to articulate the links between technological change, globalisation and the new social movements such as cyberfeminism. In this respect, Castells and Harraway have sought to outline the ambivalent possibilities and limitations of the new media age most coherently. Despite their limitations, Castells's and Haraway's analyses of the network society neither lapse into technological optimism nor pessimism. Yet, not surprisingly, other theorists such as Schiller and Virilio have chosen to concentrate upon some of the less progressive features of the new communications revolution. That is they continue to offer powerful correctives to much 'cyberdrool' which has accompanied the development of the Net within the academy. Such perspectives will continue to find a home in a world where the main driving force behind communications' development remains the requirements of the military and the market. However, while commentators concentrate on either positive or negative poles of analysis, critical debate is likely to be defined through the discourse of the other. Perhaps the main limitation here is the inability to link the arrival of new media into many of the possibilities (and of course limitations) suggested by social movements who seek to develop a political response to our rapidly changing world. The development of a new politics for a new age, which resists the temptation of fundamentalism and is adequate to the challenges of the modern world, is more likely to develop through an engagement with technological change, globalisation and gender politics than their mutual negation. For progressive and generative political forces this chapter has argued that there is no return to the certitudes of either an exclusively class politics or a less technologically complex society.

Conclusion

The Three Paradigms of Mass Communication Research

The legacy of media theory provides social theorists with complex perspectives on media practice. The current explosion of new technologies and rapid globalisation of media cultures makes such concerns increasingly relevant. As most of the writers under review accept, the exchange of media impressions now forms a permanent backdrop to the early twenty-first century. Whether we live our lives permanently in the village where we were born or restlessly travelling the globe, media cultures are almost certainly present. They provide the microscopic web that weaves together the patchwork we call globalisation. More modestly, they help to carve out, sustain and occasionally transform transnational, national, regional and local identities. The noisy flux of cultures that technologies of communication help transmit reminds us that fundamentalist and separatist ambitions are almost bound to fail. The pervasive tentacles of the mass media point to the extent to which human kind is permanently mixed in with one another. Indeed, the quicker we accept the symbolically cosmopolitan and irredeemably material nature of human existence the better. To survey the front of the morning newspaper – which McLuhan (1994) likened to a collage – is to become aware of the global reach of international news agencies. The juxtaposition of different news stories is an example of the forms of cultural connection routinely made available in modernity. These cultural figurations, dramatic reversals aside, will it seems be with us for some time to come.

Against those who would seek to explain social life in terms of one paradigm, the global flows of information permanently decentre the subject. The system of communications is too vast to be subordinate to one agency of control.

Oppositional views leak through, contradictory formations are circulated and messages are contradicted. Media cultures are irredeemably plural in their owner- ship, technology, messages, form and reception. If this is true, mass communication systems are also potentially too powerful to be left unregulated and in the hands of large conglomerates. Media cultures are prey to hegemonic strategies and ideological instances. Yet we do not have to make a *choice* between the three research paradigms on offer. Indeed, many of the writers under discussion combine at least two of the different approaches that are available. For instance, Jameson (1991) merges a critical approach with an understanding of the technological nature of modern cultures, and Stuart Hall (1986) theorises a notion of hegemony along with critical readings of the audience. It is safe to summarise that all three approaches contribute to our understanding of modern electronic, print and oral cultures. Their continued relevance will depend upon the empirical contexts to which they are being applied, and the questions we are trying to raise.

The study of the media of mass communication treads a thin line between views that overstate its importance and those that don't credit it with enough. Those whose concerns sever the media from other domains of social practice and others who press its capacity to bind subjects ideologically to certain core beliefs are guilty of the former. Alternatively, those who make the latter mistake argue that the media form just another leisure activity in late capitalist society, or suggest that they have little impact on the prejudices of the audience. These seem to me to be false oppositions, which this text should have gone some way towards deconstructing.

The emergence of global communications has accompanied the rise of certain powerful groups who have sought to present perspectives and technologies in accordance with their interests. The widespread development of communication technologies has gone hand in hand with the growth of capitalism and its restless search for new markets. The cultural forms produced have been utilised by large- scale concerns seeking profit maximisation as well as ideological and cultural dominance. This has led certain writers to accredit the media as the dominant ideological force of consumer capitalism creating new needs and desires. A more dialectical focus reveals cultural processes that resist commodification and ideological strategies. The notion of the public sphere, journalistic values of truth, objectivity and balance, and the conception of the creative artist are some of the ways in which these formations have resisted being colonised by money and power. More interpretative focuses on the audience have found that Western forms of media production often have unintended consequences and are semiotically open. The split between those that produce the message and the audience that consumes it means that the media text is often viewed in a variety of contexts and in a number of different ways. Yet we could not even talk of such issues unless certain technological prerequisites were satisfied. That cultural forms are capable of storing information and shifting it through space and time is presupposed by the previous discussion. The media neither passively serve the interests of hegemonic formations, nor are they economically, politically and culturally innocent. Similarly the technologies of communication are structured by the capacities of private capital and public power, while the media themselves retain certain capabilities. For example, a telephone has common features whether it is publicly or privately owned and operated. To follow Castells (1997), whatever economic system we adopt we will have to learn to live with the Internet. Thus, in modern settings, communication technologies are the focus of certain opportunities and dangers. They are often unpredictable in their cultural effects, while remaining linked to the operation of social power. They are both dominatory and subject to the plural practices of the audience. Finally, they provide global levels of interconnection while causing more fragmentary effects.

These different paradigms intend to persuade us that the study of mass communication is central to an understanding of contemporary society. Any notion that refuses the temptation of making media practices overly central or peripheral is in accordance with my aim. However, despite the disagreements evident between the three traditions of media studies, they would all stress different reasons as to why the study of the media should be undertaken. Ultimately, despite their very different histories and trajectories, any comprehensive approach to mass communication cannot afford to ignore any of the three paradigms evident in the literature.

The reason why the study of mass communication is important for understanding contemporary society has three parts, each of which articulates a different arena of media practice. These theoretical formulations are also concerned with a number of unanswered questions. Inevitably, not all of these can be readdressed, and some will have to be left to other critics. The first approach offers a *critical theory* of mass communication. This theory has sought to examine the ways in which media cultures have become a form of social power in contemporary societies. There is much dispute as to how effective they are in this. The intellectual traditions represented in this volume remain undecided on the extent to which media strategies culturally penetrate the life-world. In addition, these traditions have sought to connect the media with other domains of social practice: economics and politics. The extent to which the cultural has become dominated and managed by commodification strategies and state power remains an open question. The reasons usually given for the importance of these issues concern notions of authority and democracy. It is commonly argued that modern democracies are dependent upon their citizens being presented with a diverse range of opinions so that they can make creative and reflexive inputs into democratic debates. This is crucial, as in a democracy authority is meant to be invested in the people. They are the body with the power to remove their elected representatives. But, as most critics are aware, democratic decision-making processes have to work within less than ideal conditions. In recent years, Western democracies have faced a crisis of legitimacy as a result of a decline in participation in the main political parties, faltering turnouts in general elections and widespread awareness of the ways in which money and power seek to guarantee that certain outcomes are decided in their favour. The mass media, in this context, are seen to ideologically maintain the status quo and marginalise critical voices.

The concept of hegemony has revealed that the domination of information flow is nearly always uneven. It certainly favours the voices and perspectives of the powerful, but it also provides space for critical reflections and other inter-subjective relations. As this study has shown, steering mechanisms systematically distort the presentation of images, voices and historicity. But they have not successfully colonised the life-world or managed the unpredictable circulation of media cultures. For instance, the world media certainly represent human crises in the Third World in an ethnocentric manner, with little regard for local economic, political and cultural contexts. But without the presence of the global media the public would be unlikely to take any of the action needed to attend to mass suffer-ing. Of course, the media will soon refocus their attention and the global forms of redistribution and the institution-building needed may not happen. And yet, without the television images, the press reports and radio interviews most people would be unaware of the obligations we have to those spatially absent from the small corners in which we live. The global media have the capacity to publicly shame leaders of the Western world into action, despite many of the dominant frameworks that the reporting will undoubtedly reproduce. In short, while the media of mass communication have many of the features the critical approach outlines, the consequences of such media strategies are often unintended and more contradictory than most theories of hegemony suppose.

The second main strand of media research is provided by more interpretative approaches. Audience research, despite its shortcomings, articulates many of the ambivalent processes evident within media cultures. Such research has impressed that media interactions nearly always take place in domestic settings and involve complex symbolic work on the part of watchers, viewers and listeners themselves. Yet there remains a considerable amount of disagreement about how best to proceed in investigating the audience. We saw that David Morley (1992) and Ann Gray (1992) were more interested in the viewing context itself than in the specific text that was being interpreted. On the other hand, John Fiske (1987b) and Ien Ang (1985) were concerned with what made certain cultural forms popular and with their semiotic and subversive temper. In bringing such acts to conscious-ness, audience theory of all types under-theorises the totality of economic, political and cultural relationships and the way in which they cut into ordinary processes of reception. However, this perspective has allowed for the emergence of many interesting questions. Why are soap operas so popular? How can we account for television's dominance in contemporary leisure activities? The question of how important the media is has been answered with reference to the texture of the practices of ordinary life. That is, the media remain a crucial field of study because people construct a sense of identity and enter into relations with others through their various interactions with communicative forms. Media cultures matter because of the enthusiastic engagements of ordinary members of the public. What these perspectives seem to value about mass communication is the capacity of human beings to participate within a culture. If critical media theory emphasises the media's role in democratic forms of participation, audience theory upholds the rights of subjects to take part in popular commercial cultures. For critical media theorists, such as Habermas (1989) and Williams (1974), we become mature human beings to the extent to which we are able to reflexively interrogate previously held traditions and beliefs. Similarly, audience theorists, despite their evident focus upon domestic rather than public contexts, hold up the capacity of social subjects to think against the grain of media texts. They are joined together by their shared emphasis on the complex symbolic capacities of the subject. However, the issue of concern to the theorists of reception is usually less the realisation of republican virtues than the enthusiastic fan. Yet we could equally claim that so-called republic perspectives more often than not neglect the gendered forms of power and perspective that much audience research has brought into the open. Here the less *grand* ways in which media cultures are lived and practised is the focus of attention. This area of theoretical practice has enabled professional researchers to identify themselves and the audience as more contradictory subjects than was previously presumed. Political identities and more popular constructions seem to overlay one another. These more pleasurable and private engagements are an important component of modern living and have a symbolic rather than an informational or instrumental focus. Viewed positively, they allow us to participate in a plurality of popular narratives out of which we construct a sense of selfhood and imagined community. Reconceptualised less generously, the privatised practices of home consumption are themselves indicative of the processes of atomism and depoliticisation evident in Western democracy. Taken together, they speak of the deep ambivalence evident in popular media cultures.

Those who have focused on the *media of communication* have built the development of media cultures into the history of modernity. In their various ways, against those who have reduced the study of media cultures to a secondary status, they have argued that such processes are central features of modern societies. In common with certain branches of post-structuralism, they view the operation of the media as no less real and profound than the study of employment patterns or child-care arrangements. The shifting of time and space by predominantly one-way forms of communication is a central feature of our daily lives. This approach emphasises that media cultures are social practices like any other. The materialist case, which often reduces the operation of such cultures to the imprinting of a wider social structure, misses this point. Media cultures are both autonomous from and yet interwoven into other activities and practices, which in turn have a structuring impact upon them.

The development of the technological means of image and information exchange has had a profound effect upon society. From a nineteenth-century print and oral culture there has emerged an electronic culture that has helped sustain intersubjective relations across time and space. Today our daily experience is permeated with images and perspectives that are distant from the places where we live, work and love. At different moments the technical means of communication can provide a social glue offering details of events that everyone is talking about. This could be a missing baby, an earthquake, or the election of an American President. One of the effects of mass communication has been to unify diverse communities and social groups across time and space. These imaginary communities may be transitory experiences that hold our attention for short periods, or equally they can be the site of more intensive feelings of identification. The mass media ritually give us information of forms of life radically different from our own. The escape into them can give rise to misrecognition, hegemonic manipulation or voyeuristic amusement, as well as a sense that there are many different ways to live our life. Yet, as most commentators are aware, the more communications technologies have developed the more fragmented the audience has become. Communication technologies help foster processes of unification and fragmentation across the spatial contours of the local, national and the global. Its intersecting threads seem to hold the world together while progressively pulling it apart. The explosion of the amount of media culture available in different forms and genres means that the audience is continually involved in selection. The decision to watch the police drama, finish a novel or listen to the opera unites us with other viewers, readers and listeners while dividing us from others. The technical means that have enabled these transformations are worthy of study to the extent to which they continually transform such social relationships.

The functioning of the technical apparatus of communication also has had certain implications for the other two modes of media study. The centralisation of media technology with the arrival of national television, radio and press impressed concerns in the sociological literature with notions of a mass society. It was felt that the control of certain technologies by capital and the state could engender ideological forms of incorporation. The provision of video equipment, the increase in the number of television and radio channels, and the proliferation of the magazine industry has shifted the balance between the producer and the consumer. While ideological processes are still evident, the development of cultural communications has increasingly focused attention on the audience. The capitalisation of sophisticated communication technology has contributed to audience fragmentation. Technologies such as video recorders and personal stereos have had an individualising effect, allowing the audience to make choices about the way they receive media cultures that were not so evident within earlier technological waves. Audiences have become progressively more interesting to research the further technology has gone in allowing them to make cultural inputs.

This area of research also has its own blind spots; these are suggested by the other two kinds of mass communication theory. Both Baudrillard's (1988a) and McLuhan's (1994) concern for the medium was abstracted from wider social contexts (capital and state policy) and ignored the semiotic capabilities of the audience. The focus on the technological media should be reintegrated into more socialised contexts and concerns. If this is done, it could lead to an interesting set of questions. Are some technological forms intrinsically more democratic than others? Will the development of more interactive technology supplement democratic processes or further undermine public forms of discussion? What structuring effects do electronic cultures have on cooler, more rational forms of debate? I have indicated the directions answers to these questions might take, although they remain open issues for discussion.

The debate between those who would defend versions of modernity (Williams and Habermas), radicalised modernity (Giddens) or postmodernity (Baudrillard and Jameson) pervades the background of each of the three paradigms. While my sympathies lie with those who would seek to defend a modernist project aimed at the democratisation of the media of mass communication, it cannot be denied that certain aspects of postmodernism have at least a descriptive relevance. Take Baudrillard's (1988a) and McLuhan's (1994) concept of implosion. It is certainly true that media cultures routinely reverse many of the processes of specialisation evident within modernity. The fast turnover of media events in media cultures, the rapid commercialisation of media systems and attempts by political elites to monitor media output has changed our perception of the real. The media, it could be said, does not just report the news, it goes some way towards making it. In addition, semiotic capitalism's historical shifting of regimes of signification, and simulation of the real, has altered the focus of media cultures. If the media were to feature a news item on a convention of Elvis fans, this could indeed be described as a simulacrum. The fans themselves, who probably grew up listening to their favourite star's records, watching his films and reading popular stories about him, have become a media event in themselves. This example shows that the relationship between the media and the social world is not a stable one. And yet other cultural processes are at work. The mass development and circulation of tabloid newspapers speaks of a different cultural logic. The polarisation of newspapers into quality and tabloid forms has created two parallel markets. The quality press, as we saw, tend to be concerned with wide-ranging forms of public discussion on matters of public interest. The tabloids, on the other hand, deal in sensational reports, the absurd, and individualised conceptions of the world that speak of privatisation and depoliticisation. In terms of the media, therefore, it is tempting to speak of combined and uneven development. While implosion and simulation have certainly had an impact on media cultures, they have not reversed other more deep-seated trends that can be associated with modernity. The media then can be said to be imploding and differentiating information markets at the same time. Again this illustrates the plural rather than the homogeneous nature of media cultures.

Throughout this book I have made arguments for the meaning and use of certain theories. We are now in a position to see that while media critics have their own points of emphasis, all of the three areas of concern are interdependent. My aim in making this suggestion is not falsely to unify diverse areas of theoretical practice – it is, after all, the more fruitful for being a field in critical tension. But it is possible to reconcile the concerns of the different fields. They share the same object of study, while highlighting different aspects of its performance. Whether we are concerned with institutional modes of domination, identity formation or the shifting of time and space, these perspectives articulate some of the central problems with which social theory is associated. The reasons why social theorists, or anyone else for that matter, should take the media seriously are already available to us. They are articulated by complex fields of theoretical practice that have made known the hybrid and plural nature of media cultures. That these concerns are currently incomplete, and perhaps always will be, is the subject of the following reflections.

Possible Futures

The study of the media of mass communication has recently taken a new turn. The development of the Internet and super information highways has refocused the energies of many on the study of media cultures. This has had a number of combined and often contradictory effects that research programmes have only just begun to unravel. As we saw in Chapter 6, the development of the information society thesis marks the further implosion of what I have termed 'the three paradigms of mass communication'. This is a development to be welcomed as approaches, which include critical theory, the study of audiences and different technological media try to make sense of the transformation of contemporary media cultures. Whether the arrival of an information society involves a 'second' media age or merely the further intensification of commodification and the cultural penetration of the market is of course open to question. It is likely here that we will be concerned for some time to come with a debate that seeks to focus on the genuinely new elements of the current situation. Whether the Internet actually offers new possibilities for democratic exchange or simply allows space for more regressive political forces while engulfing most of its participants even further within the society of the spectacle is already a matter for heated debate. It is evident, as we have seen, that these debates will increasingly look to many of the recent developments within social theory in order to make sense of these changes.

That the arrival of new media is being driven along by transnational media conglomerates is difficult to obscure. Protest movements, as recent events within Seattle and Prague have shown, are increasingly targeting large corporate bodies as a focus for their campaigns. The threats posed to the capacity of the state to regulate systems of communications has become common fare amongst a wide range of political and social perspectives. These changes have impacted upon the frameworks and theoretical models we have to hand to make sense of these changes. Broadly speaking we can view the arrival of new media cultures as the intensification of modernity whereby the market gradually replaces the state as the main agent of governance. The commodification of everyday life pushes critical perspectives to the margins as our cultural lives become subordinate to the dual logics of money and technological reason. Such developments will eventually witness the end of public-funded broadcasting, the erosion of citizenship, the dominance of technological rationality, and an entrenched fear of more creative forms of politics and aesthetics. In the most technologically innovatory of times, we are faced with a politics of media and communication that asks us to struggle to preserve the best of more traditional media cultures. We are entering into a mediated environment where the possibility of democratically funded systems of communication is less likely than before. Unless politicians, citizens and academics are able to find new ways of relying this message then we are increasingly likely to live in a world where are communicative futures are determined by the market. This will lead to a world where ordinary people's horizons are both more reactive and less utopian in their political and cultural appetites and perspectives. These are very real possibilities. Yet they remain under-appreciative of other concerns. The development of new technological forms, the globalisation of communication and the development of reflexivity has meant that people's horizons are less determined by the state than ever before. New interactive sites, spaces for opinion and identity formation are growing within the belly of global capitalism. Mediated zones of activism, as we have seen, including the development of cyberfeminism and post-colonial criticism, potentially gives space to voices that have been traditionally excluded by older existing forms of communication. These developments point towards a politics that is not exclusively concerned with commodification but seeks to make space for more complex cosmopolitan viewpoints that are poorly captured by more traditional political concerns. These agendas are likely to be motivated by human rights, cross-cultural dialogue, the mediation of difference and more ambivalent zones of contact. This critical agenda, which is likely to take a less moralistic stance in respect of the semiotic plurality of audience, is also more likely to be concerned with questions of representation and the possibility of interaction than it is by blanket commodification. The development of critical agendas related to ambivalence, hybridity and cyborgs points towards a cultural agenda motivated by new political hopes. Perhaps if we put these frameworks (and others) together this points towards the emergence of future frameworks that take refuge in neither remorseless optimism nor predictable pessimism, but will seek to find space for more ambivalent and less culturally fixed horizons and possibilities. Within such a venture, then, we are likely to need reliable guidebooks to past thinking, and an openness towards new transformations and what they might eventually bring. Media cultures continue to have much to learn from voices and perspectives such as feminism and post-colonialism, which join together diverse pleasures, publics and politics. These agendas, as we have seen, are poorly understood by research questions that always privilege capitalism and class. We can no longer assume that critical questions are solely dependent upon the capacity of radicals to think of new institutional arrangements, and yet nor can we assume that the conservatism of our own current age will be addressed unless we grasp the nettle of thinking through a diversity of questions that involve linking a demo-cratic media to issues concerned with identity. Here I hope I have demonstrated that, whichever turn our thinking takes, we continue to be guided by the need for fresh perspectives and to attend to perspectives that were formed in ages different from our own.

Glossary

Please note glossary terms appear in bold in the text on first use.

Agency The ability to be able to act within a social and cultural context while making a difference to the flow of events. Agency should not be thought of as the opposite of structure, but dependent upon rules and resources generated by social structures. To have agency is defined by the ability to be able to actively intervene.

Audience The audience may exist in a number of senses. The first is in the imaginations of advertisers and programme makers who symbolically shape their message in order to reach a certain segment in the population. The audience in this respect is always allusive as broadcasting institutions can never be certain (despite advances in new technology) as to who is actually watching. The other way of thinking about the audience is more sociological. Here the audience is assumed to be able to make active sense of different symbolic forms (films, advertisements, etc.) often reading them against the grain. Further, sociologists have also sought to investigate the different sets of public and private relationships entered into in the consumption of the media.

Bias News reporting that is accused as being unbalanced, inaccurate and partial.

Civil society Usually refers to an intermediate zone between private life and the state, where relatively independent organisations are able to operate and circulate information relatively autonomously. This term is usually thought to offer a different understanding of the media to one which refers to control by the state or the market.

Commodification   Refers to the extent to which media messages and symbolic goods have become products to be bought and sold on the market.

Cosmopolitanism   Literally, a citizen of the world. Can also refer to a set of perspectives that have sought to jettison viewpoints that are solely determined by the nation, or their geographical standing within the world. A cosmopolitan viewpoint would need to carefully investigate whether or not it was reaffirming prejudice towards the West or Western nations.

Critical theory   An approach to the study of mass media that seeks to link media institutions and the analysis of texts in order to reveal relations of domination or emancipation. A critical theory of the media will usually seek to offer a historically informed account of modern society and the cultural industries, and suggest how they might be democratically reformulated.

Cultural imperialism   Demonstrates how the global domination of a few multi-national organisations (usually from the USA) is dominating the consumption of the media in less powerful nations. The term is also linked to the idea that the world is increasingly becoming a monoculture whereby cultural diversity is being displaced by the homogeneity of consumer culture.

Culture   There are many different definitions of this term. Has been used to indicate the spread of civilised ideas and beliefs. This usage is no longer acceptable. Here is used more neutrally to describe the symbols, meanings and practices that can be associated with living within a media-dominated society.

Cyborg   The emergence of organisms either in reality or within the imagination that call into question the boundaries between humans, animals and technology.

Discourse   Particular ways of talking, writing and thinking that can be organised into identifiable patterns of usage across time and space. Whether we are analysing a news broadcast or chat show we might be able to identify a number of different codes or ways of speaking that are more prevalent than others.

Feminism   A political and social movement that aims to foster a society where men and women can live together equally while respecting their differences. Within media studies its main influence (so far) has been on developing more critical understandings of media audiences, and different textual readings of media products.

Globalisation   Describes a process whereby the world's financial markets, political systems and cultural dimensions form increasingly intense relationships. There are a number of different consequences that may result from such processes. Some commentatators view globalisation mainly negatively as media markets are increasingly owned and control by a handful of large media conglomerates, resulting in the privatization of public space and the commodification of the public sphere. Others are less pessimistic seeing the possible emergence of a new politics that aims for a more responsible world society based upon communication rather than domination.

Hegemony Implies a view that domination in society depends upon winning the active consent of the people. The mass media in this view either conceals or marginalises critical voices in order to reaffirm the status quo. However, within most accounts hegemony is always in process and employs military metaphors such as 'strategy' or 'war of position', implying the possibility of challenge and change.

Hybridity Process whereby new cultural forms and identities come into being by combining different cultural elements. This term can be linked to globalisation (the increasing movement of peoples and cultures) and/or media technological implosion whereby different technological elements combine to produce new hardware.

Hyperreal Connecting to the increasing number of 'real' life stories, confessional forms and 'real' time cultural forms that are currently available on mainstream television. The hyperreal aims to demonstrate that what passes for 'reality' actually depends upon certain cultural conventions. This process tends to become exaggerated in a media culture whereby programme makers/advertisers have to compete with increasing levels of competition, and where a great deal of faith is still invested in ideas of the authentic.

Identity Not something which is either natural or fixed but evolves within a cultural context. Usually depends upon ideas of personal selfhood and other characteristics including class, sex and gender, race and nation.

Ideology Can be taken to mean a particular set of ideas or a belief system. Yet has also a long history in mass communication research as referring to symbolic processes that either leave unquestioned or reaffirm relations of dominance.

Implosion The eradication of barriers that define separate social spheres. This usually occurs through the impact of media technology. For example, the idea that in the modern world politics has become entertainment and entertainment has become politics. That is, it would be hard to argue that soap operas are not a political phenomenon, as advice is offered on the raising of children, masculinity is problematicised, personal ethics and relations are discussed, and of course they may be watched to avoid more troubling subjects. Further, that politics in the age of spin-doctors, image manipulation and media proliferation will all attempt to construct a certain image, as do products sold in supermarkets. To say they have imploded is to say they are becoming more alike.

Information society The argument that we have entered into a society different from that which came into being during the industrial revolution. Here information and knowledge become the key resources in determining economic success or failure. Further, such developments are also connected to the growth of the service sector and the enhanced role of culture in questions of social exclusion.

Internet The worldwide system of computer-based interactive networks that support the growth in web pages, e-mail, interactive forms of communication and economic activity.

Intertextuality Refers to the ability of media texts and readers to make connections to one another across different genres. This might include advertising's ability to associate itself with a well-known film, or the ability of fans to take on characteristics of their heroes.

Liberalism A political philosophy that emphasises the capacity of individuals to make autonomous and informed decisions. In terms of mass media, it was thought that a free media enabling individuals to maximise autonomy would be best delivered by the market rather than by state control.

Marxism A social theory which argues that the major ills of modern society can be attributed to its capitalist nature. In respect of the media, this means that large multinational companies are currently constructing the cultural horizons of most of the world's citizens in their interests. However, other Marxists have argued that the media's main significance is not in terms of ideological control, but in the commodification of everyday life. This ultimately means that most of the media-related material we consume would be done so for the profit of a few rather than the community as a whole.

Mass culture The idea that the increased bureaucratic and capitalist control over culture is producing a world of sameness, alienating technology, efficiency and commodification.

Mediums of communication The possibility that different mediums (radio, television, or the Internet) have a direct and differentiated impact on shaping human society.

Network   A set of interconnected points within a circuit, which may involve actors (human, animals, technology) or organisations.

Objectivity   The idea that you can gain accurate information about the world that is not tainted or informed by your social or cultural location.

Ominopolis   The view that new media has not so much opened up a diversity of new realities, but has lead to a reduction in the field of vision. The media, in this respect, has imposed upon us a culture of speed and immediacy that has blunted the human senses.

Political economy   A view of mass communications that emphasises it should be studied in terms of its institutional make up, in historical context, in ways which are also alive to different mixes between commercial and public forms of regulation. More broadly the term refers to the determining power of economics and politics.

Postmodernism   The ideas that features that were associated with modern society have come to an end. Currently postmodern societies are witnessing the inter-mixing of the popular and educated forms of culture, the end of ideology/utopias (the death of socialism), and the idea that language mirrors rather than produces reality. Some versions of postmodernism believe this spells the end of critical politics, whereas others welcome a cultural context that is more ambivalent and less certain.

Public sphere   The existence of a social space (whether real or mediated) where matters of public importance can be discussed to determine the public interest.

Reflexivity   The ability to be able to revise your actions in the light of new information. The argument is often made that information societies are becoming reflexive societies. That is as the world becomes defined through information overload rather than information scarcity, it is argued, it also becomes increasingly reflexive. This means opening up questions on nature, gender, sexuality, etc. that were repressed in previous historical eras.

Simulation   The idea that media age changes the relationship between fabrication and reality, and image and truth. The development of new technologies produce their own worlds and different reality effects that can no longer be contradicted by pointing to brute data.

Surveillance   New media technologies are increasingly being used to make visible the activities of citizens within public and private contexts. These activities are usually connected to powerful agencies that attempt to normalise and thereby control the behaviour of ordinary people.

Time-space compression   The idea that new technologies have made it possible to go travelling without leaving home. The arrival of real time media experiences mean that we are able to view an event irrespective of our geographical location and without any noticeable time delay. Within the economy this has introduced the possibility of 'just in time' forms of production, and within urban contexts the 24-hour city.

Virtual reality   The development of new human experiences (involving all the senses) through the use of computer technology.

Notes

Introduction

1. For this see the excellent Denis McQuail (1992), *Mass Communication Theory: An Introduction*.

1 Marxism and Mass Communication Research

1. Leavis's influence on Williams's thought was at its most marked directly after the Second World War. Williams and Leavis were both tutors during this period at Cambridge University. Williams, however, increasingly developed a respectful scepticism about Leavis's aesthetic theory while remaining connected to this tradition. While Leavis remains important, Williams's theory of cultural materialism is strongly influenced by Althusser, Gramsci and Volosinov.
2. Williams had previously discussed hegemony in 'Base and superstructure in Marxist cultural theory' (1973).
3. This point retains a crucial criticism of anti-humanism (Foucault and Althusser) popular on the Left in the late 1970s.
4. Webster argues that Jews as well as Arabs are often dehumanised by being represented as animals.
5. Hobsbawm undoubtedly overstates the reactive nature of the new nationalism. For a more positive reading see Neil Ascherson, 'In defence of new nationalism' (1991).
6. A similar approach is offered by David Morrison (1992).
7. Hall has remained consistently critical of Althusser's specific formulations. See Stuart Hall, 'Thatcherism amongst the theorists: toad in the garden' (1988b).
8. It is the lack of theoretical fit between the signifier and the signified that allows Laclau and Mouffe to argue that ideological discourse has no necessary belongingness.
9. In particular, Hall's work found a wide Left audience through the pages of *Marxism Today* throughout the 1980s.

2 Habermas, Mass Culture and the Public Sphere

1. The work of John Fiske is discussed at length in Chapter 3.
2. This point has been brought out well in the clash between Channel 4, the state and the Royal Ulster Constabulary over the TV series, *Dispatches*. For an outline of this conflict see David Cox, 'Caught in the act' (1992).
3. This will become more clearly apparent in Chapters 4 and 5.

3 Critical Perspectives within Audience Research

1. This point was more extensively discussed in Chapter 1, pp. 48–56.
2. A similar point is made by Peter Dews in conversation with Laclau. According to Dews, Laclau's version of the subject seems to be self-determining, and constructed through language. See Ernesto Laclau, *New Reflections on the Revolution of Our Time* (1990: 209–10).
3. See Chapters 1 and 2 respectively.
4. Here Fiske falls into precisely the same trap as Raymond Williams. As we saw in Chapter 1, he accuses Williams of assuming that a literary theorist would read the popular in the same way as the audience. Here I am suggesting that Fiske is assuming the audience would always read the popular as an enthusiastic fan might.
5. I am particularly grateful to Charlotte Brunsdon (1997) for her perceptive criticisms of the first edition of this book. I have tried to rework my ideas in respect of audience theory, feminism and the public in light of her reflections.

4 Marshall McLuhan and the Cultural Medium

1. These intellectual connections could probably be accounted for by the fact that both Williams and McLuhan were strongly influenced by the literary critic F.R. Leavis. Meanwhile, the early Frankfurt school, as is now widely recognised, had a marked impact on a wide range of American postwar academic criticism.
2. This probably explains Baudrillard's enthusiasm for McLuhan. Both writers share a desire to analyse the technological development of the mass media, media of communication, and notions of implosion.
3. Here Giddens differs from the analysis previously offered by Habermas. Habermas argues that expert cultures are progressively being decoupled from a culturally impoverished life-world, whereas Giddens suggests that systems of expertise are routinely caught up in everyday practices. These views are not necessarily irreconcilable, and both characterise important features of modern experience. If we take an issue like AIDS, Giddens would point to the fact that most people are aware that sexual activity within modernity involves different degrees of risk. In making informed, or not so informed, choices we will make use of so-called expert advice that stems from the medical profession, the media, lesbian and gay activists, etc. A more Habermasian approach would point to the way in which community-wide discussion of AIDS has been distorted by the operation of money and power. For instance, some of the tabloid press ran sensationalistic stories that bracketed off wider forms of rational debate.
4. Lefebvre explicitly criticises post-structuralist writers such as Derrida and Barthes

whom he views as having reduced space to the metaphoric operation of language. This creates a theoretical dualism between physical space and social space. The conversion of space into a language that needs to be read abstracts from the ways in which space is constructed through social practices. This is why Lefebvre puts so much emphasis on the production of space.

5 Baudrillard's Blizzards

1. These works have not yet been completely translated. Here I am reliant on the selections in Baudrillard (1988a).
2. The Durkheimian implications of this argument should be obvious. Mauss is not offering a nostalgic critique of the sort Baudrillard proposes. Instead, he argues that collective forms of solidarity could be promoted by the provision of unemployment insurance and other welfare measures.
3. Baudrillard's remarks on death and dying have much in common with the recent work of Zygmunt Bauman (1992b).
4. Although as Sadie Plant (1992) points out, the situationists were seeking to provide a critique of the spectacle which would lead to transformation of real social relations. In addition, the situationists fully expected their actions to be reincorporated into the system. It is not clear that the same could be said of Baudrillard.
5. This essay was originally written in 1968.
6. Jameson argues that each respective phase of capitalist production has a corresponding regime of space. See Jameson (1988b).
7. I would like to thank Sean Homer for helping me come to a more informed appreciation of Jameson's writing. The influence of his thinking is particularly marked in the preceding section.

6 New Media and the Information Society

1. Whether Castells should be connected to the tradition of critical theory is a complex issue. Please see Frank Webster's (1995) first rate discussion of Castells and his intellectual context.
2. I continue to be grateful to Nina Wakeford for her conversations on the subject of cyberfeminism. That she is now a leading thinking within this particular field is not a surprise to me.

References

Abercrombie, N., Hill, S. and Turner, B. (eds) (1980) *The Dominant Ideology Thesis,* London, Allen and Unwin.

Adam, B. (1990) *Time and Social Theory,* Cambridge, Polity Press.

Adorno, T. (1974) *Minima Moralia: Reflections from Damaged Life,* London, Verso.

Adorno, T. (1991) *The Culture Industry: Selected Essays on Mass Culture,* London, Routledge.

Adorno, T. and Horkheimer, M. (1973) *The Dialectic of the Enlightenment,* London, Allen Lane.

Alasuutari, P.(1999) 'Introduction: Three Phases of Reception Studies', in Alasuutari, P. *Rethinking the Media Audience,* London, Sage.

Albright,J.(2001) 'Of Mind, Body and Machine: Cyborg cultural politics in the age of hypertext' http://www.eff.org/pub/Net_culture/Gender_issues/cyberfeminism.article

Althusser, L. (1977) 'Marxism and humanism', in *For Marx,* London, Verso.

Altusser, L (1984) 'Ideology and ideological state apparatuses', in *Essays on Ideology,* London, Verso.

Anderson, B. (1983) *Imagined Communities,* London, Verso.

Anderson, B. (1992) 'The last empires', *New Left Review,* 193: 3–13.

Anderson, P. (1964) 'Origins of the present crisis', *New Left Review* 23.

Anderson, P. (1979) *Considerations on Western Marxism,* London, Verso.

Anderson, P. (1980) *Arguments within English Marxism,* London, Verso.

Anderson, P (1983) *In the Tracts of Historical Materialism. The Wallek Library Lectures,* London, Verso.

Anderson, P. (1992) *English Questions,* London, Verso.

Ang, I. (1985) *Watching 'Dallas': Soap Opera and the Melodramatic Imagination,* London, Methuen.

Ang, I. (1991) *Desperately Seeking the Audience,* London, Routledge.

Arendt, H. (1958) *The Human Condition,* Chicago, University of Chicago Press.

Armitage, J.(2000a) 'Introduction', in Armitage, J. (ed.) *Paul Virilio; From Modernism to Hypermodernism,* London, Sage.

Armitage, J.(2000b) 'From modernism to hypermodernism and beyound: an interview with Paul Virilio', in Armitage, J. (ed.) *Paul Virilio; From Modernism to Hypermodernism*, London, Sage.

Ascherson, N. (1991) 'In defence of new nationalism', *New Statesman*, 20 and 27 December.

Ballaster, R., Beetham, M., Frazer, E. and Hebron, S. (1991) *Women's Worlds: Ideology, Femininity and the Woman's Magazine*, Basingstoke, Macmillan.

Bannister, N. (1994) 'Cable firms stake superhighway claim', *Guardian* 28 July: 15.

Barbero, J.M. (1993) *Communication, Culture and Hegemony: From Media to Mediations*, London, Sage.

Barbook, R. (1992) 'Broadcasting and national identity in Ireland', *Media, Culture and Society*, 14(2): 203–25.

Barrett, M. and Phillips, A. (1992) *Destabilising Theory: Contemporary Feminist Debates*, Cambridge, Polity Press.

Barthes, R. (1973) *Mythologies*, trans. Annette Lavers, St Albans, Paladin.

Baudrillard, J. (1975) *The Mirror of Production*, trans. with introduction by Mark Poster, St Louis, Telos.

Baudrillard, J. (1981a) *For a Critique of the Political Economy of the Sign*, St Louis, Telos.

Baudrillard, J. (1981b) 'Requim for the media', in *For a Critique of the Political Economy of the Sign*, St Louis, Telos.

Baudrillard, J. (1982) 'The Beauborg effect: implosion and deterrence', *October*, 20, (Spring): 3–13.

Baudrillard, J. (1983) 'The ecstasy of communication', ed. and introduced by Hal Foster, in *Postmodern Culture*, London, Pluto Press.

Baudrillard, J. (1985) 'The masses: the implosion of the social in the media', *New Literary History*, 16(3): 577–89.

Baudrillard, J. (1987a) 'When Bataille attacked the metaphysical principle of economy', *Canadian Journal of Political and Social Theory*, 11(3).

Baudrillard, J. (1987b) *The Evil Demon of Images*, The First Mari Kuttna Memorial Lecture, Power Institute Publications Number 3.

Baudrillard, J. (1988a) *Selected Writings*, ed. and introduced by Mark Poster, Cambridge, Polity Press.

Baudrillard, J. (1988b) *America*, trans. C. Turner, London, Verso.

Baudrillard, J. (1990a) *Fatal Strategies*, trans. Philip Beitchman and W.G.J. Niesluchowski, London, Pluto Press.

Baudrillard, J. (1990b) 'Mass media culture', in *Revenge of the Crystal: Selected Writings on the Modern Object and its Destiny, 1968–1983*, ed. and trans. Paul Foss and Julian Pefanis, London, Pluto Press.

Baudrillard, J. (1991) 'The reality gulf', *Guardian*, 11 January, p. 25.

Baudrillard, J. (1993a) *Symbolic Exchange and Death*, trans. Iain Hamiltion Grant, with an introduction by Mike Gane, London, Sage.

Baudrillard, J. (1993b) *Transparency of Evil: Essays on Extreme Phenomena*, trans. J. Benedict, London, Verso.

Baudrillard, J. (1993c) 'Games with vestiges', interview with Silvatore Mele and Mark Titmarsh, in M. Gane (ed.), *Baudrillard Live*, London, Routledge.

Baudrillard, J.(1998) *Paraoxysm: Interviews with Phillipe Petit*, London, Verso.

Bauman, Z. (1992a) *Intimations of Postmodernity*, London, Routledge.

Bauman, Z. (1992b) *Mortality, Immortality and Other Life Strategies*, Cambridge, Polity Press.

References

Bauman, Z. (1993) *Postmodern Ethics*, Oxford, Blackwell.

Beck, U. (1992) *Risk Society: Towards a New Modernity*, trans. M. Ritter, London, Sage.

Beck, U. (1998) *Democracy Without Enemies*, Polity Press, Cambridge.

Beetham, M.(1996) *A Magazine of Her Own? Domesticity and Desire in the Woman's Magazine, 1800–1914*. London, Routledge.

Benhabib, S. (1992) *Situating the Self Gender, Community and Postmodernism in Contemporary Ethics*, Cambridge, Polity Press.

Bell, D. (1973) *The Coming of Post-Industrial Society*, New York, Basic Books.

Benjamin, J. (1988) *The Bonds of Love*, London, Virago.

Benjamin, W. (1973) 'The Work of Art in an age of mechanical reproduction', in *Illuminations*, London, Fontana.

Benton, T. (1984) *The Rise and Fall of Structural Marxism*, London, Macmillan.

Benton, T. (1993) *Normal Relations: Ecology, Animal Rights and Social Justice*, London, Verso.

Bhaskar, R. (1991) *Philosophy and the Idea of Freedom*, Oxford, Blackwell.

Bird, S.E. (1997) '"What a Story!" Understanding the Audience for Scandal', (eds) Lull, S. and Hinerman, S. *Media Scandals*, Cambridge, Polity Press.

Blumler, J. (1992) *Television and the Public Interest: Vulnerable Values in Western European Broadcasting*, London, Sage.

Bobbio, N. (1987) 'Democracy and invisible power', in *The Future of Democracy*, Cambridge, Polity Press.

Bourdieu, P. (1984) *Distinction*, London, Routledge.

Bourdieu, P. (1990) *In Other Words: Essays towards a Reflexive Sociology*, Cambridge, Polity Press.

Bourdieu, P. (1991) *Language and Symbolic Power*, ed. and with an introduction by John B. Thompson, Cambridge, Polity Press.

Bourdieu, P and Passeron, C.P (1977) *Reproduction in Education, Society and Culture*, London, Sage.

Boyd-Barrett, O. (1977) *Mass Communications in Cross-cultural Contexts: The Case of the Third World*, Milton Keynes, Open University Press.

Boyle, M. (1994) 'Building a communicative democracy: the birth and death of citizen politics in East Germany', *Media, Culture and Society*, 16 (2): 183–215.

Braidotti, R. (1986) 'Ethics Revisited: Women and/in Philosophy', in C. Pateman and E. Cross (eds), *Feminist Challenges: Social and Political Theory*, Hemel Hempstead, Allen and Unwin.

Braidotti, R.(2001) 'Cyberfeminism with a difference' http://www.let.ruu.nl/womens_studies/rosi/cyberfem.htm

Breazeale, K. (1994). 'In spite of women: *Esquire* magazine and the construction of the male consumer'. *Signs: journal of women in culture and society* 20, 1–22.

Brooks, P. (1976) *The Melodramatic Imagination*, New Haven, Yale University Press.

Brunsdon, C. (1997) *Screen Tastes: Soap Opera to Satellite Dishes*, London, Routledge.

Burchill, J. (1986). 'Lad overboard'. *The Face* 70, 28–31.

Cannadine, D. (1983) 'The context, performance and meaning of ritual: the British monarchy and the "invention of tradition", *c.* 1820–1977', in E. Hobsbawm and T. Ranger (eds), *The Invention of Tradition*, Cambridge, Cambridge University Press.

Carey, J.W. (1969) 'Harold Adams Innis and Marshall McLuhan', in R. Rosental (ed.), *McLuhan Pro and Con*, Harmondsworth, Penguin.

Carey, J.W. (1989) *Communication as Culture: Essays on Media and Society,* London, Unwin Hyman.

Castells, M. (1989) *The Information City: Information Technology, Economic Restructuring and Urban-regional Process,* Oxford, Blackwell.

Castells, M. (1996) *The Rise of the Network Society; The Information Age: Economy, Society and Culture, Volume 1.* Blackwell, Oxford.

Castells, M. (1997) *The Power of Identity; The Information Age: Economy, Society and Culture, Volume 2,* Blackwell, Oxford.

Castells, M. (1998a) *End of Millennium; The Information Age: Economy, Society and Culture, Volume 3,* Blackwell, Oxford.

Castells, M. (1998b) 'Information Technology, Globalisation and Social Development', UNRISD Conference On Information Technologies and Social Development, Plais des Nations, Geneva, 22–24 June 1998.

Castells, M. and Hall, P. (1994) *Technopoles of the World: The Making of Twenty-First Century Industrial Complexes,* Routledge, London.

Castoriadis, C. (1987) *The Imaginary Institution of Society,* trans. Kathleen Blamey, Cambridge, Polity Press.

Castoriadis, C. (1991) *Philosophy, Politics, Autonomy; Essays in Political Philosophy,* Oxford, Oxford University Press.

Chapman, R. (1989). 'The great pretender: variations on the new man theme', in R. Chapman and J. Rutherford (eds), *Male Order: Unwrapping Masculinity.* London, Lawrence & Wishart, 225–48.

Chapman, R. and Rutherford, J. (eds) (1989) *Male Order: Unwrapping Masculinity.* London, Lawrence & Wishart.

Chartier, R. (ed.) (1989) *The Culture of Print: Power and the Uses of Print in Early Modern Europe,* Princeton, Princeton University Press; Cambridge, Polity Press.

Chodorow, N. (1978) *The Reproduction of Mothering,* Berkeley, University of California Press.

Cox, D. (1992) 'Caught in the act', *New Statesman and Society,* 24 July.

Cumberbatch, G. (1986) 'Bias that lies in the eye of the beholder', *Guardian,* 19 May.

Cumberbatch, G., McGregor, R., Brown, J., with Morrison, D. (1986) *Broadcasting Research Unit Report,* London, Broadcasting Research Unit.

Curran, J. (1990) 'The "new revisionism" in mass communications research', *European Journal of Communications,* 5 (2–3): 135–64.

Curran, J. (1991) 'Mass media and democracy: a reappraisal', in J. Curran and M. Gurevitch (eds), *Mass Media and Society,* London, Edward Arnold.

Curran, J. and Seaton, J. (1985) *Power without Responsibility: The Press and Broadcasting in Britain,* London, Methuen.

Dahlgren, P. (2001) 'The Transformation of Democracy?', in Axford, B. and Huggins, R. (eds) *New Media and Politics,* London, Sage.

Dahrendorf, R. (1990) *Reflections on the Revolution in Europe* (Chatto Counterblasts Special), London, Chatto and Windus.

Davis, A. (1988) *Magazine Journalism Today,* Oxford, Focal Press.

De Certeau, M. (1984) *The Practice of Everyday Life,* Berkeley, University of California Press.

Debord, G. (1987) *Society of the Spectacle,* Detriot, Blach and Med. Debord, G. (1990) *Comments on the Society of the Spectacle,* London, Verso.

Dews, P. (1986) (ed.) *Habermas: Autonomy and Solidarity,* London, Verso.

References

Downey, J. (2000) 'Inequality and the Information Age: the Recent Work of Manuel Castells', *Key Words* 3, 45–58.

Doyal, L. and Gough, I. (1991) *A Theory of Human Need,* London, Macmillan.

Eagleton, T. (1989) 'Base and superstructure in Raymond Williams', in T. Eagleton (ed.), *Raymond Williams: Critical Perspectives,* Cambridge, Polity Press.

Eagleton, T. (1990) *The Ideology of the Aesthetic,* Oxford, Blackwell.

Eagleton, T. (1991) *Ideology: An Introduction,* London, Verso.

Edwards, T. (1997). *Men in the Mirror: Men's Fashion, Masculinity and Consumer Society.* London, Cassell.

Ehrenreich, B. (1983) *The Hearts of Men: American Dreams and the Flight from Commitment,* New York, Anchor Press.

Elliott, A. (1992) *Social Theory and Psychoanalysis in Transition: Self and Society from Freud to Kristeva,* Oxford, Blackwell.

Elliott, A. (1994) *Psychoanalytic Theory: An Introduction,* Oxford, Blackwell.

Elliott, G. (1987) *Althusser: The Detour of Theory,* London, Verso.

Elliott, P., Murdock, G. and Schlesinger P. (1983) *Televising Terrorism,* London, Sage.

Enzensberger, H.M. (1976a) 'The industrialisation of the mind', in *Raids and Reconstructions,* London, Pluto Press.

Enzensberger, H.M. (1976b) 'Constituents of a theory of the media', in *Raids and Reconstructions,* London, Pluto Press.

Evans, W.A. (1990) 'The interpretive turn in media research: innovation, iteration, or illusion?', *Critical Mass Communication,* 7: 147–68.

Fejes, F. (1981) 'Media imperialism: an assessment', *Media Culture and Society,* Vol. 3(3): 281–9.

Ferguson, M. (1990) 'Electronic media and redefining time and space', in M. Ferguson (ed.), *Public Communication, the New Imperatives: Future Directions for Media Research,* London, Sage.

Ferguson, M. (1991) 'Marshall McLuhan revisited: 1960s zeitgeist victim or pioneer postmodernist?', *Media, Culture and Society,* 13(1): 71–90.

Finkelstein, S. (1968) *Sense and Nonsense of McLuhan,* New York, International Publishers.

Fiske, J. (1982) *Introduction to Communication Studies,* London, Routledge.

Fiske, J. (1987a) 'British cultural studies and television', in R. Allen. (ed.), *Channels of Discourse,* London, Methuen.

Fiske, J. (1987b) *Television Culture,* London, Methuen.

Fiske, J. (1989a) *Understanding Popular Culture,* London, Unwin Hyman.

Fiske, J. (1989b) *Reading the Popular,* London, Unwin Hyman.

Fiske, J. (1992) 'Popularity and the politics of information', in P. Dahlgren and C. Sparks (eds), *Journalism and Popular Culture,* London, Sage.

Fiske, J. (1993) *Power Plays, Power Works,* London, Verso.

Fiske, J. and Hartley, J. (1978) *Reading Television,* London, Methuen.

Flax, J. (1990) *Thinking Fragments: Psychoanalysis, Feminism and Postmodernism in the Contemporary West,* Berkeley, University of California Press.

Forgacs, D. (1989) 'Gramsci and Marxism in Britain', *New Left Review,* 176: 70–88.

Foucault, M. (1977) *Discipline and Punish: The Birth of the Prison,* trans. Alan Sheridan, Harmondsworth, Penguin.

Foucault, M. (1980) *Power/Knowledge: Selected Interviews and Other Writings, 1972–1977,* New York, Pantheon.

Fraser, N. (1992) 'The uses and abuses of French discourse theories for feminist politics', in M. Featherstone (ed.), *Cultural Theory and Cultural Change*, London, Sage.

Fraser, N. (1994) 'The case of Habermas and gender', in *The Polity Reader in Social Theory*, Cambridge, Polity Press.

Fraser, N. (1995) 'False Antitheses', in S. Benhabib, J. Butler, D. Cornell, and N. Fraser, *Feminist Contentions; A Philosophical Exchange*, London, Routledge.

Frazer, E. (1992). 'Teenage girls reading *Jackie*', in Scannell, P., Schlesinger, P. and Sparks, C. (eds), *Culture and power*, London, Sage, 182–200 (originally published in *Media, Culture and Society* 9 (1987), 407–25).

Frisby, D. (1981) *Sociological Impressionism*, London, Heinemann.

Frow, J. (1991) 'Michel de Certeau and the practice of representation', *Cultural Studies*, 5(1): 52–60.

Gane, M. (1991a) *Baudrillard: Critical and Fatal Theory*, London, Routledge.

Gane, M. (1991b) *Baudrillard's Bestiary. Baudrillard and Culture*, London, Routledge.

Garnham, N. (1986a) 'Contribution to a political economy of mass communication', in R. Collins *et al.* (eds), *Media, Culture and Society: a Critical Reader*, London, Sage.

Garnham, N. (1986b) 'Extended review: Bourdieu's distinction', *Sociological Review*, 34.

Garnham, N. (1990) 'The media and the public sphere', in *Capitalism and Communication: Global Culture and the Economics of Information*, London, Sage.

Garnham, N. (2000) 'Information society as theory or ideology', *Information, Communication and Society* 3:2, pp.139–52.

Geertz, C. (1973) *The Interpretation of Cultures: Selected Essays*, New York, Basic Books.

Geraghty, C. (1991) *Women and Soap Opera: A Study of Prime Time Soaps*, Cambridge, Polity Press.

Geraghty, C. (1997) 'Feminism and Media Consumption' in J. Curran, D. Morley and V. Walkerdine (eds) *Cultural Studies and Communications*, London, Edward Arnold.

Geras, N. (1983) *Marx and Human Nature; Refutation of a Legend*, London, Verso.

Geras, N. (1987) 'Post-Marxism?', *New Left Review*, 163 (May–June): 40–82.

Geuss, R. (1981) *The Idea of a Critical Theory: Habermas and the Frankfurt School*, Cambridge, Cambridge University Press.

Giddens, A. (1984) *The Constitution of Society: Outline of the Theory of Structuration*, Cambridge, Polity Press.

Giddens, A. (1985) *The Nation-State and Violence*, Cambridge, Polity Press.

Giddens, A. (1987a) 'Out of the Orrey: E.P. Thompson on consciousness and history', in *Social Theory and Modern Sociology*, Cambridge, Polity Press.

Giddens, A. (1987b) 'Structuralism, post-structuralism and the production of culture', in *Social Theory and Modern Sociology*, Cambridge, Polity Press.

Giddens, A. (1990) *The Consequences of Modernity*, Cambridge, Polity Press.

Giddens, A. (1991) *Modernity and Self-Identity: Self and Society in the Late Modern Age*, Cambridge, Polity Press.

Giddens, A. (1994) *Beyound Left and Right; The Future of Radical Politics*, Cambridge, Polity Press.

Gilroy, P (1987) *There Ain't No Black in the Union Jack*, London, Hutchinson.

Giroux, H. (1999) *The Mouse that Roared; Disney and the End of Innocence*, Rowman and Littlefield Publishers, Maryland.

Glasgow University Media Group (1976a) *Bad News*, London, Routledge and Kegan Paul.

Glasgow University Media Group (1976b) *More Bad News*, London, Routledge and Kegan Paul.

Glasgow University Media Group (1982) *Really Bad News,* London, Writers and Readers Publishing Cooperative.

Glasgow University Media Group (1985) *War and Peace News,* Milton Keynes, Open University Press.

Goffman, E. (1971) *Relations in Public,* London, Allen Lane.

Golding, P (1990) 'Political communication and citizenship: the media and democracy in an inegalitarian social order', in M. Ferguson (ed.), *Public Communication: The New Imperatives,* London, Sage

Golding, P. (1993) 'The mass media and the public sphere: the crisis of the information society', Discussion paper for panel at The Public Sphere conference, University of Salford, 10 January.

Golding, P. (2000) 'Forthcoming features: information and communication technologies and the sociology of the future', *Sociology,* Vol 34, No1: 165–84.

Golding, P. and Murdock, G. (1979) 'Ideology and the mass media: the question of determination', in M. Barrett *et al.,* (eds), *Ideology and Cultural Production,* London, Croom Helm.

Golding, P and Murdock. G. (1991) 'Culture, communication, and political economy', in J. Curran and M. Ourevitch, (eds), *Mass Media and Society,* London, Edward Arnold.

Goody, J. (1977) *The Domestication of the Savage Mind,* Cambridge, Cambridge University Press.

Goody, J. and Watt, I. (1968) 'The consequences of literacy', in J. Goody (ed.), *Literacy in Traditional Societies,* Cambridge, Cambridge University Press.

Gramsci, A. (1971) *Selections from Prison Notebooks,* London, Lawrence and Wishart.

Gray, A. (1992) *Video Playtime: The Gendering of a Leisure Technology,* London, Routledge.

Gray, A. (1999) 'Audience and reception research in retrospect: The trouble with audiences', in P. Alasuutari (ed.), *Rethinking the Media Audience,* London, Sage.

Habermas, J. (1976) *The Legitimation Crisis,* London, Heinemann Educational.

Habermas, J. (1981a) *The Theory of Communicative Action, Vol. 1: Reason and Rationalisation,* Boston, Beacon Press.

Habermas, J. (198 lb) 'Modernity versus postmodernity', *New German Critique,* Winter.

Habermas, J. (1983a) *The Theory of Communicative Action, Vol. 2: The Critique of Functionalist Reason,* Cambridge, Polity Press.

Habermas, J. (1983b) 'Walter Benjamin: consciousness-raising or rescuing critique', in *Philosophical-Political Profiles,* London, Heinemann Educational.

Habermas, J. (1989) *The Structural Transformation of the Public Sphere,* trans. Thomas MacCarthy, Cambridge, Polity Press.

Habermas, J. (1990a) 'What does socialism mean today? The rectifying revolution and the need for new thinking on the Left', *New Left Review,* 183: 3–21.

Habermas, J. (1990b) *Morality and Ethical Life: Does Hegel's Critique of Kant Apply to Discourse Ethics? Moral Consciousness and Communicative Action,* Cambridge, Polity Press.

Habermas, J. (1993) *Justification and Application: Remarks on Discourse Ethics,* trans. C.P. Cronin, Cambridge, Polity Press.

Habermas, J. (1994) 'Citizenship and national identity', in B.V. Steenbergen (ed.), *The Condition of Citizenship,* London, Sage.

Hall, S. (1972a) *External Influences on Broadcasting: Television's Double Bind,* CCCS Occasional Paper 1.

Hall, S. (1972b) 'The determinations of news photographs', *Cultural Studies, 3.*

Hall, S. (1973) *Encoding and Decoding in Television Discourse,* CCCS Occasional Paper, Birmingham.

Hall, S. (1975) *Television as a Medium and its Relation to Culture,* CCCS Occasional Paper 34, Birmingham.

Hall, S. (1977) 'Culture, the media and the ideological effect', in J. Curran (ed.), *Mass Communication and Society,* London, Edward Arnold.

Hall, S. (1980) 'Encoding and decoding', in *Culture, Media, Language,* London, Hutchinson.

Hall, S. (1982) 'The rediscovery of "ideology": return of the repressed in media studies', in M. Ourevitch, *Culture, Society and the Media,* London, Methuen.

Hall, S. (1983) 'The great moving Right show', in S. Hall and M. Jacques (eds), *The Politics of Thatcherism,* London, Lawrence and Wishart.

Hall, S. (1986) 'Postmodernism and articulation' interview by L. Orossberg, *Journal of Communications Inquiry,* 10 (2): 45–60.

Hall, S. (1988a) *The Hard Road to Renewal,* London, Verso.

Hall, S. (1988b) 'Thatcherism amongst the theorists: toad in the garden', in C. Nelson and L. Orossberg (eds), *Marxism and the Interpretation of Culture,* London, Macmillan.

Hall, S. (1991) 'Old and new identities, old and new ethnicities', in A. King (ed.), *Culture, Globalization and the World System,* London, Macmillan Education.

Hall, S. (1996) 'Introduction: Who needs identity?', Hall, S. and du Gay, P. (eds), *Questions of Cultural Identity,* London, Sage.

Hall, S. and Jefferson, T. (eds) (1976) *Resistance through Rituals,* London, Hutchinson.

Hall, S., Critcher, C., Jefferson, T., Clarke, J. and Roberts, B. (eds) (1978) *Policing the Crisis: Mugging, the State, and Law and Order,* London Macmillan.

Haraway, D. (1991) *Simians, Cyborgs and Women: The Reinvention of Nature*, Routledge, London.

Haraway, D. (1997) *Modest_Witness@Second_Millennium.FemaleMan_Meets_Onco-Mouse,* London, Routledge.

Haraway, D. (2000) *How Life a Leaf; An Interview With Thyrza Nichols Goodeve,* London, Routledge.

Harcourt, W. (2000) 'World Wide Women and the Web', Gauntlett, D. (ed.) *Web.Studies: Rewiring Media Studies for the Digital Age,* London, Arnold.

Hargreaves, I. (1993) *Sharper Vision: The BBC and the Communications Revolution,* London, Demos.

Harris, D. (1992) *From Class Struggle to the Politics of Pleasure: The Effects of Gramscianism on Cultural Studies,* London, Routledge.

Harrison, M. (1985) *Television News: Whose Bias?* Berkshire, Hermitage.

Hartley, J. (1992) *The Politics of Pictures: The Creation of the Public in the Age of Popular Media,* London, Routledge.

Harvey, D. (1989) *The Condition of Postmodernity: An Enquiry into the Origins of Cultural Change,* Oxford, Blackwell.

Hebdige, D. (1989) 'After the masses', *Marxism Today,* January.

Held, D. (1989) 'Legitmation problems and crisis tendencies', in *Political Theory and the Modern State,* Cambridge, Polity Press.

Hermes, J. (1996). *Reading Women's Magazines.* Cambridge, Polity Press.

Hermes, J. (1997) 'Gender and media studies: No woman, no cry', Corner, J. and Schlesinger, P. (eds) *International Media Research*, London, Sage.

Hobsbawm, E. (1990) *Nations and Nationalism since 1780,* Cambridge, Cambridge University Press.

Hodge, B. and Tripp, D. (1986) *Children and Television,* Cambridge, Polity Press.

Innis, H.A. (1950) *Empire and Communications,* Oxford, Oxford University Press.

Innis, H.A. (1951) *The Bias of Communication,* Toronto, University of Toronto Press.

Jackson, P., Stevenson, N. and Brooks, K. (2001) *Making Sense of Men's Magazines,* Cambridge, Polity Press.

Jameson, E (1977) *Aesthetics and Politics,* London, Verso.

Jameson, E (1991) *Postmodernism or, The Cultural Logic of Late Capitalism,* London, Verso.

Jameson, F. (1988a) 'Postmodernism and consumer society', in E.A. Kaplan (ed.), *Postmodernism and its Discontents: Theories, Practices,* London, Verso.

Jameson, F. (1988b) 'Cognitive mapping', in C. Nelson and L. Grossberg (eds), *Marxism and the Interpretation of Culture,* London, Macmillan

Jenson, J. (1990) *Redeeming Modernity: Contradictions in Media Criticism,* London, Sage.

Jessop, B., Bonnett, K., Bromley, S. and Ling, T. (1984) 'Authoritarian populism, two nations and Thatcherism', *New Left Review,* 147 (September–October): 32–60.

Katz, E. and Liebes, T. (1985) 'Mutual aid in the decoding of *Dallas:* preliminary notes from a cross-cultural study', in P. Drummond and R. Paterson (eds), *Television in Transition: Papers from the First International Television Studies Conference,* London, British Film Institute.

Keane, J. (1988) *Democracy and Civil Society,* London, Verso.

Keane, J. (1991) *The Media and Democracy,* Cambridge, Polity Press.

Keane, J. (1996) *Reflections on Violence,* London, Verso.

Kellner, D. (1981) 'Network television and American society: introduction to a critical theory of television', *Theory and Society,* 10(1): 31–62.

Kellner, D. (1989) *Jean Baudrillard. From Marxism to Post-Modernism and Beyond,* Cambridge, Polity Press.

Kellner, D. (2000) 'Virilio, war and technology: Some critical reflections', in Armitage, J. (ed.) *Paul Virilio; From Modernism to Hypermodernism,* London, Sage.

Key Note Market Report (1996) *Men's Magazines.*

King, A. (ed.) (1991) *Culture, Globalisation and the World System,* Basingstoke, Hampshire, Macmillan.

Kline, S. (1993) *Out of the Garden: Toys and Children's Culture in the Age of TV Marketing,* London, Verso.

Laclau, E. (1977) *Politics and Ideology in Marxist Theory,* London, Verso.

Laclau, E. (1990) *New Reflections on the Revolution of Our Time,* London, Verso.

Laclau, E. and Mouffe, C. (1985) *Hegemony and Socialist Strategy,* London, Verso.

Laing, S. (1991) 'Raymond Williams and the cultural analysis of television', *Media Culture & Society,* 13 (2): 153–9.

Lash, S, and Urry, J. (1994) *Economies of Signs and Space,* London, Sage.

Lee, S. (1990) *The Politics of Free Speech,* London, Faber and Faber.

Lefebvre, H. (1991) *The Production of Space,* trans. Donald Nicholson-Smith, Oxford, Blackwell.

Lefebvre, H. (1992) *Critique of Everyday Life, Vol. 1,* London, Verso.

Lichtenberg, J. (1991) 'In defence of objectivity', in J. Curran and M. Gurevitch (eds), *Mass Media and Society,* London, Edward Arnold.

Lister, R. (1991) 'Citizenship engendered', *Critical Social Policy,* 32 (Autumn).

Lovibond, S. (1990) 'Feminism and postmodernism', in R. Boyne and A. Rattansi (eds) *Postmodernism and Society,* London, MacMillan.

Lull, J. (1991) *China Turned On; Television, Reform and Resistance,* London, Routledge.

Mader, R. (1993) 'Globo Village: Television in Brazil', in T. Dowmunt (ed.), *Channels of Resistance: Global Television and Local Empowerment,* London, BFI Publishing

Mann, M. (1970) 'The social cohesion of liberal democracy', *American Sociological Review,* June.

Mann, M. (1988) *States, War and Capitalism,* Oxford, Blackwell.

Marcuse, H. (1977) *The Aesthetic Dimension: Towards a Critique of Marxist Aesthetics,* London, Macmillan.

Marquand, D. (1994) 'Reinventing federalism', *New Left Review,* 203:17–26.

Marshall, T.H. (1992) *Citizenship and Social Class,* London, Pluto Press.

Mattelart, A. and Mattelart, M. (1992) *Rethinking Media Theory: Signposts and New Directions,* trans. J.A. Cohen and M. Urquidi, Minnesota, University of Minnesota Press.

Mattelart, A., Delcout, X. and Mattelart, M. (1984) *International Image Markets,* London, Comedia.

Mauss, M. (1990) *The Gift: The Form and Reason for Exchange in Archaic Societies,* London, Routledge.

McLuhan, M. (1951) *The Mechanical Bride: Folklore of Industrial Man,* London, Routledge and Kegan Paul.

McLuhan, M. (1962) *The Gutenberg Galaxy; the Making of Typographic Man,* London, Routledge and Kegan Paul.

McLuhan, M. (1969) *Counterblast,* New York, Harcourt, Brace and World.

McLuhan, M. (1994) *Understanding Media: the Extensions of Man,* London, Routledge.

McLuhan, M. and Fiore, Q. (1967) *The Medium is the Message,* Harmondsworth, Penguin.

McLuhan, M. and Fiore, Q. (1968) *War and Peace in the Global Village,* New York, Bantam Books.

McLuhan, M. and Powers, B.R. (1989) *The Global Village,* Oxford, Oxford University Press.

McNair, B. (1994) *News and Journalism in the UK: A Textbook,* London, Routledge.

McQuail, D. (1992) *Mass Communication Theory: An Introduction,* 2nd edition, London, Sage.

McQuigan, J. (1992) *Cultural Populism,* London, Routledge.

McRobbie, A. (1978). '*Jackie*: an ideology of adolescent femininity'; reprinted as '*Jackie* magazine: romantic individualism and the teenage girl', in McRobbie, A. 1991. *Feminism and Youth Culture.* London, Macmillan, 81–134.

McRobbie, A. (1991). *Jackie* and *Just Seventeen*: girls' comics and magazines in the 1980s, in McRobbie, A. *Feminism and Youth Culture.* London, Macmillan, 135–88.

McRobbie, A. (1994) *Postmodernism and Popular Culture,* London, Routledge.

Melucci, A. (1989) *Nomads of the Present,* London, Hutchinson Radius.

Melucci, A. (1996) *Challenging Codes; Collective Action in the Information Age,* Cambridge, Cambridge University Press.

Menninghaus, W. (1991) 'Walter Benjamin's theory of myth', in O. Smith, (ed.), *On Walter Benjamin,* Cambridge, MA, MIT Press.

Meyrowitz, J. (1985) *No Sense of Place: The Impact of Electronic Media on Social Behavior,* New York, Oxford University Press.

Miller, J. (1971) *McLuhan*, London, Fontana/Collins.

Mintel Market Intelligence (1997) Men's Lifestyle Magazines (see www.mintel.com for details).

Modleski, T. (1988) *Loving with a Vengeance: Mass Produced Fantasies for Women*, London, Routledge.

Moore, S. (1989) 'Getting a bit of the other – the pimps of postmodernism', in R. Chapman and J. Rutherford eds. *Male Order: Unwrapping Masculinity*. London, Lawrence & Wishart, 165–92.

Morley, D. (1980) *The 'Nationwide' Audience*, London, British Film Institute.

Morley, D. (1981) 'The *Nationwide* audience: a critical postscript', *Screen Education*, 39.

Morley, D. (1988) *Family Television: Cultural Power and Domestic Leisure*, London, Routledge.

Morley, D. (1992) *Television, Audiences and Cultural Studies*, London, Routledge.

Morrison, D. (1992) *Television and the Gulf War* (Acamedia Research monograph 7), London, John Libbey.

Mort, F. (1996). *Cultures of Consumption: Masculinities and Social Space in Late Twentieth-century Britain*. London, Routledge.

Mosco, V. (1996) *The Political Economy of Communication*, London, Sage.

Mulgan, G. (1997) *Connexity*, London, Chatto and Windus.

Murdock, G. (1978) 'Blindspots in Western Marxism – a reply to Dallas Smythe', *Canadian Journal of Political and Social Theory*, 2(2).

Murdock, G. (1992) 'Citizens, consumers, and public culture', in M. Skovmand and M. Christian Schroder (eds), *Media Cultures*, London, Routledge.

Nairn, T. (1969) 'McLuhanism: the myth of our time', in R. Rosenthal, *McLuhan Pro and Con*, Harmondsworth, Penguin.

Nairn, T. (1964) 'The British political elite', *New Left Review*, 23.

Nairn, T. (1988) *The Enchanted Glass: Britain and its Monarchy*, London, Radius.

Negrine, R. (1994) *Politics of the Mass Media*, London, Routledge.

Nixon, S. (1993) Looking for the holy grail: publishing and advertising strategies for contemporary men's magazines. *Cultural Studies* 7, 467–92.

Nixon, S. (1996) *Hard Looks: Masculinities, Spectatorship and Contemporary Consumption*, London, UCL Press.

Nixon, S. (1997). 'Exhibiting masculinity', in S. Hall (ed.) *Representtion: Cultural Representations and Signifying Practices*. London, Sage, 291–336.

Norris, C. (1990) *What's Wrong with Postmodernism: Critical Theory and the Ends of Philosophy*, Hemel Hempstead, Harvester Wheatsheaf.

Ong, W.J. (1977) *Interfaces of the Word*, Ithaca, NY, Cornell University Press.

Parekh, B. (1991) 'British citizenship and cultural difference', in G. Andrews (ed.), *Citizenship*, London, Lawrence and Wishart.

Pateman, C. (1982) 'Critique of the public/private dichotomy', in A. Phillips (ed.), *Feminism and Equality*, Oxford, Blackwell.

Pateman, C. (1989) *The Disorder of Women*, Cambridge, Polity Press.

Phillips, A. (1991) *Engendering Democracy*, Cambridge, Polity Press.

Phillips, D. and Tomlinson, A. (1992) 'Homeward bound: leisure, popular culture and consumer capitalism', in D. Strinati and S. Wagg (eds), *Come on Down? Popular Media Culture*, London, Routledge.

Philo, G. (1987) 'Whose news?', *Media, Culture & Society*, 9(4): 397–406.

Philo, G. (1990) *Seeing and Believing: The Influence of Television*, London, Routledge.

Pieterse, J.N. and Parekh, B. (1995) 'Shifting imaginaries: decolonization, internal decolonization, postcoloniality', in J.N. Pieterse and B. Parekh (eds) *The Decolonization of the Imagination; Culture, Knowledge and Power*, London, Zed Books.

Plant, S. (1992) *The Most Radical Gesture: The Situationist International in a Postmodern Age*, London, Routledge.

Plant, S. (1996) 'On the Matrix: cyberfeminist simulations', in Sheilds, R. (ed.) *Cultures of the Internet*, London, Sage.

Plant, S. (1997) *Zeros + Ones: Digital Women + The New Technoculture*, Fourth Estate, London.

Poster, M. (1990) *The Mode of Information*, Chicago, Chicago University Press.

Poster, M. (1994) 'The mode of information and postmodernity', in D. Crowley and D. Mitchell (eds), *Communication Theory Today*, Cambridge, Polity Press.

Poster, M. (1995) *The Second Media Age*, Cambridge, Polity Press.

Poster, M. (1996) 'Cyberdemocracy; Internet and the public sphere', in Porter, D. (ed.) *Internet Culture*, London, Routledge.

Poster, M. (1997) 'Postmodern Virtualities' in Featherstone, M. and Burrows, R. (eds)*Cyberspace/Cyberbodies/Cyberpunk; Cultures of Technological Embodiment*, London, Sage.

Postman, N. (1982) *The Disappearence of Childhood*, New York, Dell.

Postman, N. (1985) *Amusing Ourselves to Death: Public Discourse in the Age of Show Business*, London, Methuen.

Postman, N. (1993) *Technopoly; The Surrender of Culture to Technology*, New York, Alfred A.Knot.

Potter, D. (1994) 'The present tense', interview with Melvyn Bragg, *New Left Review*, 205:131–40.

Poulantzas, N. (1975) *Political Power and Social Classes*, London, Verso.

Poulantzas, N. (1978) *State, Power Socialism*, London, Verso.

Pursehouse, M. (1987) *Life's More Fun with your Number One 'Sun' – Interviews with some 'Sun' Readers*, CCCS Occasional Paper, No 85, Birmingham.

Radway, J. (1986) 'Identifying ideological seams: mass culture, analytical method, and political practice', *Communication* , 9 : 93–123.

Radway, J. (1987) *Reading the Romance: Women, Patriarchy and Popular Literature*, London, Verso.

Ransome, P. (1992) *Antonio Gramsci: a New Introduction*, Hemel Hempstead, Harvester Wheatsheaf.

Reeves, G. (1993) *Communications and the 'Third World'*, London, Routledge.

Ricoeur, P. (1981) *Hermeneutics and the Human Sciences*, trans. and ed. J.B. Thompson, Cambridge, Cambridge University Press.

Robertson, R. (1992) *Globalisation: Social Theory and Global Culture*, London, Sage.

Robins, K. (1997) 'Cyberspace and the world we live in', in Featherstone, M. and Burrows, R. *Cyberspace/Cyberbodies/Cyberpunk; Cultures of Technological Embodiment*, London, Sage.

Robins, K. and Webster, F. (1999) *Times of the Technoculture; From the information society to the vitual life*, London, Routledge.

Ross, A. (1994) 'The new smartness' in Bender, G. and Druckrey, T. *Culture on the Brink; Ideologies of Technology*, Seattle, Bay Press.

Roszak,T.(1986) *The Cult of Information*, Cambridge, Lutterworth Press.

Rustin, M. (1992) 'Democracy and social rights', *New Left Review*, 191.

References

Said, E. (1978) *Orientalism,* London, Routledge.

Said, E. (1993) *Culture and Imperialism,* London, Chatto and Windus.

Saussure, E de (1974) *Course in General Linguistics,* London, Fontana.

Sayers, J. (1986) *Sexual Contradictions: Psychology, Psychoanalysis, and Feminism,* London, Tavistock.

Scannell, P. (1986) 'Broadcasting and the politics of unemployment 1930–1935', in R. Collins *et al.* (eds), *Media, Culture and Society: a Critical Reader,* London, Sage.

Scannell, P. (1990) 'Public service broadcasting: the history of a concept', in A. Goodwin and G. Whannel (eds), *Understanding Television,* London, Routledge.

Scannell, P. (1992) 'Public service broadcasting and modern public life', in P Scannell *et al.* (eds), *Culture and Power: a Media, Culture and Society Reader,* London, Sage.

Schiller, H. (1970) *Mass Communication and American Empire,* New York, M.E. Sharpe.

Schiller, H. (1986) 'Electronic information flows: new basis for global domination?', in P. Drummond and R. Paterson (eds), *Television in Transition,* London, British Film Institute.

Schiller, H. (1991) 'Not yet the post-imperialist era', *Critical Studies in Mass Communication,* Vol 8: 13–28.

Schiller, H. (1996) *Information Inequality; The Deepening Crisis of America,* London, Routledge.

Schlesinger, P (1978) *Putting 'Reality' Together,* London, Constable.

Schlesinger, P. (1990) 'Rethinking the sociology of journalism: sources, strategies and the limits of media-centrism', in M. Ferguson (ed.), *Public Communication: The New Imperatives,* London, Sage.

Schlesinger, P. (1991) *Media, State and Nation – Political Violence and Collective Identities,* London, Sage.

Schlesinger, P., Emerson Dobash, R., Dobash, R.P. and Weaver, C.K. (1992) *Women Viewing Violence,* London, British Film Institute.

Schudson, M. (1993) *Advertising, the Uneasy Persuasion: Its Dubious Impact on American Society,* London, Routledge.

Segal, L. (1999) *Why Feminism?,* Cambridge, Polity Press.

Seidler, V.J. (1991) (ed.) *The Achilles Heel Reader; Men, Sexual Politics and Socialism,* London, Routledge.

Siune, K. and Truetzschler, W. (1992) *Dynamics of Media Politics: Broadcast and Electronic Media in Western Europe,* London, Sage.

Smart, B. (1992) *Modern Conditions, Postmodern Controversies,* London, Routledge.

Smart, B. (1993) 'Europe/America: Baudrillard's fatal comparison', in C. Rojek and B.S. Turner (eds), *Forget Baudrillard?,* London, Routledge.

Smith, A.D. (1990) 'Towards a global culture?', in M. Featherstone (ed.), *Nationalism, Globalisation and Modernity,* London, Sage.

Smythe, D. (1977) 'Communications – blindspots of Western Marxism', *Canadian Journal of Political and Social Theory,* 1(3): 1–27.

Soja, E. (1989) *Postmodern Geographies: The Assertion of Space in Critical Social Theory,* London, Verso.

Soothill, K. and Walby, S. (1990) *Sex Crime in the News,* London, Routledge.

Soper, K. (1979) 'Marxism, materialism and biology', in J. Mepham (ed.), *Issues in Marxist Philosophy: Materiallsm,* Brighton, Harvester.

Soper, K. (1990) *Troubled Pleasures,* London, Verso.

Sparks, C. (1987) 'Striking results', *Media, Culture & Society,* 9.

Sparks, C. (1992a), 'Popular journalism: theories and practice', in P. Dahlgren and C. Sparks (eds), *Journalism and Popular Culture,* London, Sage.

Sparks, C. (1992b) 'The popular press and political democracy', in P. Scannell *et al.* (eds), *Culture and Power: a Media, Culture and Society Reader,* London, Sage.

Squires, J. (1996) 'Fabulous feminist futures and lure of cybercultures', in J. Dovey (ed.) *Fractural Dreams; New Media in a Social Context,* London, Lawerence and Wishart.

Stallabras, J. (1996) *Gargantura; Manufactured Mass Culture,* London, Verso.

Stevenson, N. (1995) *Culture, Ideology and Socialism: Raymond Williams and E.P Thompson,* Aldershot, Avebury Press.

Stevenson, N. (1999) *The Transformation of the Media; globalisation, morality and ethics,* Harlow, Longman.

Street, J. (2001) *Mass Media, Politics and Democracy,* Houndmills, Palgrave.

Taylor, C. (1989) *Sources of Self: The Making of Modern Identity,* Cambridge, Cambridge University Press.

Taylor, C. (1991) 'Language and Society', in A. Honneth and H. Jonas (eds), *Communicative Action,* Cambridge Polity Press.

Tester, K. (1999) 'The moral consequentiality of television' *European Journal of Social Theory* 2(4):469–83.

Thompson, E.P. (1978) 'The peculiarities of the English', in *The Poverty of Theory and Other Essays,* London, Merlin; New York, Monthly Review Press.

Thompson, J.B. (1984) *Studies in the Theory of Ideology,* Cambridge, Polity Press.

Thompson, J.B. (1990) *Ideology and Modern Culture: Critical Social Theory in the Era of Mass Communication,* Cambridge, Polity Press.

Thompson, J.B. (1994) 'Social theory and the media', in D. Crowley and D. Mitchell (eds), *Communication Theory Today,* Cambridge, Polity Press.

Thompson, J.B. (1995) *The Media and Modernity: A Social Theory of the Media,* Cambridge, Polity Press

Thompson, J.B. (1997) 'Scandal and social theory', in Lull, S. and Hinerman, S. (eds) *Media Scandals,* Cambridge, Polity Press.

Tomlinson, J. (1991) *Cultural Imperialism,* London, Pinter.

Tuchman, G. (1978) *Hearth and Home: Images of Women and the Media,* New York, Oxford University Press.

Turner, B.S. (1993a) 'Contemporary problems in the theory of citizenship', in *Citizenship and Social Theory,* London, Sage.

Turner, B.S. (1993b) 'Cruising America', in C. Rojek and B.S. Turner, *Forget Baudrillard?,* London, Routledge.

Turner, B.S. (1994) 'Postmodern culture/modern citizens', in B.V. Steenbergen (ed.), *The Condition of Citizenship,* London, Sage.

Turner, G. (1991) *British Cultural Studies: An Introduction,* Boston, Unwin Hyman.

Urry, J. (2000) *Sociology Beyond Societies; mobilities for the twenty-first century,* London, Routledge.

Van Dyk, T.A. (1991) *Racism and the Press: Critical Studies in Racism and Migration,* London, Routledge.

Van Dijk, J. (1999) *The Network Society,* London, Sage.

Van Zoonen, L. (1998) 'The ethics of making private life public', Brants, K., Hermes, J. and van Zoonen, L. (eds) *The Media in Question,* London, Sage.

Virilio, P. (1989) *War and Cinema: The Logistics of Perception,* London, Verso.

References

Virilio, P. (1994) *The Vision Machine*, trans. Julie Rose, Bloomington and Indianapolis, Indiana University.

Virilio, P. (1995) *The Art of the Motor*, trans. Julie Rose, Minneapolis, London, University of Minnesota Press.

Virilio, P. (1997) *Open Sky*, London, Verso.

Virilio, P. (1998) 'Military space', in Der Derran, J. (ed.) *The Virilio Reader*, Oxford, Blackwell.

Virilio, P. (1999) *Politics of the Very Worst – An Interview by Philippe Petit* trans. Micheal Caraliere, Semiotext(e), Columbia University, New York.

Virilio, P. (2000a) *The Information Bomb*, London, Verso.

Virilio, P. (2000b) *Polar Inertia*, London, Sage.

Virilio, P. (2000c) *Strategy of Deception*, London, Verso.

Volosinov, V.N. (1986) *Marxism and the Philosophy of Language*, trans. L. Matejka and I.R. Titunik, Cambridge, MA, Harvard University Press.

Wakeford, N. (2001) 'Networking women and girls with information/communication technology: surfing tales of World Wide Web', in Bell, D. and Kennedy, B.A. (eds) *The Cybercultures Reader*, London, Routledge.

Webster, R. (1990) *A Brief History of Blasphemy*, Southwold, Orwell Press.

Webster, F. (1995) *Theories of the Information Society*, London, Routledge.

White, C.L. (1970) *Women's Magazines, 1693–1968*, London, Michael Joseph.

White, S. (1988) *The Recent Work of Jürgen Habermas: Reason, Justice and Modernity*, Cambridge, Cambridge University Press.

Wilding, F. (2001) 'Where is Feminism in Cyberfeminism?' http://www-art.cfa.cmu.edu/www-wilding/wherefem.html

Williams, R. (1952) *Drama from Ibsen to Eliot*, London, Chatto and Windus.

Williams, R. (1961) *Culture and Society (1780–1950)*, Harmondsworth, Penguin.

Williams, R. (1962) *Communications*, Harmondsworth, Penguin.

Williams, R. (1965) *The Long Revolution*, Harmondsworth, Penguin.

Williams, R. (1973) 'Base and superstructure in Marxist cultural theory', *New Left Review*, 82.

Williams, R. (1974) *Television: Technology and Cultural Form*, London, Fontana/ Collins.

Williams, R. (1978) 'Problems of materialism', *New Left Review*, 109: 3–17.

Williams, R. (1979a) *Politics and Letters: Interviews with 'New Left Review'*, London, Verso.

Williams, R. (1979b) *Marxism and Literature*, Oxford, Oxford University Press.

Williams, R. (1980) *Problems in Materialism and Culture*, London, Verso.

Williams, R. (1982) *Culture*, London, Fontana.

Williams, R. (1985) *Towards 2000*, London, Penguin.

Williams, R. (1987) 'The press we don't deserve', in J. Curran, *The British Press: A Manifesto*, London, Macmillan.

Williams, R. (1988) 'Culture is ordinary' (1958), in *Resources of Hope*, London, Verso.

Williams, R. (1989a) 'A defence of realism', in *What I Came to Say*, London, Hutchinson.

Williams, R. (1989b) 'Isn't the news terrible?', in *What I Came to Say*, London, Hutchinson.

Williams, R. (1989c) *The Politics of Modernism: Against the New Conformists*, London, Verso.

Williams, R. and Orrom, M. (1954) *Preface to Film*, London, Film Drama.

Willis, P. (1990) *Common Culture*, Buckingham, Open University Press.

Winship, J. (1987) *Inside Women's Magazines*. London, Pandora Press.

Index